TACTICS ON TROUT

ALFRED A. KNOPF  1969 NEW YORK

Tactics on Trout

by RAY OVINGTON

ACKNOWLEDGMENTS

The author wishes to thank his many publishers of books
and magazine articles for the use of certain writing that
has been published by them under his by-line. Thanks go
to *Field & Stream, Outdoor Life, Sports Afield, True,
Argosy, Man's Day, Fishing World, Fishing Magazine,
The Fisherman, Hunting & Fishing, Outdoors, Elks,
American Legion, Pennsylvania Angler, Florida Wildlife*
magazines and book publishers Little, Brown and Company, The Stackpole Company, Cornerstone Library,
Thomas Nelson's Sons, and J. L. Pratt and Co.

Contents

Introduction   vii

CHAPTER 1   *The Midstream Rock*   3
CHAPTER 2   *Two Center Rocks*   15
CHAPTER 3   *Three Center Rocks*   23
CHAPTER 4   *Deep Center Current*   31
CHAPTER 5   *Curved Center Current*   39
CHAPTER 6   *Shelving Riffle*   47
CHAPTER 7   *Undercut Bank*   57
CHAPTER 8   *Sharp-Angle Pool*   65
CHAPTER 9   *Corner Bend*   73
CHAPTER 10   *Split Riffle*   83
CHAPTER 11   *Head of Pool I*   93
CHAPTER 12   *Tail of Pool I*   101
CHAPTER 13   *Head of Pool II*   111
CHAPTER 14   *Tail of Pool II*   119
CHAPTER 15   *Head of Pool III*   127
CHAPTER 16   *Tail of Pool III*   139
CHAPTER 17   *Ledge Pool*   147
CHAPTER 18   *S-Shaped Pool*   155
CHAPTER 19   *Bridge Pool I*   163
CHAPTER 20   *Bridge Pool II*   169
CHAPTER 21   *Stream Snags I and II*   181
CHAPTER 22   *Shallow Flat Water*   189

CHAPTER 23   *Deep Flat Water*   195

CHAPTER 24   *Stream Tributary*   203

CHAPTER 25   *Below Tributary*   209

CHAPTER 26   *Waste Water*   217

CHAPTER 27   *Rock Eddies*   223

CHAPTER 28   *Stream Split*   229

CHAPTER 29   *Stream Rejoin*   237

CHAPTER 30   *Road Pool*   243

CHAPTER 31   *Big Boulders, Fast Runs*   249

CHAPTER 32   *Little Streams (Four Types of Water)*   257

CHAPTER 33   *Step Pools*   267

CHAPTER 34   *Watching the Trout*   273

Appendixes   287

Index   *follows page* 327

Introduction

The concept of this book is vastly different than most fishing books that deal with generalities about tackle, technique, and voluminous information which the angler-reader has to assimilate and then use selectively as his demands on the stream call it forth. Our approach here—yours and mine—is one of stepping from the brush, considering the stream condition as it flows by us, ascertaining the manner of approach, and then the use of various techniques by which we hope to catch a good creel of trout.

So, let's not waste time in the library, the tackle shop, or even on the water itself, thinking about generalities, theories, or dogmas. Let's go fishing together—right now.

Our "angling laboratory" is a composite of many trout streams as it ranges in size from big brooks to little rivers. In all, we have detailed the problems and ways of fishing some thirty-four basic situations. We've laid out a stream for us to fish in much the same way as a designer of a golf course creates his fairways, bunkers, and greens. These basic problems exist on all trout streams and we will fish them together at all seasons of the year and under typical weather and water conditions, making note of the fly hatches, water temperature, levels, and other elements which go into the coffer of the mind to produce the decisions as to just how to proceed in the art of catching trout with all kinds of flies—streamers and bucktails, wet flies, nymphs, and dry flies.

The writer of any kind of "how-to" book is always confronted with the basic problem of just how much or how little his reader knows about the subject in actual practice. In this book, we can assume two extremes: that the angler has been fishing for many years and considers himself an expert. He'll have fun with us, either agreeing or disagreeing with our approach to the problems. On the other hand, the beginner will not be left ashore unable to follow us in our use of sometimes complicated techniques, because, since we are fishing together, he will learn, by application, all the new tricks as he goes along.

We have illustrated the various problem waters with drawings of the stretch of stream to be negotiated and also presented a step-by-step manner of fishing the water in question, explaining all of the casts, drifts, retrieves, and motions of the flies and lures. Throughout the text we have included line drawings of specific fishing techniques and other tips, preferring to leave the actual mechanics of casting and rod and line how-to instruction to the Appendix. The reason for this is that many readers will know how to perform the various casts and need not have to read through this instruction and can so continue their fishing with me undisturbed. For the beginner who still has to master the casts in question, the Appendix is there for him and his reference whenever it is needed. Also in the Appendix are listed the dressings of many of the author's favorite flies, some of them his own creations. Much basic material, then, will be found in the Appendix, so we have really two books in one.

Read as a book, during the off season, these situations and their approach will recall many instances to the reader of his own experiences; the times when he has failed and the times of success. They will offer a *modus operandi* for the next time he goes to the waterside in search of fun with trout. It is hoped that some of the techniques and approaches will be remembered and practiced when he makes his first cast on the next Opening Day.

Actually, the entire book is one long monologue and I suppose, it should be enclosed in quotation marks, since we are fishing together and I'm doing all the talking while you have no chance to agree or disagree with me. I've tried to anticipate your questions and possible alternatives to different techniques and approaches used here. Therefore, I make no claims that what I have written in step-by-step are the ONLY ways of fishing these waters. I have tried, however, to call on thirty years of angling successes and failures on just such stream problems and present what I believe are basic and productive means and methods under the circumstances outlined and illustrated.

Our only dogma demands astute observation before entering the water; to decide the best manner of approach the selection of the proper leader and lure for the time and conditions and then the use of the best ways we know how to present our fraud in such a way that the trout falls for the imitation and finds himself securely hooked.

I have attempted to write a book which I wish I could have read many years ago. Throughout those years I have bought or borrowed almost

This is the "blank" that most of us see when we go fishing—now, let's get a closer look, and learn how to fish it.

every book available on the varied aspects of trouting, and, without wishing to be classed as a critic, I found most of them interesting, informative, yet not truly instructive in the actual steps and procedures which angling requires to be successful. The problem was to try to create a trout stream on blank white paper, and then invite the reader to whom I could talk and instruct to fish with me.

So, my years of trouting have been wonderful ones and bounteous. As a writer on outdoor subjects I have had the pleasure for many years of janitoring a daily column "Outdoors" for the now-defunct New York *World-Telegram and Sun.* That "job" enabled me to not only fish everywhere in the Western Hemisphere, but allowed me to meet and talk with anglers, tackle salesmen, manufacturers, guides, woodsmen, and fellow sportsmen from Argentina to Alaska, from New Jersey to Labrador, with a generous portion of fishing in our Western states. Most of the really sophisticated trout that have had me at my wits end have been encountered in the waters of New England, New York, and Pennsylvania. I also had the coaching of millions of listeners to my "Rod and Gun Club of the Air," which was broadcast for more than ten years over the Mutual Radio Network. Thousands wrote us every week with tips and hints and experiences which we in turn shared with the audience.

I have also thoroughly enjoyed teaching classes of youngsters as well as so-called mature people in the art of casting, fishing, and fly tying. I find no real difference in the ages, since all of us become little boys when we go fishing.

Finally, before we don our waders, pick out a favorite and appropriate fly rod, and go forth to the stream, I want to thank good souls and good anglers such as Jim Deren, to whom I'll always be eternally grateful for what I absorbed from him and his cronies that harbored daily in the Angler's Roost; Angus Cameron, my present editor, who finally turned me loose to write and illustrate this effort—a man of infinite patience who trudged me through the pains of my very first book, *How to Take Trout,* when he was an editor of Little, Brown and Company; and John Lowell Pratt, who also showed me infinite patience with my book ideas and final productions for him in the paperback field, many of these distributed by the Outdoor Life Book Club. He was also my editorial supervisor for a series we created for Thomas Nelson's Sons— the Young Sportsman's Library.

To the reader, please forgive me for making all the editorial *faux pas* that could drive the orthodox reader out of his mind. Remember, you are not supposed to be "reading" this book. The reading of instruction can be exceedingly boring. You are, rather, meant to "listen" with me and wet waders with me on some of my favorite and frustrating bits of trout water. These are not dreamed-up situations—they are actual ones, just as the elements carved them out of rocks, gravel, and the whole of nature.

Remember, that when we refer to a specific type of cast or retrieve technique which is a matter of rod handling rather than fishing technique, please refer to the Appendix. You'll also find a good deal of other pertinent information therein.

SPECIAL NOTE ON THE APPENDIX

The purpose of this book is to take you fishing with a minimum of basic initial instruction of rod handling and the other mechanics of fly fishing. Throughout the text we make references to specific casts, rod techniques in line with the problem at hand. If we were to detail the actual mechanics of these fishing techniques, we would not be fishing but instructing you as we might with a rank beginner. So, what we have done is to take you fishing in the main part of the book, but if you have yet to learn the mechanics of rod handling and basic line handling, this is data led for you in the Appendix, along with other vitally needed information. I trust that this is a satisfactory arrangement and that you will find both the text of the book and the appendix equally informative.

TACTICS ON TROUT

Figure 1. The Midstream Rock.

CHAPTER 1

The Midstream Rock

IT is a wet, cold, almost forbidding early dawn on the first day of the trout season. We've just enjoyed a good breakfast and have donned heavy clothes. We're warm and comfortable in our waders, fishing jacket, and hat. The path leading through the woods emits smells of the good thawed earth after its long winter freeze.

It's been raining off and on for a week before the big day and is still drizzling a bit. A slight wind is rustling the bare limbs of the trees and, as we approach the stream with our rods assembled and pointed forward down the path, a song sparrow bubbles a cheery phrase, a blue jay squawks at our intrusion, and a phoebe flits from the willows. The first cold draft of wind coursing up the valley drops a fine, chilling rain. The welcome sound of rushing water greets our ears as we emerge from the brush and place our feet on the boulders that grace the stream edge.

The water is high and slightly discolored. The level is about a foot above normal, and, perhaps two feet above what it will be after the first dry spell when the water clears in May to offer the fine hatches that we can anticipate on this stream.

Looking upstream we see the run is about a hundred feet wide, flowing smoothly, uninterrupted for quite a spell in both directions. Right opposite us is a large midstream rock and below this the typical wash-wake streak contrasting with the syrupy rolling of the currents. It's a simple setup, seemingly, yet one which most anglers fish too casually, or overwork simply because they neglect to make each cast count. A minimum of line disturbance is hoped for and can be accomplished only by our studied approach.

The choice of flies is a very easy one generally. (In the Appendix at the back of this book is a complete listing of my favorite flies, their natural insect of bait equivalent, and our personal recipe for tying.) As we

4

approach our stream today underwater flies such as streamers, bucktails, or nymphs are called for, since there is no sign of a hatch. Even the earliest May fly, the Quill Gordon, will not hatch until noon, if then, depending on the amount of light that the heavy rain clouds will allow, and a rising temperature. With no flies hatching, no nymphs drifting in the surface film, we can assume that nymphing or working a bucktail might be appropriate.

Let's try a bucktail first, because in this first chapter we want to perform together some rod casting tricks, line manipulation, presentation techniques, and natural drifts which we will need to have mastered, since they will be used throughout our travels on this classic stream of ours.

Figure 2. Bucktail Flies.

A. *Typical streamer fly made of rooster hackles, generally only two, inside-to-inside tie. Sometimes the feathers are reversed so that they fan out instead of sticking together. This makes for more active movement in the water.*

B. *The hair bucktail, made of deer hair or other suitable hair such as polar bear and black bear in combination. Both these types generally are dressed with a jungle-cock eye to represent the shine of the head and eyes.*

C. *The bucktail streamer is a combination of both streamer feathers and hair and is very good for heavy-water fishing or night work. It is a good dressing for weighted flies.*

Our bucktail is an imitation of the dace minnow, a common and abundant species. Our leader is nine feet long tapered to 3X and our hook size is long shank number 12. The dace has a silver-tinsel body and the conventional white, brown, and black bucktail, sparsely tied and topped with jungle-cock eye.

We approach the streamside and head for position 1 in figure 3 (page 6). From here we can cast to the trout that are resting just ahead of the rock in the dead water that is created by the slipstream of the current. We will also work the outer edge of the froth-line wake below the rock for as long a distance as it is practicable.

Oh, yes. I forgot one of our other dogmas—that of fishing with as short a line as possible. Seldom do we recommend long casts or long-line fishing, fun though it may be and good exercise, since we will see

Figure 3. Cross-Section View of Midstream Rock.

This is the underwater cross-section view of the rock, showing the terrain of the bottom, the slipstream of the water in front of, beside, and below the rock. Note, too, the various positions of the trout. Those on the bottom are resting in the quiet water and are reached by deeply drifted flies. Those on the surface are there mainly because there is sufficient food drifting on the surface, such as a hatch. Study the current swings and you can see that your fly must be handled properly in the drift, and can, if it is manipulated properly, be made to rise up from the depths right in front of the trout's nose.

the importance of line and lure control—an art that cannot be mastered with a line that is too long to control at every second.

From this position alongside a shallow beach, we see that the water straight out from us is much too deep to wade. The distance from 1 to the rock is a nice, easy thirty feet. There is also enough backcast room from this angle if we keep the backcast high over the streamside willows behind us.

Our objective is to place the fly so that it will drift down from C to B and, on the retrieve, through A. We also need to allow enough time for the fly to sink a few inches before reaching the "hot spot."

So, now, we make our first cast to a point directly across stream, above C. In order to allow the fly to sink quickly, we make the cast and very shortly pull another three feet of line from the reel and rollcast the additional line in a modified upstream bend (see Appendix, page 301), so that the current, flowing fast as it is, will not jerk the line downcurrent ahead for the fly. With the loop of line drifting now, well above the fly, the rod is then raised to about the ten-o'clock position and as the lure travels toward C we raise the rod tip as high as we can reach in the stature position, keeping the left hand on the line that's coming down from the first guide. This is our trigger in case of a strike. (See Appendix, page 296, for casting instructions.)

Our fly, according to our view of the end of the line where it joins the leader, is now between C and B and as it approaches B it is well underwater, right near the snouts of the trout that are surely there.

The current now takes the fly around the edge of the rock between

B and A. In order to keep the slack line from proceeding the fly down-stream, we rollcast and mend the line upstream so that the line bellies upstream (see Appendix, page 300). This can be accomplished by a deli-cate cast which will not pull the fly up from its deep drift alongside the rock, where the potential of trout seeing it is very good. On this cast we do not try to cover all the water below, but rollcast forward. As the fly comes to the surface we begin our backcast and the fly comes out with a minimum of disturbance. (See Appendix, Roll-Pickup, page 304.)

Our next cast goes out a bit farther over the same water and the fly then drifts down between C and D and we pull it back to B and drift as before to a point just below the rock.

Now, we don't give in to the tendency to cover all the available hot spots from this one position, even though our tackle has a vastly greater ability to perform for us. Sure, we could cast to the side of the rock below A and drift the fly down to outer wash, but again that would be

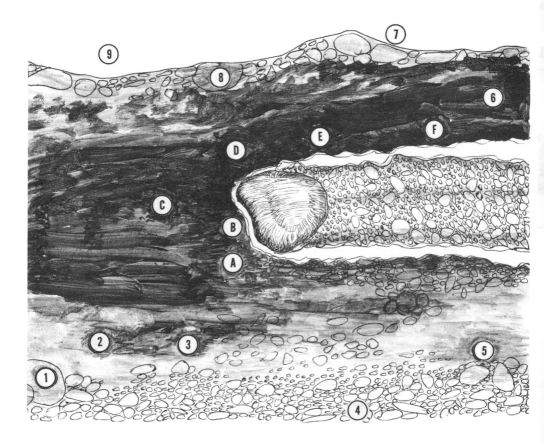

Figure 4. Center Stream Rock.

unnecessarily long-line fishing. Because of the fast current on our side of the rock wash, the line would be largely uncontrollable. We also resist the temptation to fish the far side of the rock, preferring to save that for later on. I have shown position 2 as a wading alternative if the rock is farther out than thirty feet. It will be used later when we fish our nymphs.

Let's try now from position 3. We make a similar upstream-and-across cast to a point above C and let the fly drift on an almost straight line to just above D and then pull it in short jerks right across in front of the rock and drift to the side of the rock. In a simple forward rollcast, with the line held off the current between us and the wash, the leader and the fly are allowed to drift on the inside of the wash for the length of line we have out. The fly is then retrieved in short minnow-like jerks across the deep water over to the shallow and is then picked up. It is not retrieved over the deep, since this would scare any trout that might be lying there.

Proceeding now to position 4 or into the edge of the current out from it, we are now able to present our fly to a spot just above and between A and B. Here, fishing as we are slightly upstream, we have to hold the line off the water so that it does not belly downstream ahead of the fly and whisk it away from the hot spot. When it drifts down below the rock to a point directly opposite us, we mend the line in a modified rollcast and have a belly of spare line upstream to be absorbed so that the fly will sink and perhaps bounce along the outside, and later on the inside, of the wash (see Appendix, page 305).

We don't change position yet. There is another good cast ahead of us right here. This we direct to a point just below the rock, short of E, and work the wash on the other side. Our next cast might target at the center of the downstream side of the rock and be allowed to drift down the center of the shallow. A slight twitching motion could be given to the fly as it travels. The amount of this water to be covered depends upon how high off the water you are able to keep the line so that the current does not catch it and so whisk the fly away from its mission.

Proceeding to 5, we have the opportunity to fish the bucktail as we would a dry fly—upstream. Casting to A the fly drifts along the wash and sinks rapidly as we gather in the slack. Hold that rod high now to avoid line belly and downstream drag because of too much slack. Before we leave 5 we can shoot a good cast to the center of the lower edge of the rock and then jerk the fly through the wake line, rollcast a loop upstream, and work the water below the picture as the fly travels downstream.

Our final shot from 5 is between E and F and an across-stream drift through the wash and down.

Note now, as we return upstream for a workout with nymphs, that we have made precious few casts; the water has been disturbed to an absolute minimum and we have given the trout every chance to hit a natural-moving minnow imitation. The next fisherman to work this water after us would find that the fish had not been put down by our actions.

So, since no other angler is presently fishing downstream toward the rock, we'll retrace our steps to point 1 and change over to a nymph rig that is appropriate for this season of the year.

Cigarette?

Walking leisurely, we remember that the Quill Gordon nymph is about the most potential hatch that can come off at this time of the year. The water is cold, about 48 degrees, and, with luck, even a light hatch might come off if the clouds part and let the sun and light show through. Light at this time of the year is sometimes as important as water temperature when it comes to the point of a hatch developing. The Quill Gordon nymph is of the clinging variety and as such is found in the faster rock- and boulder-strewn currents in company with the various stone-fly nymphs. Also, on many of the Eastern streams, a green caddis larvae is active now, prior to hatch. Due to the roiliness of the water, these insects are constantly being disturbed from their sticky bases on the rocks and gravel of the stream bottom.

So, just for experimental purposes, we'll rig up with a two dropper and tippet leader. On the very end we'll tie on a medium-sized stone-fly nymph; on the lower dropper, a green caddis-worm imitation and on the top, a Quill Gordon, since its tendency before the hatch is to drift for quite a spell before reaching the surface film (see Appendix, page 305).

Our leader is rather heavy, tapered to only 3X because of the use of the three flies. Here you have the opportunity to use some of my weighted nymphs or you apply wrap-around lead to your leader as your alternative. If you choose the latter, the best way to ensure no catch-up during the cast is to place one piece of lead ahead of the top tippet and one below the second so that the leader does not double back on itself.

With this rig, our line will, of necessity, be shorter. From position 1 we cast the rig to a point above C and once the flies have begun the descent, we throw an upstream loop of line in similar fashion as we did with the bucktail. But now, attempting to create a natural dead drift, we raise the rod tip high off the water and follow the drift with it as it goes, keeping in constant touch with the line in this manner to avoid missing the very soft strike. As the flies approach the rock, we strip in about three feet of line, still holding the rod high. The nymphs rise toward the surface in a most natural manner right at the hot spot. The same procedure is followed to a point above A and B with the drift continuing down into the wash as far as is practicable.

In order to work the slip of current alongside the wash—a very good area for early-season nymphing, by the way—we take up a position as far out as water speed and depth permit. We merely drop the rig into the water below us and slowly feed out the line as the flies almost bump along the bottom. In this instance we do not raise the rod tip-high but point the tip directly to the water, at a right angle to the line, so that between the sensitive reaction of the rod tip and the trigger of spare line in our line hand we will feel the slightest bump of the trout as it mouths the nymphs as they rise to the surface. Many hits are missed or not even noticed unless this procedure is followed. More times than we care to mention, trout have tasted and rejected our lures without our being aware of the fact.

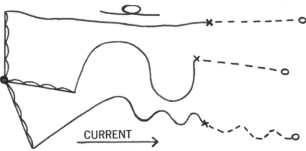

Figure 5. The Rod at Right Angles to the Line.

Shown here are three typical drifts downstream where it is imperative that the rod be kept at right angles to the line as it leaves the rod. The line as such is used as an indicator or bobber. It will float relaxed and on the surface and the slightest twitch or hit from a trout will be seen as well as felt. Also, the line drift as it goes down is controlled by enlarging or reducing the size of the gap or bulge as the case may be. As the line begins to straighten out, you can release more line, saving the bulge and thus be sure that no tension will meet the fly from your line manipulation. This is a subtlety of fishing that you will seldom see performed on the stream.

CODE
fly lights ×
pickup •
roll extra line ℓ

From here the nymphs swing to the shallow and the pickup does not disturb the water in the least and several drifts can be made to entice the trout. If a fish takes one of the flies, it is my usual procedure to replace the other patterns with the successful one and so approximate a group of the same species moving in the water. As we proceed in the above manner, gradually working our way to 5, we have carefully nymphed the water on the side of the wash and its potential deep run.

On the other side of the stream we can proceed with the same routine as before. The water is deeper and the current does not proceed the flies. A weighted bucktail is recommended or any one of the arrangements shown in figure 6.

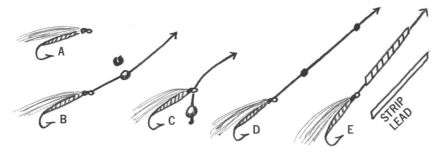

Figure 6. Weighted Bucktail Flies.

A. *Weighted bucktail with wrap-around lead tied into the dressing.*

B. *BB shot clamped onto the leader about three inches above the fly.*

C. *BB shot hanging free below the fly. This offers excellent freedom of action for the fly and can be easily removed and the fly retied.*

D. *Two BB shots for extra-fast and deep-water fishing.*

E. *Wrap-around lead strip placed on leader without knots so that it can be slipped up or down for ease in casting.*

Now let's skip a couple of months and revisit the "rock." We will be in the prime days of fly hatches and can enjoy some good wet-fly, nymph, and dry-fly action all in the same day, if we keep our eyes sharp for the signs of the hatches. In figure 7 you will see two approaches to the rock, one from the upstream down, and the other from the downstream position up, working only the limited area around the rock. The valuable left and right "curve cast" is detailed in the Appendix because many casts will be only mentioned by name throughout the book.

The water level is down, the water clear and adequately warm for hatches, the deeper side of the rock will obviously be the main point of concentration and will now be about the same depth and speed as the shallow side was in early spring. Most of the flow of insects and land drop-ins will be filtered and shuttled by the currents to that side. During the day when there is no apparent action it might be a good idea to scan the water carefully for bottom-feeding trout that flash while feeding on the caddis larvae and nymphs.

Also, at this point may I refer you, as I will often, to the chapter "Watching the Trout," since your ability to spot exactly what is happening will in great measure determine whether to fish the top, the surface film, or underwater. We'll fish some typical fly hatches in our next problem, that of two center rocks . . . a vastly more involved bit of fisherman's fairway.

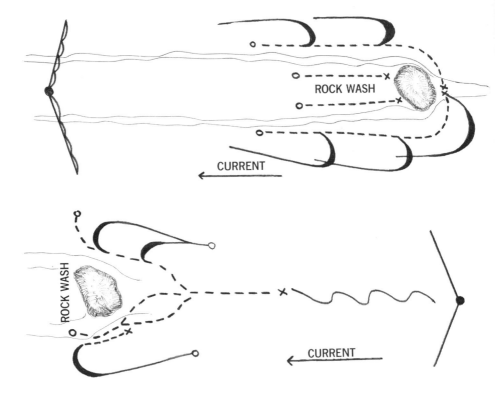

Figure 7. Rock Wash Current.

A. *The angler is situated about fifty feet below the rock and his objective is to work both sides of the wash, landing his fly first above the rock to let it drift down in as natural a manner as possible. The cast to the left of the rock and above it is made with the right-hand curve cast as described in the Appendix. The fly drifts down with the wash, but the line is about to drag the fly under, so you throw a loop of line by a modified rollcast forward at the first point in the drift as indicated in the diagram. When the fly drifts below on this slack, you throw another additional bit of line and fish the fly down until it is absorbed and then retrieved.*

The same general technique is used on the right-hand side of the rock. The casts in the middle of the rock and below it are made in the usual directly upstream manner. Due to the bubbles and fractions of light on the surface of the water, the drifting line is of less trouble and carries with it less chance of scaring the trout. It would be impossible to throw a loop here as the washes would carry it away too quickly anyway.

B. *Now we see the angler fishing the rock from the upstream position and he makes a short cast with a slack line so that the fly drifts down to and alongside the rock. To extend the drift beyond the first layout of the line, a loop of line is rolled ahead of the fly and slightly to the side and it is absorbed in the natural drift. Done in this manner, the rock can be fished several times without any disturbance, and the pickup or retrieve can be made well out from the fishing area. Watch the next ten anglers you see work this type of problem. Most of them will muff it completely. That's why there are always some good trout there! The dead-drift method as described is a real killer with nymphs that are weighted. You can drift them as far as necessary and they will be traveling underwater. Then you raise them up by merely tightening the line.*

CODE

fly lights X

pickup o

drift ----

CHAPTER 2

Two Center Rocks

HERE we have a situation similar to that of the preceding chapter, but infinitely more complicated as far as actual fly delivery and presentation are concerned. As we stand on the shore near position 1, we can see that to make a natural drift will be quite a trick, faced as we are with unwadable deep water in front of us; current which will whisk the leader and fly from its objective unless we can figure a way to beat it.

The temperature today is about 50 degrees and should reach 65 or even 70 by noon. The level has fallen to near normal height and flow. The water is clear. Ashore on a nearby lawn magnolias are in full bloom, a sure sign that the popular and quite heavy Hendrickson hatch is due. The day is quiet, with a mild spring breeze ruffling the water once in a while. Billowy white clouds are overhead, many songbirds migrating northward flit about in the willows along the stream. The warm sun gently toasts the back of the neck as we set out for position 1. Even if we don't catch a trout, it is the kind of day that makes one feel that it is good to be alive.

The Hendrickson nymph is abundant in this stream and the wet-fly version or my own pattern, originally tied by Ed Sens, is sure medicine. This insect drifts in the current sometimes for several miles after it leaves the bottom of the stream, bent on hatching that day (see Appendix, page 320), so we decide to rig up with two of these nymphs on a long fine leader tapered to 4X. Since the nymph is a drifter and so completely helpless in the water, our presentation will approximate this as nearly as possible. Later, if the sun warms the water sufficiently, we'll have a good hatch and work this water over generously with the dry fly.

Before approaching the rock, we'll try to affect the drift in the stretch below position 1. We have a long drift to 3 in which to work. Wade quietly with me, stand by my side facing downstream, and on the first "cast" merely drop the flies in the water about fifteen feet away with five feet of slack as we did in the previous chapter. This is the simplest way to fish for trout and sometimes the most effective. In this situation, we will develop skill in drifting the fly in mid-water and cause it to rise to the surface to dawdle a bit before the recast, imitating the rising and hatching nymph. The first cast then lands about fifteen feet downstream and we feed out the slack from our rod tip as it is pointed directly downstream toward the line. Only our trigger finger is employed on the line from the first guide to trigger the strike. Contact here is direct with the fly despite the fact of its uncontrolled drift. We feed out the line now, as the pull of the current dictates. After letting it down about ten feet, we snub the feed line, raise the rod tip slightly, and watch the lower, drifting line reappear on the surface. We see the knot at the top of the leader appear. Finally, the fly swings back and forth right on the surface. Its action has been one of the natural rise of the insect, and on that rise the trout usually strike.

In order to vary the technique and work the same water, we cast the next try slightly out toward the rock so that the lure drifts into the center of the fast run, but we are careful not to allow the current to grab the line and whisk the fly from its course. We can work down as far as forty feet this way, and even fifty, since it is all controlled drift.

Now, to the rock. Still in position 1, we try a direct cast across stream similar to the one described in the preceding chapter and work the near side and lower side of the rock and its wash. Our casts from position 2 are apparent as are those from position 3. Position 4 calls for the right- and left-hand casts upstream for the dry-fly drift.

The real excitement is ahead of us as we cross over to position 5. If we can handle this properly, we can not only bring up some good trout but can fish the problem almost endlessly right through the day. It is a veritable fish market during the twilight hours when the shadows begin to lengthen and spread their protective darkness over the twin rocks.

As we glance out into the water, we can see the bottom plainly since the sun is directly at our back. The Hendrickson nymphs are drifting on the top just under the surface film and several trout are surfacing in their rush to feed on the succulent nymphs. Their actions, with occasional rises, give away their feeding positions, so we just stand where we are for a moment and take in the scene. There are three trout in the dark strip between the rock washes. There is a short rise followed by a tail-flipping splash on our side of B. Several good surface disturbances are also being made quite constantly along the deep side of the central rock wash. All this gives us a choice. We can first work the rises in the center strip with our two nymphs, because it is not yet time to switch to the dry fly, since very few duns have been seen hatching or drifting down from above. Since we cannot wade into the water, we must rollcast the entire time from 5, since the background brush will not allow backcast room.

Our first cast to A is angled to the left-hand corner of the nearby rock, and as soon as the fly lights we rollcast an additional bit of line upstream of it for the drift. Holding the rod high, we follow the line down the center of the run toward 4. This cast can be made several times, since the shallow area seemingly contains no fish at the moment, the trout having left here for the food-carrying currents.

After working the center run between the rocks quite a few times, we lengthen the rollcast and head for the left side of the near rock and work the outside of the wash, rolling an additional curve of line above the fly at least three or four times during the drift. On the good runs, we can work the water right to the edge of the pictured area.

Taking our next position at 6, right opposite the rocks, we can fish the entire area from a slightly different angle, taking the center strip first, making a short rollcast to B and then, as the fly passes the rock on the far side, allowing it to fish the run. We can also cast to a position above 4 and fish the section there to rest the area above for a few minutes. But the best is yet to come.

From 6 we make a rollcast to a spot about ten feet above A and quickly throw another roll above the spot with spare line to be absorbed in the drift toward us into the V between the rocks and to B and back to us. This one is loaded with possibilities so I suggest at least four tries. When the line reaches our feet, we roll it again and fish the center run to give the A and B section a slight rest before recasting.

Moving to position 7, we have the slight advantage of an upstream position and can also work the far side of A and drift the fly down so that the line touches the nearby rock. We retrieve with a roll and skip the fly to the lower section of the central run, all almost in the same movement. Picking our shots, we have worked the line well, with a minimum of disturbance, a witness to the fact that the fish are now breaking the water freely since the nymphs are drifting right in the surface film. The rises are very similar in their rise to the actually hatching nymph.

From position 8 we can dead-drift again, working the water from as near as we can cast to 1, drifting in an escaping-form-of-life type of retrieve to A and then letting the flies drift by below B right in front of the inshore rock—and what a potent bit of water this is!

The duns are now floating down from a hatch above and a glance into the water shows the nymphs drifting in the film. Keep your eye on them and you can see them actually popping their shucks and flying into the air, if they are lucky enough to escape the maws of trout and minnows.

The whole stream is alive as the hatch reaches its peak. Flotillas of Hendrickson duns are sailing on the water, some drifting quietly, some flexing their wings. It's time to switch to the dry fly, so we walk downstream to position 5, work in typical upstream technique, and then move to 4 and finally to 3, working up to 2 before the hatch has completely quit.

That's about four hours of fishing. We have cast carefully, quietly, and accurately and our creel of experience and trout is heavy with proof that a sound approach figured on the angles and various combinations of casting and lure presentation pays off. It is far better to fish this way, we agree, than to cast hither and yon without any idea of what is happening. In the space of four hours, we have fished with nymphs, deep down, and finally enjoyed the finest part of trouting, the dry fly.

We return to this spot in June, when the hatches are about to come off at twilight. Since there are so many flies hatching at this time of the year, usually at least four species of May flies, several caddis, and sporadic drift-ins from the nearby woods, a brace of wet flies, fished the

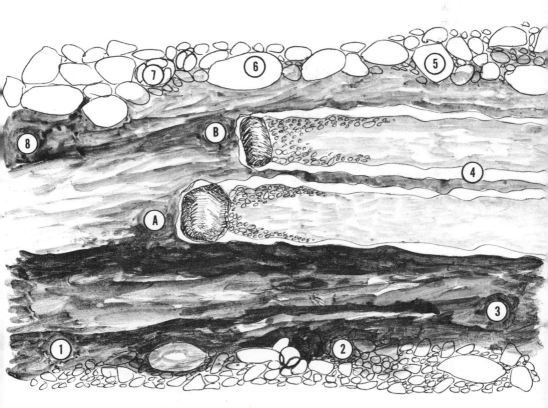

Figure 8. Two Center Rocks.

old-fashioned way, can give us a pleasant diversion from concentrated working of the specific runs.

We just enjoy casting tonight. We've a Dark Cahill and a Hendrickson wet fly on the leader and we just play around, starting in from 8 and casting with no rhyme or reason until we end up at position 1. If the spirit moves us, we can switch to the dry fly as the curtain of night begins to draw itself across the runs. Big dry flies such as the Wulff varieties are my special favorites, since they are easy to see. They imitate the stone flies, big May flies, and moths and millers that find their way to the water. Tonight we enjoy ourselves in an adlibbing mood. It's fun just to fish and cast, to enjoy the aroma of the twilight coolness, to take in the sounds of birds and wonder at the size of the trout that can be in this potent stretch. Over the years, we will return with very specific ideas and techniques and at other times merely throw casts left and right with abandon. We'll catch fish either way.

From the point of view of specific background information, nymph fishing and wet-fly fishing are closely related, as you will see as we angle over many different situations and make the selection between the two fly types and in some cases seemingly confused techniques. While wet flies are basically designed to imitate nymphs among other types of insects, the reason for the closer "nymph" imitation is that during a specific hatch the trout tend to become finicky and when feeding on one particular insect species they are more selective. I've proven this over and over again while using two flies on the leader—one a wet fly, and the other a nymph of the same general size and color. The silhouette and shape was evidently the deciding factor that made the fish select one or the other. So to meet this situation the imitation must go beyond simulation to the faithful reproduction of the nymph in size, shape, and coloration. Most of all, free action in the water is required in line with the type of nymph and its characteristics of movement when off the bottom and bent on hatching. When the rises signify a hatch, the nymphal imitation is preferred over the more general wet-fly pattern. True, wet flies do produce during these periods too, but I've come to realize that trout, like humans, can become specialists. The wet fly is generally a better producer when a hatch is not in progress or even expected, or when the hatch is long over and the dead flies or wash-in flies from the land are being swirled in the current. The wet fly is often used as a "fish finder" when no action is forthcoming, while a nymph would get no response at all.

The artificial nymph, when properly tied (see Appendix, page 316), is deadly because it represents the underwater or nymphal stage of our principal stream-bred insects, the most constant and varied all-season food readily available to the trout.

Nymph fishing, as you will see, is most productive just before a hatch since the trout follow their course as the insects leave the safety of their rocks, gravel, or mud and drift and swim in the current toward the surface film and begin their transformation into the dun, or first flying stage. That branch of trout angling rivals any other, including the much over-rated dry-fly fishing, for its demands are great; that you give the trout not only what he wants but in a way that will make it look natural to him.

In this "actual fishing" book we detail ways of fishing some very difficult water fairways. You'll often see trout rising freely, yet acute observation will show that they are not really surface-feeding. I'd been confounded by this phenomenon many times, and I remember borrowing a pair of binoculars to enable myself to scrutinize the water carefully. What those glasses revealed sold me once and for all on the sport of nymph fishing and the need to tie imitations that might not be exact to the human eye, but exact AS THEY MOVE AND APPEAR IN THE WATER TO THE TROUT.

The development of nymphal imitations started to gain a foothold in this country about thirty-five years ago when anglers began taking an interest in more "researchful" fishing. It is very unfortunate that much of the angling literature, especially from the earliest British writers, has been taken as gospel over here, for it has created much unnecessary confusion and has influenced even the present generation. English fishing techniques are innocently followed today in America where the fish and streams are so different as to make the whole idea seem like idiocy. With all due respect to those thorough British writers and especially to my friend, the late G. E. M. Skues, whose major work was *Minor Tactics on a Trout Stream*, we must eliminate theories not based on localized conditions, and most of all, we must become beatniks to traditions and dogma to pierce the unknown with our own being, senses, and tools and learn the basics of American trout and American streams. We must not attempt to fight the Indians the way General Burgoyne did and become inoperative.

As is the case in exact imitation in dry flies, only a small percentage of the thousands of insects found in or along the stream are of serious consequence to the angler. To be able to recognize these and know their habits is for all practical purposes sufficient. With this knowledge the angler can take just a few minutes before the first cast or during a lull to examine the specimens from the stream, match the artificial to them, and confidently proceed to fish.

At first glance one would imagine this to be all-conclusive, leaving no loopholes; that to proceed to fish this way would lead to limit catches every time. I do not wish to convey this impression, however. Nature has a bag of tricks well designed for the protection of her creations.

There is, however, one constant on which we can depend: the development cycle of a basic few types of stream-bred insects throughout a given season on a given stream. Though the weather may play tricks, the cycle proceeds close to schedule and the angler can join in at any point and detect the nymphal species active or potentially so. This will be a great help in deciding what fly, where, and how to fish it.

There are four distinct types of May-fly nymphs classed according to their physical build and habits. They are burrowers, like the Green Drake, for example; the clamberers, like the Hendrickson; the clingers, like the Quill Gordon; and the swimmers, like the Leadwing Coachman.

The clinging nymphs are found mainly in and around the rocks of the stream, on the underside and protected sides, in the sheltered ledges and the shady and downstream side of refuse, old stumps, and whatnot. These little flies are equipped with powerful and wide legs and strong claws and in some species there are suction discs on the abdomen to help them hold to the rocks. Their bodies are generally thin and flat, shorter and more bulky than those of the clamberers. They are largely inaccessible at this stage except where the trout can root around the rocks and grab at the unwary ones. About the only time they are available before their drift to emergence is when the rocks are rolled or dislodged by sudden spring freshets. This is one reason why nymph fishing and sunken wet-fly fishing is excellent during the early season of high waters and just before the insects actually hatch.

When the clingers are about to hatch, they leave the shelter of the dark rock crevices and undersides to drift in the current, staying close to the bottom. When this "downstream migration" is taking place the drifting insects avoid the faster currents of the surface. Sharp observance will point out the quiet, still waters and even reverse currents beneath the fast, bubbly surface—comfortable places where the trout lie in wait for the insects to come downstream to them. These are the important places to fish, such as the areas behind the rocks and directly in the slipstream in front of them on the current side.

At the time of emergence the clingers drift up toward the top in much the same manner as the clamberers. They, too, are unable to swim in the true sense, but kick their way as they rise. They emerge from the nymphal shuck usually below or right beside a rapids or rock wash, attracting the attention of any trout in the area. Bulges and swirls of actively feeding trout will tip off the action.

The duns will appear just to the side of the swift water and drift into the quieter sections to clumsily take off into the air. The spinner transformation then follows in the afternoon or evening and wet-fly fishing, using a dappling technique, can be most effective in this type of stream situation.

CHAPTER 3

Three Center Rocks

WITH the experience of working the one- and two-rock setup, this impressive bit of water doesn't look so difficult, yet there are subtleties which if recognized will render many more possibilities for connecting with some really good trout. The whole point here is to concentrate on specific runs and presentation which will allow the fly to do its work without having the line disturb the water for future tries.

Our time to fish this for the purposes of executing some dry-fly tricks is the second week in June. From our notebook of past experience, we know the Light Cahill fly (see Appendix, page 323) hatches in the late afternoon and into the twilight—sometimes in droves. Like the March Brown and the Quill Gordon, this fly in its nymphal form lives in the fast aereated water—the heads of pools or around midstream rocks, such as we have before us as we enter the arena at 1. This evening we'll extend our short-line fishing to give you the opportunity of spot casting at distances up to fifty or sixty feet with a single dry fly, the Light Cahill on a number 14 hook. The fly is sparsely dressed for the high riding that is necessary in such bubbly water. I also tie this pattern for deeper riding on quiet water, but we'll fish that type in another chapter.

As we look out over the stream we see that a few of the Light Cahills are hatching, but still not action from other than dace minnows and other bait fish. We can learn a great deal from watching this insect in its emergence. In some cases, such as the Hendrickson and Green Drake, the insect usually makes a clean getaway from its shuck. In the case of the Quill Gordon, March Brown, and Light Cahill, the insect seems to struggle a bit on the surface before taking off secure on the wind and away from the danger of becoming food for trout. Note that the insect flutters on the surface bouncing into the air, dropping back, fluttering

24

on the surface, taking off again, and finally getting its flight pattern established. All this activity lends itself to dramatic trout-feeding action as we will see in a few minutes when the trout turn from feeding under the surface film to taking the floating insects from the surface. Right now, if you will look closely, you can see the trout rolling to the rising nymphs about a foot below the surface. See those swirls on the surface? They are not the rises of trout to emerged flies, but are the follow-through motions of the trout feeding underwater. They will change shortly and you'll see actual surface rises as the nymphs begin to cast their shucks.

But to get us started on the actual technique of fishing the three rocks let's unlimber the dry-fly rod and the weight-forward line. Our leader is twelve feet long, tapered to 5X for extra-fine fishing. We'll not be able horse the fish or strike too hard with this rig, so we are in for some excitement if we can connect with even medium-sized trout.

From position 1 the most obvious first cast is to 8, you might say. But, now, take another look. Always make it a practice to work the area nearest you first without disturbing the area for future casting. If you were to make that cast first, you'd be drifting the line near B and A and the two potent runs. Your fly would then be skirting across the water and the line would be slapping unmercifully. All but the most bold of the trout would be put down.

So, instead, let's turn downstream in the direction of 2 and merely drop our fly in the run and let it drift to the extreme, rollcast the pickup and try a couple of more casts before heading for a spot just above A to place the fly there and allow it to slide in the current along the near side of the rock. Once around the curve, we roll a spare length of line in a curve above the fly so that the bellying line will not precede it down the run. We can drift it now to a point near 2, let it swing across the current to be retrieved, and the water will still be virgin. The next try would be to a spot some ten or even fifteen feet above A, allowing the fly to drift right to A and decide for itself which way it will slide by the rock. If it goes to the far side into the double wash, then a forward roll of about a three-foot length of line will be in order to ensure a drag-free drift for about ten feet. You'll have to roll the line over the rock or else it will become caught up.

Nice spot to hoop a lunker!

And that's just where you'll find one, so try the cast a few times.

Now, let's make that same cast again from 1 but slightly farther out toward B, so that the fly will course by the near edge of rock B and down that same center washline. Let's rollcast and make a partial pickup cast in order to bounce the fly to A and then let it drift down the near side of the rock for another try there. Nice bit of rod handling and manipulation? Yes, and that water has hardly been scratched. We haven't moved from our good position 1 and we've worked carefully over half of the stream section and over potentially hot trout in the first stages of the hatch.

Now we can try that first idea, the cast to 8 and the drift right over the area where several trout have been busting the surface. Now look. There are quite a number of Light Cahills on the water fluttering for their ascent into the air. Place that fly near 8—quickly. Throw a slight curve of line in an upstream mend so that the line will not precede the fly in the downstream drift and allow it to be guided right into the center wash—right by the rock again. There must be a trout in there as long as your arm!

Try it again, but to rest the run, throw extra line so that the fly will head for B, and now roll and retrieve the fly almost to the pickup stage and flip it forward to drift on the far side of the center rock. Hold your rod high, roll again forward and the fly will head down the far wash toward 4. Before it gets there, stop it. Don't disturb all that water in between with a slapping, drifting line. You'd have lost control anyway even if a trout were to hit the fly from this position.

Now, you can do the conventional thing. Cast as you go to place the fly just behind rock A and move to position 2. From here you can perform the usual dry-fly cast upstream and across, drifting the fly right down to your position.

From here on it's easy. The spots where the biggest trout are rising are quite obvious. Look closely. The fish are making two types of rise: the gentle, where you merely see the quietly floating fly disappear from the surface and the rainbow-like curl on the surface, to a fluttering fly in the bubbles. From 3 you work both sides of rock A, the wash between rock A and rock B, and the wash in position 4.

It is shallow at 3 and you are able to wade upstream, casting to both sides and drifting in conventional manner until you reach 4. A tricky one to start with now is the target area on the left side of rock B and the drift down the left wash. To perform this, you throw a left-hand bend to position the fly and then roll in a right-hand bend to remove the line from the drift. Try that one a few times. It is not easy but well worth the trouble here so that the fly will then be in position for a mend to the left, and with your rod held high you may be able to manage a drift over to the left side of rock A. It's a real pro who can manage that one with skill. Remember, that area has not been touched since you first started an hour ago. There are some nice rises there at the moment.

Now, staying right where you are, work the left and right sides of rock B and the left side of rock C, a comparatively easy routine.

Now work that deep run to the right of rock C. There's the main current of the entire river and flies are drifting now in profusion right in

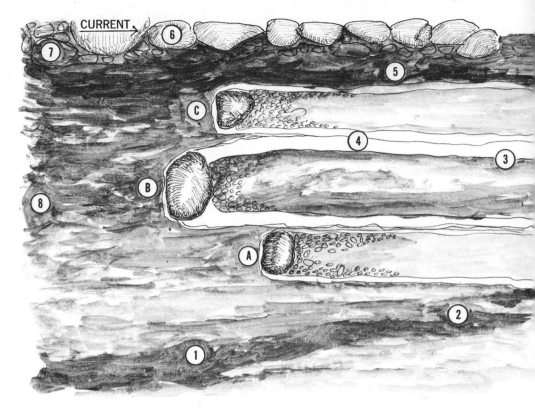

Figure 9. Three Center Rocks.

the center of the run. From 5 use the left- and right-hand curve cast as described in the last chapters and gradually wade up to a position where you can work the rocks at 6 without throwing too long a cast with resultant impractical slack line. Don't fall for the performance urge. Make your casts short and wade up rather than reach too far upstream.

From 6 you have virtually what you had at 1, and from 7 the roll downstream with the dry fly, or merely a short flip cast and extended drift right to the lips of the rocks.

Along about this same time of the season, the Little Marryat or Pale Evening Dun is on the water (see Appendix, page 324).

This is strictly very-small-fly fishing. The nymph is barely a quarter of an inch long, and the emerged dun, likewise, yet the trout go for this insect like kids for a bar of candy. The only specimens of the nymph I have ever taken have come from trout gullets, because while drifting in the water they are difficult if not impossible to see in the late-evening light or to catch even in a fine screen.

The Little Marryat emerges along with the Light Cahill and I've seen trout that were stuffed to the gills with these tiny insects, proving that upon occasions the trout prefer them to the bigger Cahills and other insects such as the caddis, either of which might be equally available and plentiful in the same run of water and at the same instant. The trout's preference to this pale little dainty fly will be especially evident when the water has been very warm during the day and the fish have congregated in the fast water that is pocketed and aerated at the head of pools and in and around midstream rocks and ledge drop-offs.

Though I carry the dry-fly imitation I find it very difficult to follow in the semi-darkness while fishing the fast broken water and prefer to work the nymph downstream, using a short line, allowing the fly to drift close to the surface and giving the rocks and little current runs particular attention. Another good spot is along the stream edges where the current swirls and slashes under an overhang, for quite often a surprise strike will come from water of this fast type that is only a foot or so deep.

The upper reaches of the feeder streams leading to our larger-trout waters seem to have an abundance of these hatches and it is quite often that the main stream finds them in great numbers even though the hatch appeared some distance from the main course.

If the water is not too deep you can wade into position 8, but I'd reserve that one for later on, after the hatch, when it would put you in good position for working a big bucktail fly to entice the large trout that come out in the early night to forage for eatin'-size meals.

There are two schools of thought when it comes to fishing the bucktail. There is the dead-drift theory, where the fly is handled similarly to the drifting Atlantic salmon fly and then there is the escaping-form-of-life technique involving all sorts of erratic movements, jerks, and quick, flashy movements of the fly. Since both, and the variations in between, seem to catch trout, let's try a bit of each in a specific situation. We'll learn how to manipulate this very deadly fly under all circumstances (see Appendix, page 309).

Our three rocks and their environment offer a grand laboratory for experiment.

I would suggest you duplicate my rig, that of a stiff-tipped rod, heavy butt leader, tapered only to 2X. The reason why it should not be tapered to a finer tip will become apparent in a moment. First of all, we are after big fish. We want to make fairly long casts and be able to absolutely control the drift of the fly. What is more important, we want to be able to make the fly move and react quickly to the rod motion and hand tension on the line as we activate it in its runs through the water. A light, long leader or a soft-tipped rod would not offer us what we need.

Our bucktail need not be a large one, despite the heaviness of the

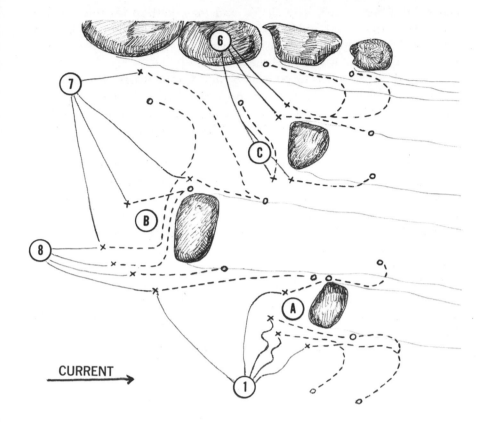

Figure 10. Typical Casting Targets.

Shown here are some typical casting targets and the planned retrieves from various stations at the head of the rocks. Note that fully half the time the fly is in the water it is dead drifting. At the beginning of the action retrieve, the fly is jerked in zigzag motion if the current is fast, or pulled upwards and dropped down quickly to accentuate the movement that imitates a wounded minnow thrashing toward the surface. Using the weighted bucktail makes this type of action easier to create. The stiff-rod tip, the stiff leader plus the additional tugging with the free line as it comes from the first guide makes sure that the action you are trying to impart actually gets to the fly. More often than not, the soft-tip rod, the thin leader, and lack of line twitching minimize the actual movement the fly receives so that whatever slight action does reach the fly under these conditions is bound to be largely ineffective.

Code
   fly lights X
   pickup o
   drift and retrieve _ _ _ _
   cast line ⌒⌒

leader. I'd choose a 10X long shank, and for a pattern for this evening fishing I'd select a red and white bucktail with a silver body. It need not be weighted, although our fishing over this very same stretch in the morning will require a weighted one.

So armed, we go forth to position 7 and try our wares. The diagram (figure 10) on page 29 is easier to understand than a lot of words, so study it for a moment and see the variations that can be accomplished in light of the experience we have just had in recognizing the problems of the layout of rocks and currents and the ways to handle our line.

A good sleep behind us and we are back on the water in the early morning. The deep current will be our working area starting from 7 and down to 5. We will proceed to 1 and then try, if the water is not too deep, to take up the position at 8. Each cast is made short below us and we allow the bucktail to sink down in the current. About every five feet we raise it up from the deep and skitter it on the surface—let it sink again and up to the surface, drawing with it the attention of the trout.

What's the reason for the weighted bucktail now rather than at night? Remember that last night the trout were already active, feeding on the Cahill hatch. Today, perhaps after a good midnight snack, they are down deep. Certainly a sharp eye can check this fact. The only way, then, to rouse them is to get right down to their level and entice them up. They usually hit when the fly is skittered on the surface. Obviously they saw it on their own level before and followed it up. When it looked as if the minnow was going to escape, or they decided that it was wounded, they pounced.

Look at that rise—smack! There's nothing like the hit of a big trout to a fast-working bucktail when the action takes place on the surface!

CHAPTER 4

Deep Center Current

DRAB-LOOKING is this water, and entirely unimaginative. Most anglers would bypass it, or, at best, merely scan the water by making casts while they are walking to the next pool or inviting bit of water. Yet this type of problem, if handled properly, can and does yield many good fish at practically any season of the year, any time of the day.

Fishing it properly, however, is another story, so let's rig up, this time with a couple of small wet flies—or small nymphs, if you prefer.

Conditions? Midseason: nothing much happening; not even a rise other than the small rings made by chubs. No hatch. The sun is bright, the water clear. Everybody else is either fishing the pool above or they have gone in for lunch. We are going to catch a nice trout for our late lunch!

A short line is called for as we begin, for we are not going to try to cover the entire seventy-five-foot stream from one position—like most anglers would attempt to do. We'll fish it carefully, remembering that the most important thing is to present our drifting wet flies as naturally as possible to the trout.

Where are the fish? Look closely. They are all in the deepest part of the run. Some are flashing on the bottom, uprooting caddis larvae and other nymphs that live on the bottom. It's logical, then, that some of the fish are on the feed, and that the flies must get down to them, though not necessarily right to the bottom.

Our biggest problem in delivery is that we must cast over slow-moving water and keep the flies moving right in the deep, fast stretch. The action of the current is exactly opposite from our intention. The water fans out and toward us from the very center as indicated on the illustration by the herringbone stripe markings.

Figure 11. Cross-Section View of Water.

This is the cross section of this type of water. Note that the trout will often nurse the bottom of the stream during the off-periods when there are not hatches or drifting insects to draw them up. Rocks on the bottom offer the trout resting places where they do not have to constantly fan their fins. It is an easy trip to the top when something lifelike comes along on the current. In the evening, especially during the summer months and conversely in the very high waters of early spring, the trout will feed right up against the bank into the willows. That's where the wash-in worms, grubs, and whatnot come from.

If you wade the center of the stream, you disperse the trout in all directions. Don't wade there at all. Fish from the side and learn to handle your lines and drifts as described.

Now, at 1 we cast in the direction of 5, allowing the flies to light in midcenter. We hold the rod high immediately and roll forward a couple of feet of slack line upstream of the flies. As they drift down, we follow them with the rod tip, keeping in touch with the line. We allow no slack, yet do not restrict the drift of the flies. As they reach a point well below, say about thirty feet, we snub our line, flip the rod tip up and back, and skitter the flies on the surface, letting the current drag them toward the shore at about 2. We retrieve in the waste water and try again, starting the flies out a bit downstream and allowing a longer drift before activating and retrieving.

Now comes the tough problem—that of working the far side of the deep stretch from our position. We must cast the flies over the fast, deep center. The bulk of our line, however, will land in the deep current and will whisk the flies away from their path almost before we can get in any drift at all.

So, we solve this by making a long cast and actually overshooting the fringe of the far side of the current. Once the flies have landed, we pull them back to the fringe and roll the surplus in an upstream mend. The rod is immediately held high and any slack is kept to a minimum by our rod hand. As the rig floats down, we point the rod in its direction, keeping our line hand alert to snub any rise that might be forthcoming. The fan-out of the current aids us now and takes the flies toward the far shore in the current's natural flow.

Repeat this process with at least ten good casts between positions 1 and 2. Here, we will invest in some upstream wet-fly fishing. We cast into the center of the current opposite 1 and retrieve the slack as it comes down to us, rollcasting forward and then beginning our pickup. We NEVER drag-retrieve in the conventional manner, since such line disturbance is death under clear-water or low-water conditions. A good lay for a cast is directly across from our position and here we can experiment with the surface dappling and zigzag bucktail-type of retrieve. This sometimes will activate the fish on the bottom, particularly if there is a hatch in prospect.

Now, for a change of action, we'll work this water with the dry fly. No hatching insects; not a rise from any fish in the stretch. But any angler who has fished trout for several years knows that quite often, especially on this type of water where the trout are almost always headed upstream and generally easily triggered, a dry fly will draw them up.

Since the light is coming from the direction of 3, we'll take up that position so that we can see into the water and better spot our artificial as is graces the currents. Several trout are flashing on or near the bottom and we'll try for them. Adhering to our principle of working the nearest water first, we cast to the fringe of the deep water, throwing a right-hand bend in the line so that the drifting line will not precede the fly.

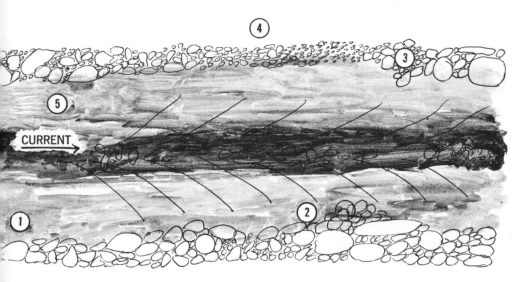

Figure 12. Straight Center Current.

As slack develops, we throw it upstream of the fly using the same bend technique. As the fly begins to be drawn out into the shallow water we rollcast and then pickup to eliminate any unnecessary line disturbance and recast a bit farther upstream.

Our next try is sighted for the center of the run, with the fly planned to drift toward the other shore. As it does, we again roll a bend well upstream from it and allow a good long drift of about ten feet. Our retrieve, as usual, is the roll and quick backcast as the leader catches up with the fly.

How often have you ever seen such rod handling and line manipulation?

Not very often.

Yet, we have not disturbed the water. Light a cigarette and look again. Those fish are still flashing right under the very place you have been fishing.

Since we have had no action from a typical and seasonal dry fly, let's try a trick that might catch us an unwary trout. Whenever I get really anxious to bring home a good one, I resort to the most outlandish creation yet devised to snare trout—the Royal Coachman. It doesn't look like any natural insect on the trout stream, yet the fish seem to go for it when all else fails.

We'll pick a nice, plump fanwing. That ought to raise some action. The sunlight will flash on the wings of the beast and the slight breeze will activate it on the surface—what else can they possibly want?

So, out it goes right up the middle. Watch that drift. In a second I'll throw an upstream bend. Wham! Missed!

Another cast quickly. Ah, that's it. Only a little fellow, but enough proof that the Royal does it when all else fails—sometimes!

Bucktail water?

Yes.

Now, you can really get in some exercise on this next treatment. Let's fish it when the water is high and cold—like on a day soon after the opening of the season. Theory has it that trout stay close to the bottom in cold water and feed little, or at least are not yet active on or near the surface.

Rubbish!

Here's the medicine that will take trout, and more important, raise the brows of the heretics.

Make your cast high and long—right across the fast center current. Don't let that fly stay still an instant. Retrieve it just as fast as you possibly can and let it make a good disturbance in the process. Use a heavily dressed fly so that the fuss on the water is noticeable. Save the sparsely dressed one for later on. Jerk that fly—flip it back over the water it has just been dragged through. Work the dickens out of that center current.

But watch your step. A strike to that fast-moving fly will hit like a ton of bricks, so have spare line handy. Big rainbows move through this type of water in the spring, and if your stream harbors them this technique will rouse them, no matter how cold the water.

Bucktailing in the evening?

Just the reverse. Take this stretch in late July when the stone flies are hatching. Your small, sparse bucktail will imitate them as well as the dace minnows. Work directly up or down stream, leaving the center of the current alone until well after dark. The trout will be nosing the shallows and looking for minnows and stone flies about to hatch in the shallows. Work quietly and with a short line. Wade carefully upstream rather than down so that your footsteps and wake will not drive the fish into the center and thus take their minds off their business.

One last word before we go in for a warm lunch. Notice that we have hardly entered the water in this situation. Watch the area when other anglers are working it. Know where they'll be wading? Right up the center, driving the trout well up or down from them, but beyond any interest in their flies. That's good . . . it means that within an hour, you'll have the chance to fish the water properly.

I never fish this type of water, particularly in the early spring, without carrying my streamer fly book along in my jacket pocket. It gives me a feeling of security, for I know that I can always depend on either a streamer or a bucktail for a lunch-sized trout. The collection houses a veritable spectrum of color—brilliant reds, greens, pastel blues, yellows, silver, and gold. It is very pleasant to contemplate using these gay fellows, for they offer a welcome contrast to the more somber patterns of the nymphs and dry flies.

The manner of fishing the streamer has its special attraction too, for the technique used is unlike that of casting dainty number 12's and 14's. Because of this the stream, particularly the one pictured in this chapter, seems to acquire a new mood; it appears and feels different when a Mickey Finn or a Parmachene Belle is on the end of a stout leader. There is the ever-present expectation of a hefty strike that has its appeal in this type of fishing.

You'll see, from our actual experiences to come, that it is much more than rumor that big trout are taken on streamers and many a whopper that has found itself mounted on some angler's den wall or in the dining room of a sporting camp fell victim to this ruse. Yes, there is a very broad and practical use for the streamer fly in trout angling, whether it be in lake or stream fishing. It is the uninitiated angler who believes that streamer fly fishing for trout is any less scientific than other forms.

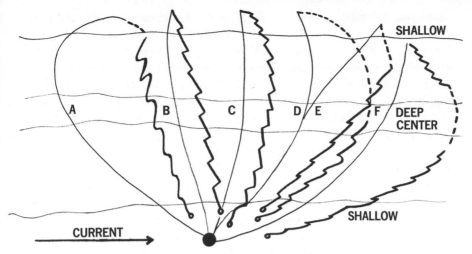

Figure 13. Bucktail Retrieves.

Here are six retrieves to practice. When mastered and used at the right time they can take trout right out from all the other anglers on the water.

A is made upstream with a slight right bend. The fly is allowed to drift only briefly and then is retrieved without jerks but in a curved course just under the surface. This is good when there is a wind blowing.

B is much the same in direction but the cast is more erratic and with sharp jerks and quick stops as the current carries the fly downstream.

C is the usual across-stream cast but retrieved VERY FAST and literally dragged along the surface in an almost steady course. This is a good one in the spring for big rainbows.

D and E are both drift-and-under-surface retrieves with speed that can vary.

F is on the downward course of the current and the retrieve is a jerky one, good when in the mood for almost direct downstream angling. It is a preferred way to work over shallow broken water.

When it is realized that almost all trout streams and lakes contain bait fish on which the larger trout feed, the killing qualities of the streamer fly, properly presented, will be recognized.

Big trout obtain most of their food from beneath the surface, and therefore the streamer fly can be fished in a stream or lake any time when the trout are not actively feeding on a surface insect hatch. Many devotees of wet-fly and nymph fishing know from experience that there are periodic "dead spots" between fly hatches and dead spots during the hours of daylight and so rely on the streamer rather than resort to bait or spinners.

As we discover the subtleties of the currents, fishing as we do with all kinds of flies, certain feed lanes are havens for trout.

Streamer fly fishing was first popular in this country in the state of Maine, where it was proven effective in the lake regions and wilderness streams on landlocked salmon and brook trout. These flies were tied to represent the small smelt and minnows upon which the trout feed.

The conventional streamer fly is tied in two distinct types, feather streamer and bucktail. The feather streamer consists basically of long rooster hackle feathers tied parallel to the top of the hook shank extending to or slightly beyond the hook bend.

The bucktail streamer is tied of bucktail hairs, or, for that matter, doe hairs or any combination of animal hair that lends itself to attractive action in the water. The material is tied on a long-shanked hook.

Both types are called streamers because of their streaming, undulating appearance in the water, an attempt to imitate the varied colors and actions of minnows and small bait fish (see Appendix, page 326). Most modern anglers concede that the exact imitation *per se* means less in streamer fishing than in wet-fly, nymph, or dry-fly fishing. The only exception in my books is the dace minnow, a bait fish that is common in most Eastern trout streams where cold water and fast runs are the rule (see Appendix, page 326). I like them tied sparse, in any pattern, the only exception to this being the weighted flies cast to rainbows in the deep, fast runs of early-season swollen streams. The other exception, of course, is the Marabou.

Figure 14. Marabou Fly—Dry, Wet.

Fast, active surface-disturbing retrieve with bulky dressed bucktail. (A fluffy and full Marabou, brown and black, would also be good medicine.)
   A—*fly when dry.*
   B—*fly when wet.*

But, we've lots of streamer fishing ahead of us, so let's proceed to the next section of stream. We'll work a favored bucktail on this enticing water.

CHAPTER 5

Curved Center Current

SEEN from above as it is in figure 15, the setup and perhaps even the procedure looks simple. Yet the subtleties built in tricky bits of water and current are there and must be mastered if we are to hold to our creed of working the water properly.

Note that the stream is, for our purposes, about fifty feet wide with a deep center current not unlike the straight stretch of the preceding chapter. The curve, however, makes all the difference in the world. It is a pretty problem to keep a dry fly acting properly on such water, and, since we've mentioned the floater, let's set out from position 1 and see just how we'll drift our artificial.

We are fishing in the late afternoon of a June day. The stream is lower than normal, the water clear. No hatches are in evidence, although as we approached through the alders and willows, many May flies were on the streamside branches in the stage of casting their dun skins. This promises a good flight of egg-laying spinners for the evening. The fly is the Leadwing Coachman (see Appendix, page 325), and as the water cools and the shadows gather, the spinners or adults will be flying over the water causing, we hope, a good rise and some excellent dry-fly fishing.

I've always liked this particular two hundred feet of water. It is on one of my favorite streams in New York State. It has skunked me many times but there have been a few instances where I've connected with some really big trout. Let's hope we can perform well for you, or, better, that you snag a big one.

Casting from 1, we'll attempt to work the underwater rocks that cause the current to swing wide from 2. Now cast out to the far side of the deep run, allow the current to pull out an additional ten feet of line, which will place the fly in the center of the current bend. By the time the flies arrive there, they will have sunk at least a foot. We can now begin a retrieve right across the front of the nearby rocks off 2, where I have taken trout before. This is good for at least three tries and if we don't pull a rise, we work the same cast but retrieve the flies downstream from the position 2 rocks. Our next venture is to place the fly directly across the stream almost to the water's edge below 7 and, holding the rod high and throwing an upstream mend, allow the flies to drift in the outer side of the deep run as far as the lip of rocks off 6. The retrieve from here is to the rocks off 2 and pick up.

Would you have fished the water in this fashion? We have worked the hot spot easily and economically. No need to wade and ruin the water.

From position 2 we can switch to the bucktail just for the practice and make our first cast into the bend downstream off 3 and, by rolling a left-hand bend, flip the fly into the deep and effect a sharp and quick surface retrieve right across the deep stretch where trout are lying way down. Our next cast is to the edge of the fast water at 6 with a drift across the jutting underwater rocks and a bellying retrieve across the fast water. An upstream shot in the direction of 7 is the next easy one with a directly across-stream retrieve. Sounds simple, but how often do anglers wade the deep and scare the trout rather than look the water over first and then see the obvious way to play the game?

You have probably noted that the deepest and best spots for trout

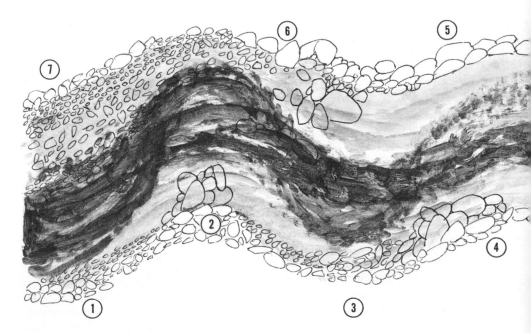

Figure 15. Curved Center Current.

to lie is in the bellies of these curves: upstream from 2 off 6 and between 3 and 4. The center strip of course holds fish when they are feeding, since there is little holding water out there in midcurrent and few if any rocks to hide behind. No matter what lure or what depth, these hot spots are the ones to concentrate on.

If you were fishing this water in the early spring, you would tend to work the shallows, since the water would be well over the now-bare rocks and usually into the willows. Strangely enough, I have never seen anglers fish their flies in the high brush at the stream edge in high water, yet that is where the trout lie. In this case the refuse of leaves and twigs hangs on the willow stems and branches—an obvious tip-off to the feeding location of the trout. Sure, the deep water may hold them, but from the bank comes their prime food, including worms and grubs.

Let's go ashore to the willows for a moment. I've something to show you that will give you some idea of the May fly and its different stages

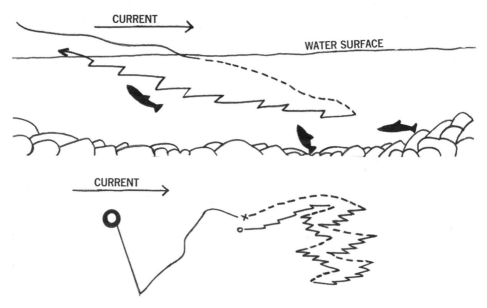

Figure 16. Cross-Section View of Typical Retrieve.

A. *This shows the cross section of the stream and the cast wet fly drifting downstream and being retrieved in short jerks back to the place of entry. Note that it is a steady jerking motion, somewhat like a small minnow or active nymph swimming in the water toward the surface.*

B. *The same cast is allowed to drift down and then in a succession of retrieves and drifts downstream a good portion of the area is worked both ways, the dead drift and the short, jerky active form. The retrieve is toward the waste water at the edge of the stream. (See Appendix for steps in making this retrieve, page 295.)*

Figure 17. Dun Transformation.

On a branch near the stream the duns (dark ones) land and begin to flex off the dun skin from their entire body and wings. This process takes almost all afternoon, and sometimes overnight. Here you see the duns in the process of changing their costume, discarding the old for the shiny new. Those in the lower right corner are the spinners riding on the surface of the stream.

of emergence. Once the May fly has hatched from the nymphal stage, it can no longer eat or feed. It flies to the nearest shade, preferably to branches and leaves near the water's edge.

Look here, on this branch. See these May flies? Look closely and you'll see that they are beginning to shed the dun skin and will soon be in what biologists call the adult or final stage. It is unfortunate, from the point of view of the angler, that biologists spend little time and offer little information on the important stage of the dun, since that is the prime food for trout after they have left their secure life on the bottom of the stream.

Here you see their undress. Tonight, at about twilight, these glassy-clear spinners will cavort and dance over the stream. They constitute the characters and cast of a dramatic ballet of the "Evening Rise," a magical hour for them, the trout, and the angler.

Instead of watching for the advanced stage of the hatch, where the insects rise up from the bottom, the invasion of the water will be noted as coming from the air. Thousands of these insects will descend from the high trees, skirt out in groups from the stream edge, and dance in their characteristic up-and-down motion. This is the mating dance and quite a sight to witness.

The imitation of the spinner is usually a very sparse dry fly. In most cases the spinners are drab of body color with cellophane-clear wings, so almost any pattern will suffice just so long as it is of the right size. The manner of fishing it becomes obvious.

So, now, with the cool of evening at hand, let's rub on a bit of insect repellant, for there are other insects active at this season that go after anglers—the no-seeums, or, in angler's terms, midges.

We approach our water from a downstream position of 5 and are armed with a stiff-action dry-fly rod, a good long leader of at least 12 feet tapered to 5X. A spinner version of the Dark Hendrickson is a good one for tonight, but let's see about size. There, on a rock, is a spinner, some half inch long in body. This calls for a size 12 sparsely dressed fly. I usually choose a multicolor fly that is wingless (see Appendix, page 319) but with a couple of turns of white at the head for better vision.

Look up into the sky. They are there now by the hundreds. See them beginning to dance high up in the sky? Now come the swallows after them; phoebes too. There's a kingbird rising out from the other side of the stream, stopping in midair to catch one and then another. Soon the bats will also join the feast.

A few of the insects are flying out over the stream now. See their up-and-down motion in a mass ballet? Soon come the creatures from the deep to add their drama as they pierce the water surface to invade the air for their evening meal: the trout, minnows, and other rough fish.

We'll wade out very quietly from 5 and throw an upstream cast toward the rocks off and below 6. The fly lights between the rocks and the deep water and drifts down. We gather the slack. The fly cocks beautifully and—bingo!—our first trout of the evening. There is a rise to a spinner

Figure 18. Dance of the May Fly.

This is the dance of the May fly of ballet fame. The up-and-down zigzag of the flies as they search out mates and join together in midair is a sight to see and one worth watching in the twilight. Later, after the brief dance, the females can be seen dipping down to the surface of the water depositing their eggs. Finally they drift, spent and dead on the water surface.

on the far side, so we direct the next cast to a spot between 2 and 3 and the fly drifts down a bit. A mend upstream with its loop allows a long drift down below 3, and just as we are about to lift for a recast, there is an explosion of water. Wow! That's a nice trout and we missed it.

Try again. Same cast to the same place. Ah, this time we connect.

The insects are now lowering their attack from high above and myriads of them are dancing up and down above the water.

The water boils. You have a question?

These flies do not feed in this stage. Therefore they must have little food value to the trout. A true statement, but the prime attraction is the eggs that they have laid. That's the food value and the actual food that the trout are seeking. They are not after the hen but the eggs.

Here. Pick one up and examine it. There's a spent spinner floating by your waders. See the egg sac at the tail of the body? That's the delicacy.

If you don't believe this, try an experiment. Take off your fly from the leader and at about five inches from the end of the tippet, tie in a square knot. Now tie one in about an inch below that one. Now one more in between there and the end, and one at the end. Now make a cast with this rig. Try it merely across stream and let it drift. See the spinners dancing right above it? You can't see what's going on but the spinners are dropping the eggs, and in many cases, they will, as you see, skuff the water surface to dislodge their cargo.

Strike! Another strike. Another. The trout were fooled by the knots —which I'm sure reminds you of the many times trout have been seen hitting the knots in your leader.

How about a cigarette on that one?

Relax now. There are so many spinners about and the run is being creased by cruising trout and busted by jumpers that a cast almost anywhere, drag or not, sloppy or not, will likely take trout. Try to keep from slapping the line on the water, and don't make the conventional drag retrieve, but remember to roll it up first and then start your backcast.

There's magic here in the evening rise and in a few minutes you'll have creeled a limit. I'll just sit by and watch the show from the gallery!

Figure 19. Shelving Riffle.

CHAPTER 6

Shelving Riffle

COME with me now to one of my favorite pools, if you could call it a pool, on a favorite Catskill trout stream. Its headwaters are born in the all-season ice atop the highest mountain in the region. From its source, the stream tumbles and crashes down the mountainside through gorges flanked with hemlock and spruce, by woodlands peppered with mountain laurel and rhododendrons, through fields and orchards along country roads until finally it slows as it flows into a large reservoir that feeds the water-hungry hordes of New York City, miles below.

Rainbows grow to a length of twenty inches or more in the reservoir, the original stock having been planted almost twenty-five years ago. Since then, no additional stocking of the species was ever necessary. Natural spawning in the wilderness-type tributary streams that never see anglers offer a haven for the spring runners, up from the ice-held lake.

Brown trout grow to enormous size in Eastern terms, and in fact they are big in any man's language, sometimes being creeled in at five pounds or more. Some brook trout drop down into the big water once in a while from their moss-lined, evergreen-shrouded spring holes high up beyond casual human interference. Small-mouth bass, sometimes in company with huge walleyes, often hole up in the headwaters of pools. I took one from the overhanging undercut bank shown in the above illustration one day not too many years ago. I've been surprised by pesky small-mouths in the deep water of that main current, especially in the closing days of the trout season. They hit dry flies like mad!

Friend, this is a good spot. There are trout in there that will make you cringe when you see them come up to a floating fly, be it your

48

creation or Mother Nature's. When you connect with one of these beauties, mark that day on your diary and remember it.

Far upstream beyond the bend where the stream goes behind those small Christmas trees is a large pool that is the end of a series of rapid drops. The river bangs between huge house-size boulders, calms itself in the deepest pool on the river, and then slides along its shallow and almost characterless way until it bends right here in front of you.

Just below the picture is another rapids of a more broken type than a waterfall, and another big pool. Anglers working their way up from the pool below usually only give this water a passing cast or two, preferring to get to the pool above as quickly as possible. That's why I like this water. I seldom find much if any company on it. About the only time anyone fishes it is when they are in the habit of working the entire stream no matter what it has to offer in pools, riffs, or runs. They almost always work it wrongly, and as a result they merely disturb the trout, not remove them. Nine times out of ten the fisherman viewing this water as you are doing here will wade right up the center of the deep, scare all the fish either way upstream or down below them. Some, of course, will scurry into the rocks on the deep side.

That's just fine.

There are times when even the most astute approach and careful presentation will yield little or not a rise even after an hour's try. The section has skunked me many times and when I reflect on it I find it almost unbelievable that this can be so—I know its moods and secrets so well.

Take a close look.

The obvious run is the deep section. In the early spring the water is well above the rocks along the shallow side and into the bushes on the right. We show it here in the late spring. It is not yet really the season. In July, half of that beach is out of water but now is filmed over with clear stream an inch or so deep right to the rocks, gradually deepening in the slithering currents until it reaches the drop-off. At this point it is about two feet deep and the ledge drops off another couple of feet to deepen further to about six at the center of the main run. The holes between those rocks on the right hold any number of good browns and once in a while a wet fly can lure out a nice little brook trout or two. The rainbows seem to stick in the center of the run unless they are seen at rare times near evening chasing minnows over the brink of the shelf. It's quite a sight to see trout boiling below the riffle and then suddenly cutting the shallow water with their dorsals, driving a school of minnows clear out of water. I've seen them race up and down that shallow like bonefish on the Bahama flats. Big trout too, make no mistake about it. On this kind of water, the trout move about a great deal due to the

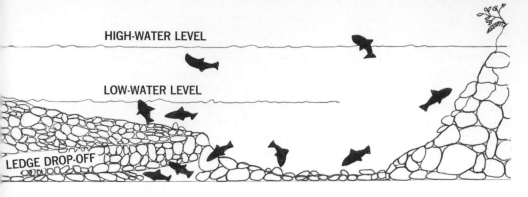

HIGH-WATER LEVEL

LOW-WATER LEVEL

LEDGE DROP-OFF

Figure 20. Cross-Section View of Shelving Riffle.

This cross-section view of the shelving riffle shows the shallow leading to the edge drop-off and the deeper bottom of the stream where the main current lies. All the water from the shelf and the main current passes through here and against the far bank with its overhang, not unlike the one described in a future chapter. At first glance the fish are everywhere, but a general rule can be laid down. During the bright light of day, the trout nurse the deepest bottom. Some do feed in the overhang and deep side of the stream edge, especially when it is in shadow. Others begin to edge up to the rim of the shelf as bits of food, and perhaps dead insects from an upstream hatch, begin to filter down. An actual hatch in this pool will come off just below the ridge of the drop-off and the trout will be seen rising right on the lip. The trout pictured on the top of the water over the deepest part are rising to drifting insects during a hatch.

variance of the light during the day, the depth of the water, the timing of the hatches.

In spring, the trout will be up in the woods on either side and bait fishermen work the brushline with success. As the water subsides, the trout gradually congregate in the deep water. There are a great many caddis larvae in that deep and as a result there are many good hatches of these insects right on the spot. As you may know, the caddis larvae do not drift in their hatching but pop up like corks once they get the message to take to the air. I've seen this water and the air alive with these insects and seen a stretch that an hour before seemed to be absolutely devoid of fish suddenly look like a hatchery pond at feeding time. The March Browns and Cahills hatch along the edge of the rip. They flutter and fuss until the big boys from the deep down below come up for their feast.

One of the best times to fish this water is in late June after a hatch has come off up in the pool above. Many of the duns will drift this far down and as they come the trout are ready for them. The mere good presentation of any typical and seasonally correct fly will bring rises even from the big rainbows—fish that seldom rise to the dry fly unless you are exceptionally careful in your wading and do not send them down from sloppy line delivery or unnecessary disturbances.

In the late season, when the shallow has become a beach, all the trout are jammed up in the main current and in the rocks at the right. They stay there all day long and seldom if ever will you lure any but the small fish to a fly. This calls for night fishing, an act of gentle art described in a future chapter.

But, now, enough observation of the potentials. Let's try for a trout.

Just to give you the lay of the water, let's fish a brace of two small bucktails—a favorite fish-finder rig I use when there is no action present or anticipated. If a caddis hatch develops or May flies begin to drift into the picture, we can quickly change if we see rises to them.

Starting from position 1, we work the center current between us and 9, just as we have worked the center current described in a previous chapter.

A cinch.

But, we have been retrieving our fly at about position 2 and have missed a potent spot for the corner-hanging trout that are there unless a passing fisherman has walked too close to the water there or, worse still, has been wading in it. That corner is a favorite holding stretch for big rainbows. So, let's sink the two flies nice and deep and bring off a rising motion of the type described for the action of a rising nymph.

Drop the flies virtually under the rod tip. Let the current carry them down and feed out the line as they go, your rod tip pointed downstream

Figure 21. Shelving Riffle.

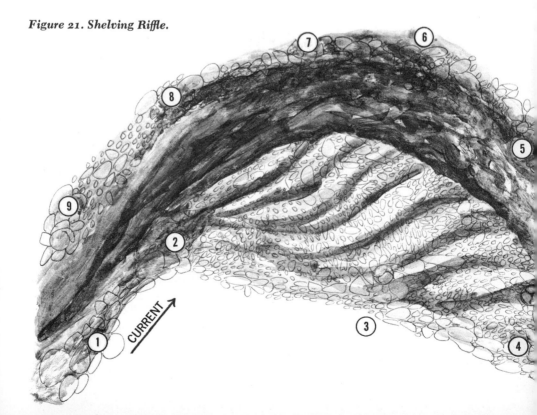

directly at the line. If they drift too far inshore, point your rod out, throw just the suggestion of a bend so that they continue to drop down just outside 2. Now, raise the rod tip, snub the free line. The flies rise right on the corner, dilly at the surface a moment and hang there swinging enticingly.

It's ten minutes later now. Isn't that a fine rainbow!

Since you had to land the fish at 2, that's as good a place as any to start in again. Let's stick to the two flies, cast them across toward 9, drift them toward 8 by means of holding the rod tip as high as you can reach, letting the flies swing in the current. Instead of sweeping across, though, drop them down with a rolled excess, drag back up, and repeat, covering the water in a broad and long zigzag. Make sure that at the beginning and end of each pause you allow the flies to slither on the surface. Oops, there's a rise, probably from a good brown. Yes! And he's hooked. Repeat that technique, moving a bit down from 2, but not too far. We don't want to disturb the fish that we will soon see are hanging under the lip of the ledge.

Now, before we leave this position for an exploratory look into the pool, let's try an upstream cast directly into the main current off 9 and allow the flies to sweep down to 8 in a completely dead drift, not unlike the type of drift used in Atlantic salmon fishing. Two small rises from little fish. Skip it for now. That water we usually reserve for the evening when hatching insects are seen drifting there from above.

While the pool seems quiet, let's leave the scene for a moment. The light is just right to see into our large aquarium from a position on a high rock behind 6. This isn't exactly fishing, but what you may learn from what you'll see will be of great value. Sometimes it is better to climb trees than to fish blindly.

Light a cigarette now that you are on your perch. Look down over the deep water toward the edge of the drop-off. See those trout? There are at least a dozen there that are flashing right against the lip. Some seem to be feeding; others just merely moving about. There are some nice ones there, aren't there?

Now, what do you suppose would happen if we were to wade in from 2 right down upon them or up from 5, even if we were careful? Sure, they'd scamper away and you'd have nothing but exercise to show for your efforts.

Now, look into the deep water right at your feet. More trout? Yes. As soon as there is a hatch or they decide to muss up the minnows that school in under the backdraft of the lower side of the ledge, we'll see some action. This usually comes off when the sun is more on the downstream side and so throws a shadow over some of the ledge.

So here we go for the most difficult line handling thus far in the book.

We are going to fish from 5, work the lower edge of the drop-off only, reserving the rest for later on.

In order to effectuate a good natural drift of the fly along that drop-off we have to place the fly on the top in the shallow. Okay, make the cast in the direction of 2, but place the fly only about five feet above the line of the drop-off. Now, quickly throw a loop of extra line upstream and to the right so that the line will not cover the area you are fishing and put the fish down or frighten them into the deep. If one is scared, he usually alerts the others. With so many trout gathered in one spot, extra care must be exercised.

Try this a few times just for the practice and the opportunity to get used to the action of the current that is coming down the deep side and that which is marrying it that is coming from the shallows. Quite a confusing bit of current to work, isn't it?

Blip! A rise and a smart tug, but you missed. Too much slack line. Try again, this time farther up the line, and throw a generous bend into the main current. Retrieve only after the flies have drifted well down and out. Do not retrieve when the line is over the deep water.

Let's move to 6 now that you have the hang of how to master the drift. Cast now from this angle still in the direction of 2 and land the fly over the ledge into the shallow. Raise the rod tip, roll a forward loop just as the fly enters the dark water. This stops it momentarily and the leader is out of water.

Wham!

You really fooled that trout and he's away into the deep water. That's a good break, for had he decided to run straight down along the edge he'd have scared the whole bunch of fish into oblivion.

Now, an easy one. Cast the flies toward 3 over the ledge, roll a mend upstream, and watch that fly course along the edge of the drop-off. I don't think you'll have to wait long for a hit.

There you go—another nice one. Bring him around to 5 and net him.

It isn't really necessary to follow you along 7 and 8 or even 9 since the routine will be quite obvious in the light of previous experiences.

Tonight will be a good time to work the dry flies, especially Light Cahills in short casts all along the deep with a once-in-a-while cast to the ledge and an appropriate drift.

But, now, quickly, a month passes. The beach is bone dry. It is late twilight or early evening, that bewitching hour that is neither one nor the other. Some tiny whitish-pinkish May flies are hatching. Several species of May-fly spinners are also about. Moths, millers, land flies are zinging about in the cool air. The swallows are dipping low to the water. Stone flies—not many, but enough—are casting their shucks from the rocks along 5, 6, 7, 8, and 9.

We begin from 2 and cast to a point upstream from 8. We are using a gray-bodied Wulff pattern of dry fly on a size 10 hook. We're after a big trout with a big fly that approximates the hatching stone and perhaps any of the land-bred insects that happen to drop into the water for a bath. Anyway, it is a good fish-finder and quite effective in the darkness, even though it is hard to follow unless it rides in a silvered reflection.

Each cast is accompanied by an upstream mend in order to extend the drift and not allow the line to precede the fly. Each cast is rolled forward on retrieve. Our long leader will not scare the fish in the middle stretch. When we see a rise in the center current below, we can shorten our casts and try for it, but a stop cast downstream drift. If the insect floating above invites a hit from a lunker upstream from us, a conventional upstream cast to him is in order. Slowly, from a path about fifteen feet from the drop-off, we cast this water, keeping our rod high so the line does not become snagged in the pebbles. We work like this all the way down to the bottom of the picture. We've kept only three of the biggest trout and go home to our room for a freshening and some liquid enticement for the body.

It's been a good day. Talking with other anglers all we hear are kicks. The water's too clear, too low, too warm. The stream is fished out—too many fishermen with spinning tackle and worms came from the big cities. Past floods have wrecked the stream. Trout fishing is doomed.

We think over our day, but make no report on it for the benefit of humanity—or even our brothers of the angle.

We'll return to that stretch of water many times before we hang up our rod for the last time. We'll catch fish there more often than not. The days that this stretch skunks us will be remembered and will be the inspiration for further sharpening of the eyes of observation and the practice of reason that is so much the delightful part of angling for trout.

As you saw from the cartoon-like illustration in our introduction of our beginner angler viewing the stream for the first time, he didn't see much within the confines of the bank. The art of observation—and the importance of it—can and will be acquired by the time you and I fish through the situations in this book. A wise old philosopher remarked one day that you cannot "do" until you can "see."

I can recall an unforgettable sample of observation that paid off for me many years ago. It really set me off to begin to look and to investigate the secrets of the currents and the mysteries of trout fishing. The occasion centered about the big brown trout of Mills Pool on a favored Eastern stream. I had never been so mad at the world. Through sheer clumsiness, I'd broken the tip of my best rod. It was bad enough to have broken it, but to make matters worse it meant that I'd have to forego the chance of taking the big brown that I'd been working over for some days and recently for a period of an hour. He was just in the mood to strike; I had seen him move toward my fly several times. I was certain that he would have taken it on my next cast.

I sat dejectedly on an old log, gloomily staring at my scowling reflection. Just out there in the current the brownie occasionally changed position to take bits of food borne by the current. As I watched intently, anger turned to interest, for here was the opportunity to observe a summer trout and his actions.

Though feeding time had long passed, the brown was not averse to sucking a nymph down below or rising to the surface if a particularly succulent insect floated by. I noted several lesser trout in the same general run, but because of his size the brownie was more distinguishable. I studied him for some time, wondering at the amount of free ranging he was doing from surface to bottom while rarely straying sideways from the current stretch. He'd eye each bit of food carefully after gliding up to it, drifting back to his former position to swallow his prey. Among other things, I learned that it is not always the choice of lure that takes fish, for here was a perfect example of a trout that seemed to sample everything, though he was not actually on a feeding spree. He took these insects because they drifted by him NATURALLY.

Another incident proved this business of planning through observation. For many years I had fished one particular pool on an Eastern stream famed for its large trout. I had taken some grand fish from that river, but I knew that there were much larger fish in the pools and runs than I had ever caught or seen caught. The pool I remember is a large, long one. The bank on the side I had never fished was steep, rock- and boulder-strewn, and brushy. Quite naturally, I had avoided that side and been content to heave long casts to the deep and broken water skirting the forbidding rocks. I'd strained every muscle, used every rod I had

Figure 22. Potent Holding Water.

Looking down on the hard-to-reach section of the stream where the big ones feed just beyond reach from the opposite bank. Note the big rocks and the current wakes from many underwater rocks. Potent holding water for the big rainbows and a monster brown or two.

CURRENT

ever owned on that effort, and more than once had waded out over the tops of my chest waders in an attempt to reach the potent runs.

One afternoon, the sight of the big 'bows and browns rising freely just beyond casting distance forced the decision to cross the stream up above and try and find a place to either cast out or wade down the good side. Finally I was able to get into the water above the area in question. I had to use both hands to hang on to rocks and stumps and brambles. Several times my footing slipped out from under me and I almost went for a bath.

At last I secured a spot from which I could cast. Looking down the run I saw several of the big fish rising and tailing on the confusing current of the water's surface. I'd have to cast short, since hemlock branches all but touched the water between me and the best fish. Somehow I managed, but only after screwing up my courage and learning from observing that almost-forbidden stretch just how to fish it.

Toward the end of the season, that same water was easier reached due to the low levels. I walked up and down the bank making a mental note of the runs and rocks. I spent the better part of that same day observing similar stretches of the river and especially areas of the big pools that had had me fooled for several seasons. Bare as it was, it revealed to me the need for study of the terrain of the bottom, the swing and sway of the currents when the water is high, and keeping your eyes open and then interpreting what you see.

Figure 23. Undercut Bank.

Undercut Bank

THIS little bit of water might be called the spot for "operation hang-up." Before we fish it, I warn that with the rig we are about to use, you may lose some flies. So be prepared. Either make more money so you can afford to buy them, or learn to tie your own. The reward, however, may be a trout big enough to mount and hang over the family mantel.

As we survey the situation we see a deeply undercut bank with its maze of overhanging foliage. Most banks are much more overhung than this one, but for artistic reasons we were more interested in showing the water and the problem than covering it up with any more twigs and snags.

Now, the reason a bank like this becomes undercut is that the direction of the strongest currents of the stream bang against it and remove all the dirt and roots necessary to clear a path downstream. Now, logic has it that since this is a strong and main current, it will also carry with it lots of food. Since the shape of the undercut, underwater, is made in a dark corner, trout will hide in it. Therefore, it behooves the smart angler to learn how to fish it properly with a minimum of hang-ups and also to make each cast count. A fly well placed and allowed to act naturally way in under there is bound to produce a rise.

A great many of the larger trout find their haven here. Those trout scared there by anglers also find a corner of safety. The rock cluster immediately out from the deep section is another good spot that we will work in a way not unlike the angles well trod in Chapters 1 and 2. The rock cluster at the tail of the overhang is another potent spot.

So, with our work laid out in front of us, let's rig up with a bucktail first. Since you have been fishing previously with a dry fly, that leader will suffice. Rather than use a heavy tippet, the light one is used here tapered to 3X, but a tippet of 4X is added, simply because if you do happen to snag you can break off the leader easily without having to disturb the water. The extra-light leader tippet will also be an advantage on the cast, as you will see in a moment.

Starting from 1, note now the extra-fast water and the broken surflike run between us and the hot spot. That will give us trouble unless we remember to keep our rod tip high on every cast in order to hold that slack line from bellying our flies away from their mission under the shadows.

To become acquainted with the beginning of the run, and also to learn how to handle a bucktail on such a light tippet, let's start our first cast from as far out from 1 as we can wade in the direction of 5. That leaves us about a thirty-foot cast to the rocks at 5. We have plenty of backcast room; besides, with this light terminal rig it would be almost impossible to rollcast accurately, although later we will use the roll-and-mend techniques as we have in almost every sequence in the book.

Our first throw goes about five feet above the rocks at 5. Note that the tippet end of the leader and the fly bunches up on the cast. This is good unless it tangles, for it will allow the fly to settle quickly, and if a trout hits it the slack will be a welcome cushion, since the pound-test is so light.

As the leader absorbs and the fly sinks, watch that line. Keep rolling it forward and with a slight mend upstream, but carefully, so that you do not pull the fly away from the run. That's quite a trick in this position, so just to get the hang of it try several casts while you are working in the clear. A bit farther downstream you'll have trouble unless you can control the works. Hold that rod high now after you make that cast.

Figure 24. Undercut Bank.

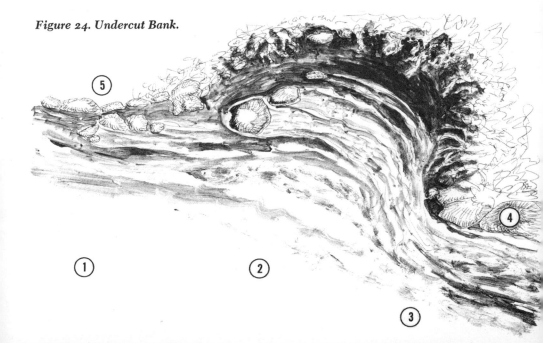

Now, with a good run past the rock, mend again and lift the fly to the surface and mend generously upstream so that the fly will slide by the big rock and down along its outer wake. Nice try. That trout certainly hit hard.

Now do you see the point of the light leader? Careful! Don't horse that trout. Rod high! Use your line hand to control him as much as possible. He's heading for the undercut, so lower your rod tip. Let the current aid you in dragging him out from there. Now use that fast water to advantage. That's it. You've turned him. Good, now wade below . . . No! Not through the pool. Go ashore, keeping a tight rod on the fish but a soft hand on the spare line. Remember you are powered only with 4X and that is a big brownie on the end. You'll land him at 3.

Meanwhile I'll sit on a rock and enjoy a cigarette.

Now, with a little taste of blood, you can quiet down for a serious bit of technique. Your next try is going to be from a point out from 2 as a warm-up for what is to come. That's the center-rock bit again, so go to work and ease off the cast for the retrieve at a point down from 3. Work the first water first. Don't skip over a hot run like that and head for the undercut quite yet. You can take another trout on the outside.

That's it . . . nice rise and you hooked him well without breaking off.

Sure, return him to the water. There are better ones to come.

Wade out a bit now . . . about up to your belt. No need to go deeper, for you still will need all the height off the water you can get, to keep the slack line out of that fast froth. All set? Now cast the fly. Wait a minute. Let me tell you first and then you can perform.

Your fly is going to land just ahead of that big rock. The leader will coil around it so that it drops down quickly. But you'll have to roll the leader over the rock without disturbing the fly, so take it easy. At that point you'll need to roll a bit of line forward as the fly is carried under the first part of the overhang. Luckily, it will be drawn in under the brush. Remember now to hold the rod high and keep mending as the fly does the circuit.

Fire away. That's it. Fine. Now, you are halfway down. The slack is being dragged by the current, so before the fly starts to be whisked out in a frightening manner, rollcast it to the surface and retrieve.

That was a solid hit. There he goes again. Lucky you didn't pull it away too quickly. Now you are into a whopper. That's okay. Let him head out and upstream. That'll tire him and you can let him sound the fast current for a while. Careful though to keep him from snagging you on the bottom. Heaven knows what's down there to file your leader.

You can creel that one. It'll feed a hungry man tonight.

Just for the sport of it, try that routine again.

The next cast can now be delivered below the rock, but this time you'll

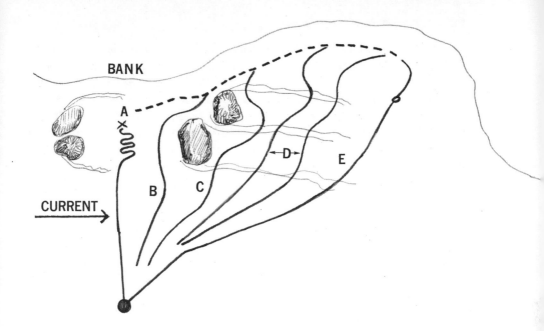

Figure 25. The Cast and Retrieve.

The fly is cast to A. It drifts to absorb the slack to a point between the rocks. Then you mend the line that is almost curled around the rock to C. A short drift here absorbs the slack, another mend and still another if needed as D. At E as the cast becomes almost too long to control you roll forward, lift the fly to the surface, and begin your backcast. In each mend, the lure has not been disturbed in its flow under the overhang and your rolls haven't snagged either.

need to roll and mend an upstream slack to the left, offering a bit more line to accommodate the swing (see Appendix).

Beautiful. Right in under the brush. Now let it work over the area. As it goes around the lower rock, mend the line well upstream so that your drift will pass 4. That's holding water for a big rainbow.

Hey, watch that slack. Look at your line, it's tightening and going under. You've hooked a good one and I bet it's a rainbow.

Sure enough, out he comes and there's no mistaking that salmon-like jump. Up he goes again. That's living.

Careful now—only 4X on that leader.

So, in a very few casts you have taken trout, and good ones on one of the most pounded streams in the East. You've fished a difficult spot and have not hung yourself up once.

Since we can't cross the stream from above let's try it below 4. We'll clean the fish there and see just what they have been feeding on. Open that rainbow and I've a dollar that says he'll be full of dace minnows.

Right? Right! That is first-rate water for a bucktail most of the time. Dry flies and surface skittered wets are the usual medicine when fly hatches are in progress. Right after a rain when lots of insects are pouring down the stream, almost anything will take trout here. But remember that under these conditions those fish will move out into the wash behind the rock and even into the center current during a hatch. You can cast a dry fly right into the fast water up from 4 or drift and skitter wets down from 5. From 5 you can also stop cast a big fluffy dry fly. Pick one that floats high and give it plenty of slack. You may miss most of the rises due to the slack line, but if one happens to connect when your line is tight, you'll have to be mighty careful to let the spare line help your sensitive rod tip cushion the hit or the trout will break off.

It is easy for the observer to tell the angler, "Keep him from snags," but quite often an entirely different thing to perform. Certainly it is a problem to be faced sooner or later in trout fishing. Browns and brookies invariably head for these locations when alarmed or hooked, and when they do, they can scare the daylights out of you, especially if you are fishing with light gear. The trick is to keep as much pressure on them as you can, but always with the rod parallel to the water, causing the line to drag in the current, further helping the cushioning of the pressure from the fish. This rod position will also tend to keep the fish from jumping, since your pull is sideways, not up.

But just how far can you push that 7X leader? The one way to find out is to dry-run a test. Rig your rod as usual, draw out about fifteen or twenty feet of line from the rod tip, and attach the hook to a tree or some stationary object. Now, with your line hand and fingers on the spare line coming from the reel, bend the rod against the pull, vibrating the tip and the pull to get the feel of the approximate amount of strain you are applying. Note, too, the bend in the rod. Now, try more pressure —more, until the leader breaks or the hook straightens out. Now you know. You had largely underestimated the 7X and so will now be more confident with THAT PARTICULAR ROD ACTION when you fish with such fine terminal tackle. You'll know just how hard to pressure your fish to keep him from the snag.

If it becomes impossible to keep a hooked fish from brush or snags, relax all tension suddenly. Stop fighting for a moment and the fish will probably drift out into the open. If it does not swim clear, take in some line and walk over as close as you can get. Have the net in readiness and also keep a couple of yards of slack in the line hand and at least a good loop in the rod hand, held next to the handle to cushion any sudden dash.

There are times in big-stream fishing when a trout will head for the jagged rocks in order to file the leader or scuff the fly from its mouth. I can recall one trout I encountered in my early days—a big she rainbow that was hooked on a wet fly in mid-current well below me. She made a dash for the side water and thrashed up the shallows, dragging the line under a large boulder. Had I relaxed the line rather than used the rock as a pulley, I would have been safe. As it was, I was forced to wade down and reach underwater to loosen the line from the rock. When I resumed the battle I knew that it was only luck that she was still on. She cost me plenty, that siren. A brand-new line was shot to pieces.

Sure, you'll lose many fish to snags—but it is fun while it lasts.

Figure 26. Sharp-Angle Pool.

CHAPTER 8

Sharp-Angle Pool

IT is time to fish a caddis hatch. I've arranged one, with the cooperation of Mother Nature.

You've seen them hatch, literally in droves. Sometimes they are so thick that it is hard to see the far bank. They get in your eyes, crawl down under your collar, swarm up your rod, land on your line. Once in a while, one gets up your nose. They come seemingly from out of nowhere. The trout feed voraciously on them, but, nine times out of ten, no matter what fly you toss at them, they will refuse it and go on feeding sometimes right under your rod—that is, if you are a careful wader.

To understand how to fish this hatch, brief and tremendous though it is, you have to know something about the caddis. There are probably more caddis worms or larvae on the bottom of most American streams than there are May flies and stone flies combined. Yet little is known about them. For some unpoetic reason, the caddis has not had the angling romance tied to it as a reputation as has the dainty May fly. Yet the caddis is a pretty little insect. There's one on your rod just above the handle, which means we had better get going. Standing here in the woods near the stream will not catch us any trout. We'll not approach this pool in the way we would walk into a supermarket. This one calls for the stealthy approach. We'll head for position 1. Our stream is an Eastern one, more specifically, one that lies within the shadow of New York City, barely fifty miles away. There are two caddis species of note on this and other nearby streams, the green or grannom caddis and the dark caddis, as it is known (see Appendix).

Our season is the second week in April. Some of the early Hendrickson May flies have hatched and more are to come. Right in the middle of this hatch, the green caddis is found in profusion all over the bottom of

66

the stream. It will not hatch for a week, so we have the opportunity today of catching fish on the larvae, and by the means of writer's magic, we'll fish the same water during the actual hatch. For experimental purposes, we'll fish a wet fly first just to snag a trout so that we can open it and show you the contents.

Better still, here comes another angler. We'll ask him if we can clean his trout, if he's caught any. Got that one on a worm, eh?

Now, look at those contents from the gullet. Green worms, yes?

Farther down in the stomach a mass of green mush, mixed with other nymphs the trout fed on during the early morning. Proof enough?

So, we'll fish three caddis worms on a leader. We'll weight the leader only slightly because the water in the pool below is not fast and the flies will sink, easily.

Since the caddis is a worm and not a clinging or clambering or swimming type of underwater insect, it can only stick itself to the surface of a stream rock or adhere to other refuse that is stationary. Once disturbed by the current or a wading fisherman's boot, it can only drift at the mercy of the current. The trout know where to look for them, right on the bottom in sheltered water. So, we'll follow their lead when we get down to the quiet water. Meanwhile, take my word for it.

Now, with our artificial selected, let's take a look at the water we will fish.

From our position 1 on the narrow but fast stream, we can drift our flies down to the lip of the current, where it suddenly stops into the dead-water of the pool. We'll not skip by that big rock below us and the shallow beach leading to the double rocks off 7. We'll let the artificial dally right on that lip—a sort of miniature shelving riffle. That pool is deep even under the fooling white water that crosses over it. It's a wonderful place for trout to harbor, being under the passing current in comparative quiet. From their vantage point they can see any and all bits of refuse and food and feed whenever they have a mind to.

It's an easy proposition to fish this downstream area, but let's handle that lip water with some subtlety.

As the flies drift down by the corner rock directly below us, we snub the line and hold them there for a few seconds, merely dangling.

Ah, that was long enough. We took a little one. Bring him back upstream. He's barely legal, but needed for the post mortem to again prove our point of stomach contents. Sure enough, six green caddis, freshly eaten!

Now, let's cross the stream very quietly and, walking to the stream from 2, take up a position by the brush upstream from the corner rock. We want to make a cast to the hole in the rocks just off 7. We could fish this with almost anything, since there are no hatches or rises. A bucktail would do, two good-sized wets would produce perhaps, and certainly our little green caddis worms will make sense. The cast goes out to just in front of 7 and drifts down in front of the rocks. We raise the rod tip, draw the flies back about two feet so that they drift down past the rock into the wake. Whammo! There we go again.

Without disturbing the water by wading down to the corner rock and into the very prize spot of the entire pool, we hold rods high and track

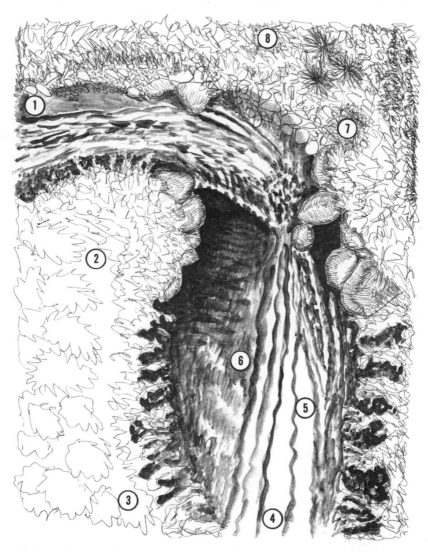

Figure 27. Sharp-Angle Pool.

through the brush to 2. Here we can now look down into the crystal-clear water and the bottom of that deep is as exposed as a home aquarium. Wait until that slight water-ruffling breeze quits and then you'll see a show. There they are, trout lying next to each other, stacked like cordwood all the way from 6 up to the flash of current.

Watch for a minute. See those trout flashing? Note what they are up to. They are nosing the bottom (see chapter on rise types) feeding on the caddis worms. There's a big one worth casting to. We'll move forward just a bit, still keeping within the cover of the brush. Our plan is to drop the flies close to the bottom until that monster sees them. There is little or no current so the action will take a bit of time. The bottom contains no snags so we don't have to worry about becoming hung up.

Darn that breeze. I can't see him, but I know that the flies are still above him. Now, they have drifted down. Careful. Don't lift that line even though it is moving on the surface almost over his head. Perhaps he won't notice it. He's moving. He sees the flies and grabs one of them. The whole pool explodes and trout shoot out like missiles in all directions. You can net him right there by the edge of the brush, that is if you are lucky enough to keep him from heading into that fast water on the far side of the pool.

Ouch, there he goes. Hold your rod high and snub him. He's headed for those snags above 5. Good. Now out in the center he'll soon tire.

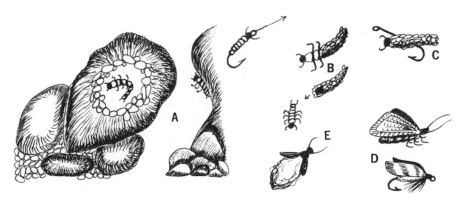

Figure 28. Caddis Types.

A. *The green caddis in its house built up of tiny pebbles. It is also found on the underside or sheltered side of rocks, sticking there bravely through the entire winter months. The imitation is shown next to it.*

B. *The stone-case caddis type and the actual insect out of the case.*

C. *A hooked caddis of the type that uses leaves and refuse for its case.*

D. *A method of hooking the caddis for casting.*

E. *The hatching caddis bagged up in its cellophane-like sac that buoys it to the surface quickly.*

Since the pool is disturbed for the moment, we can do a little biological research. Let's find the actual insect and see what it looks like. Reach down when you see a rock with a generous bit of underside. This is not the caddis that builds its house of sticks or gravel, but it clings to the underside of rocks and twigs until its day of hatching.

Here, we'll lift up this rock. They are there . . . see them, four green worms—rare steak for trout. Remember that color and shape and size. Our imitation is pretty close.

It is now two weeks later. Our green caddis is about to hatch and, in fact, examination of the leaves and bushes along the stream shows us that there was a hatch yesterday. Had we been fishing the stream in the early morning today we'd have probably connected with trout if we had used a March Brown wet fly, size 14, a good imitation of the adult flying caddis.

Now, the caddis does not hatch in the manner of the May fly. It does not drift in the current to any degree but seems to pop up from the bottom when the time comes, borne upwards by tiny air bubbles under a cellophane-like sac that makes it pop to the surface. Once there in the film it snaps out its wings without any fuss and becomes airborne within a second.

Here's one drifting a bit toward us. Catch it on your net hoop. There. See it take off. No time wasted. See those little sacs floating in the water? They must be from a hatch upstream—thousands of them coming down toward us. Soon our chance will come and the air will be filled with hatching insects.

So, let's get ready. Our imitation of the green caddis at the time of emergence is detailed in the Appendix, so for the sake of trying for a good rise, we'll tie on two of the flies on a weighted leader. Since the flies will be hatching virtually all over the pool we'll concentrate on the most obvious spot, the very center. We'll fish upstream gradually and wade quietly and slowly for this purpose so that we can be in a position to deliver the fly slightly up from 6. The technique is to let the flies drop to the bottom and as quickly as possible rollcast forward, raising them to the surface, rolling them forward for another sink, then raising them again, to approximate the rising of the natural from its security on the bottom.

Here they come. Mother Nature gave the signal. See what I mean? Once emerged they bounce right out into the air. Of the fifty or so in front of you, perhaps only five are still on the water casting their reverse parachute.

But, are the trout taking them on the surface? No. Those curls and breaks on the surface are being made by the trout taking those flies UNDERWATER, not on the top. A dry fly would be virtually useless. Try if you like and see. Here now, the water is clear for a moment. See those trout curling about? They're having a ball eating the larvae as they are rising up right in front of their noses. They are not the least interested in what's going on on the surface. That's one reason the dry-fly fisherman swears up and down during the caddis hatch. It would seem that he should be able to take trout like fishing in a barrel, but he doesn't. Few anglers know this trick about the caddis hatch. When it is known and you are able to sink the proper imitation and then raise it up sharply as we have been doing, you can fish out a pool in a half hour. Who says worm fisherman have the advantage?

The other caddis worms that live on the stream bottom build stick cases or cases made of gravel. In the early spring, if wet-fly and nymph fishing is still too subtle an art to catch enough trout in a day to keep your interest, try hooking one of the insects on to a bare hook, size 12. Drift it just like you would a wet fly, as close to the bottom as you can. That's what I call my poacher's trick, simply because I learned it from a poacher!

Now, with a limit of trout in your creel, all caught on the green caddis fly fished properly, let's go back to the neighborhood bar and see how the others made out.

This sharp-bend pool is a beautiful one to fish in the early morning with a fluffy Marabou streamer. Generally, water of this type with a pool of this design usually holds but one lunker trout that no one ever catches. At least that is what I like to think, and the romance usually pays off if I am patient enough to follow through and live the myth.

How would you fish the pool for the big one? Where would you stand and where would you cast?

I'd start from the brush at about position 7. From here, without disclosing my intentions to the trout, I can rollcast upstream for a bit and allow the Marabou to settle into the far rock and down into that black water beside it. There should be a lunker there. I can wash the edge of the rip, not all in one cast but by a succession of casts, whisking the line away before it disturbs the water below the rip. I can also work my near rocks almost under me and allow a drift down almost to the overhanging brush. After that, I can extend my cast to the center of the pool up from 6 and jerk retrieve the fly with abundant mends all along the deep side of the pool. When that's exhausted I will work the area between 5 and 6 by stepping forth now to the rocks below 7 and dropping the fly in the foam and letting it drift downstream and retrieving, after raising the fly off the bottom in a surface rise, hoping to tempt any rainbows that might be holding under the foam. As a last resort, from this position, I'd stand at my side of the rip and work my Marabou along and under the overhanging brush on my side of the stream.

I've still not disturbed the pool to any extent. I'd probably have at least four good hits from this exercise, choose to go back to camp with perhaps one good trout, to return in the early evening in time for a go at the pool with dry flies. This stretch of water is just built for dry-fly fishing over both still and fast water.

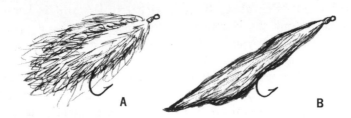

Figure 29. Marabou Fly.

    A. *Dry Marabou with feathery feathers.*
    B. *Marabou when wet imitates a fluttering minnow very well.*

I need not detail the casts, nor the drifts, from 4, 5, and 6. You can take over that pleasant duty. Use high-riding dry flies and you will come home with at least some very good stories.

I can remember fishing this stream one late afternoon. I had arrived there prematurely for the hatch that usually comes off at just before dark. There had been a sudden thunderstorm way upstream and a belt of cold water came rushing down. The sudden coolness brought on the hatch all at once and I believe that the insects and the trout were about as surprised as I. We had a good time that night and my creel didn't swing empty along the path through the alders. A night to remember.

Incidentally, the trout that you keep should be killed instantly, not let die a slow death flopping about in the creel. Dispatch them with either a blow from your net handle squarely across the butt of the head, or by snapping the head back and breaking the backbone. You can also stick a big fish with a penknife blade just where the head joins the backbone. Clean the fish on the spot. Don't wait for the post-mortem digestive juices to go to work on your meal. This action causes the fish to become soft and mushy. If the water is cold, douse the fish and then wrap in aluminum foil and stow in your creel or pouch. The original temperature and conditions will remain constant for many hours.

Figure 30. Corner Bend—Slow Water.

CHAPTER 9

Corner Bend

WHILE I was working on figure 29 a fisherman friend dropped in and said that the place looked like great wet-fly water. I've heard this kind of comment about various stretches of stream over the years: so-and-so pool is great dry-fly water; so-and-so is just built for bucktails, etc., etc.

Well, this is fine, and I discover myself thinking in the same vein sometimes. But thinking this way is so stereotyped. When man begins to classify nature, he immediately limits his outlook and also limits the bounties that nature can provide if he were to maintain a more open mind.

Sure, this is good wet-fly water. It is also good dry-fly water, and certainly you can fish bucktails and streamers. You can even use spinning lures and live bait.

Yes, I have delighted in fishing this section of the stream with wet flies. These have been the days and evenings (and an occasional morning, if I have not stayed up too late the night before playing cards or tying flies) when I've just fished for the fun of casting, working my way downstream, taking the water as it presents itself and its problems and hot spots.

That's because I like wet-fly fishing. It's nontechnical this way and I tend to forget all my research on insects, trout habits, and all the rest. One needs this exodus from the technical once in a while. The wet fly seems to offer this relaxation even more than dry-fly fishing, which, to me, is generally more work. I like to go for a walk along this stretch, sitting down on a rock once in a while and merely drifting the flies back and forth.

I grew up in the era of the purist anglers who considered wet-fly fishing as a poor second to dry-fly. This influence stuck with me for a number of years until I became a reactionary. The attitude of elite dry-fly men that wet-fly fishing is only "chuck and chance it" gets no quarter from me any more, even as a technique. I do like to chuck and chance it, as I have said above, and I've spent many an hour of chucking and chancing it with their overrated dry flies. Again, if we know the stream, the insects, and when to use a particular type of fly to its best advantage, little of our angling need be chuck and chance it.

I also don't believe that any man has learned enough about what goes on above or below the surface to justify a diploma from Nature or her trout. Wet-fly and dry-fly schools are but overlapping forms leading to the complete whole of fly fishing. They should never be considered as separate entities. It has been said that wet-fly fishing is the ideal method for the beginner. I rather suspect that this theory is based on the hand-me-down from the old-school angler who believes that dry-fly fishing is only for the experts. The basis for wet-fly casting is easy for the beginner to master—true; but to consistently take fish with the wet fly is in my opinion no easier than any other method. As a matter of fact, I have helped many people to cast and have invariably started them with the dry fly, for it is much easier for them to see their cast on the water, recognize their mistakes in delivery, and control of slack or drag when either develops. The beginner is fascinated with the floating fly because he can see it riding the currents. There is the added chance that the floater will take a small fish without too much sophisticated handling, and believe me, there is nothing so reassuring to pupil as well as teacher as a hooked fish, even if it be small.

Starting at almost any spot you can fish this bend on a cold blustery day with a wet fly securely tied to a fine leader. (Cast it well into the midstream current.) In a matter of seconds, the fly sinks, dragged under by the force of the water. Down, down it goes, whisking by rocks and snags to pause momentarily over the gravel behind a rock. A trout is resting somewhere in there—a large one. The fly moves upward with the hackles undulating in a lifelike manner. The shadow of the trout glides near and just as the fly is about to be drawn from the pocket. He lunges for it with deadly accuracy and takes it into his mouth.

Fished in many streams throughout various parts of the country, the wet fly imitates a nymph, water insect, small minnow, or almost anything that resembles food. Its coloration and general appearance fits into nearly every angling situation, making it truly the most universal of all lures in fly fishing.

Look upstream near the bend. An angler is fishing his way along, and by his casts and retrieves, he too is enjoying the chuck-and-chance-it angling, pitching the flies into likely pockets, runs, and eddies. Watching him cast into all that water, it is hard to realize that the little bit of fur, yarn, tinsel, and feathers can be the potent killer, for in a broad stream such as this with deep fast-moving stretches, the wet fly looks so small and insignificant as almost to discourage the whole idea of fly fishing. Yet, these little flies, when similar to the naturals, are just what will take trout. Though it may not be possible for us to see the artificial as it moves through the water, any trout in the area can and does.

A quick bend in the river is always a good spot to fish, for a bend constitutes a good reason for the broken bottom conditions to be found there. If there were no obstructions, there would be no bend. The corner rock under those trees has been holding out against the ravages of ice floes and spring thaws for, perhaps, centuries. Upstream and down from it there are holes, rocks, and channels where trout lie and insects live, breed, and develop. On the other side, likewise, those big rocks have stood as the cornerstone of the bend and the water below them is choked with holes and rocks. Wading in the water on either side will be a pesky problem due to all this jumble—evidence of the forces at work to try and straighten out the bend. This battle of the elements makes the grounds for excellent trout holes, resting and feeding locations. Naturally the aquatic insects gather in such water. The drifting flies concentrate at the bends, too, as the current tightens the runs where they are carried along. This concentration makes for excellent lies for trout and obviously the good spots for the angler to cast his flies.

In any consideration of wet-fly techniques, several questions always seem to pop up. When is the fly near the fish? Can it be determined whether the fish are feeding underwater if they cannot actually be seen in the act? Is the lure moving naturally? Is it the right pattern? These and many more questions arise as we survey this run, particularly with its big rocks and long broken stretches, similar to ones we have fished earlier in this book.

Under all these unaccountable circumstances and unanswered queries, are any or all of the fish we take pure luck? We are, in reality, searching the water with the fly for a trout that will come up and take it. Sure, this element is always present even if we are going about the business with all the science and technique that we have been able to acquire over the years. The best salesman in the world still has to look for and convince prospects. They are never the same twice. All he can do is draw on the accumulation of knowledge, just as the trout fisherman does and tries to increase his average.

Pattern selection, to the average angler, is often a matter of personal faith or the result of hearsay or advice. I can recall the first time I cast a wet fly to the head currents immediately upstream from those twin

Figure 31. The Fishing Technique.

Starting at A, the little circle represents our position, the solid line, the cast, the dotted the drift and active form of retrieve in skitter and also underwater zigzag up-and-down motion. The dot represents the pickup. This can only show the general outline, for all currents and runs and holes cannot be shown. It does give the idea of just how much fishable water can be covered with "chuck-and-chance-it" wet-fly fishing, and all of it, as figure 29 shows even better, is excellent fly-fishing water.

We can enter the water at A and stay close to the rocks, holding on with our left hand and casting with our right, if need be. We will be working close to the rocks, preferably on this side of the stream since the main current would obviously be pressured against this bank. If you study the first six spots and their casts you'll see it is largely short-line fishing, split-second manipulation, and short, jerky retrieves in and around the rocks and into the holes ahead of them—alongside and below. From the seventh position around to the attack on the large midstream rocks, the casts are longer and we use many of the techniques shown earlier in the book. As we work the rock, you are reminded of the situation of the midstream rock, Chapter 1, as we fish it from the upstream side at first, gradually work down until we split our interest between the lower side of the two big ones and the three little rocks farther downstream. Again, I urge you to look at each cast and retrieve carefully and see if you agree on the technique, remembering our creed of making a minimum of casts and fishing them out to the best advantage.

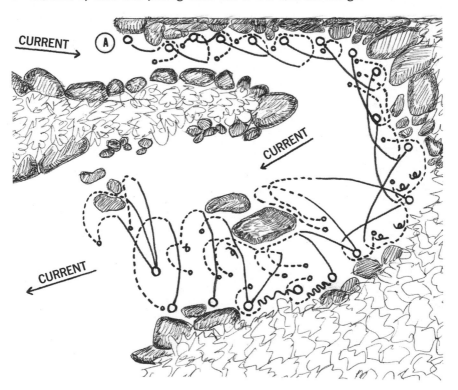

CURRENT

CURRENT

CURRENT

rocks. I had tied on two Dark Cahills in size 14. I don't know just why
I did at the time. In a matter of a few casts and drifts, I managed to
hook one trout and lose him, take a nice one, and then casting to the
white water in the shallow on the lee side of the rock, a really good
brown gave me a battle that took me well downstream. Since that day,
I've been partial to the Dark Cahill, and when I have no other point of
view to aid selection of a fly, be it in early spring or late season, I am
usually going to choose this pattern.

"What are they taking?" is a most common question asked on any
stream. Since the angler we have been watching has hooked and released
four fish since rounding that bend, let's ask him, just for fun.

"They've been hitting one of my three flies consistently," he answers.
"And what's that?"

He pointed to the rig, and I could see that a black gnat was the potent
medicine that he had been using successfully.

"Ever try a Dark Cahill?" I asked. "They are usually good at this time
of year."

"Tried 'em, but have never taken a trout on one yet" was his answer.
So there you are.

I know anglers who are three-or-four-fly men and consistently catch
fish on them and them alone. Whether it is because they fish them hard
and long enough and WELL ENOUGH that results are obtained I do not
know. Others equally successful believe that if they change patterns
often, they will find the ONE that is perfect at that particular time.

In this regard, just for kicks, we'll try an experiment on this river bend
that may prove a point to both of us.

Many anglers adhere to traditional patterns and will go to the ends of
the earth to buy a fly tied with natural blue dun and will not settle for
the dyed gray hackle, though to the average eye the color seems near
enough. Others, and I join this group, own and tie "variants" that are
made up of a combination of colors, each sparsely added.

I know that if I were limited to four wet-fly patterns and would be
forced to fish with only these for the rest of my days, I'd select the Leadwing Coachman, standard duckwing dressing, but I'd insist on the gold-
amber peacock body, not the green; the Hare's Ear, an English pattern
somewhat like the March Brown; the Cahill, either light or dark version,
and a multicolored wingless hackle fly somewhere between black, gray,
and brown, with a white turn or two of hackle in front, making it bivisible. I'd want them sized 8 to 16.

Now, to our experiment. You pick a pattern that you'll use during the
next hour of fishing. We are going to start on the right side of the stream
just as it disappears upstream around that point. You will use your three
flies and I, mine. Your three?

"Dark Cahill."

"My three will be Leadwing Coachmen."

And may the best fly win!

An hour later we end up at our position just below the rock. Neither one of us has taken a trout.

So, just for fun, let's tie on black gnats. Here's three for you and I'll use these. Fish just as carefully and this time we'll work together, alternating casts.

Five fish apiece. Nice working in the bright sun with no hatches showing, no breeze to blow in the land breds. Glad we met that angler and his gnats.

What does it all prove?

I dunno. It does prove that we had a good time trying to prove something and caught fish. If having to prove something can contribute to the fun of the day, let's dream up more exercises like that.

No, we do not always have to prove something. That is only trying to elevate our ego and the illusion that we think we are getting proficient at one-upmanship on Mother Nature.

I've fished that stretch of water and many others similar to it, at many different times of the year. Believe it or not, other than eastern brook trout, I've never taken a trout, brown or rainbow, on a black gnat since, although due to the experience I've tried them many times.

If we were arbitrarily going to chuck and chance it in the dry-fly manner, I'd pick a seasonal pattern and fish first the midstream rock, much in the way we did in the first chapter, bearing in mind that the swing of current on this side is stronger and therefore more potent than on the far side.

Being easier to reach, I'd fish it first, at any rate. My cast would come from a spot downstream. I'd also work a fly right opposite and close to the grass-draped rock on the right and, as I worked my way upstream, I'd make several passes at the rock, alternating with casts in under the brush on the right.

It is a tough stretch to wade, with hardly any flat stones or steady terrain. It is instead chocked with jagged rocks, or at least rock clusters that offer no kind of a path. This makes for excellent trout water as we discovered while wet-fly fishing. We can work the area over very carefully and fully, alternating with casts out into the middle current just to rest the area. We'd probably take an hour to reach the end of the bend where it goes behind the foliage on the point.

Then, if I could cross the stream conveniently and without much effort, I'd work a bucktail, or, in the stone-fly season, two small bucktails not much larger than conventional wet flies all along that shore. Naturally, I'd throw a couple of long casts to the vicinity of the rock. In low water it is possible to wade the clear stretch marked well in the picture, right down to the rock. That water generally offers up a fish or two, particularly in the evening.

The Green Drake hatch that originates from a quieter bit of water up above really draws up the big fish into action. I've taken some nice plump fifteen- and seventeen-inch browns on big fluffy dry flies when the Green Drakes were coming down, even if the amount of flies was very small.

Three of us worked this water, fishing almost side by side a couple of seasons ago. Between the rock and the end of the bend, we caught and released fifteen trout in the space of an hour, all keepers. Seldom have I seen such action to dry flies.

Arriving at this water as a stranger, and it is strange, even to one who has fished it many times, some very basic conditions must be known and certain facts of life well understood. For one thing, temperatures are all-important. Also, water speed, height, and clarity greatly affects the fish. At 42 degrees, digestion takes about five days. At 52 degrees, the time is about twenty-four hours. The shortest digestion period appears to be about 66 degrees. When the temperature goes up to 70 degrees or more, little feeding is done. The "therefore type" of deductions from these facts are a constant on which we can depend. Fish eat less in very cold water and few if any insects hatch anyway. When it becomes too warm, the insects do not hatch nor do the fish feed. Someone arranged this so there would be no waste!

But you know—you won't find one angler in a hundred armed with a water thermometer on the stream!

Light enters the picture too. Trout always like the shadows, particularly brook trout. Rainbows prefer the foam-feathered water and the deep currents even though they are exposed to the light. The brown trout is the only species that seems to be at home in wide-open areas and shallows just so long as there is enough oxygenated water for him and a place to hide nearby. This is why the brown trout seems to be the most adaptable to our streams where there are few banks with overhang, few stretches where the stream is arched over with evergreens or other shade-giving cover.

When some of this information is used properly, we begin to see the idiocy of the mythical approach to angling that so many authors have given the sport. From time immemorial, the trout has been glorified by anglers—his colors, his form, his power, and most of all his seemingly magical ability to detect the fraud in the most carefully made artificial fly. When hooked his determination to shake himself free is extraordinary but much overrated by too many angling scribes. (A small-mouth bass of the same weight will show a trout to be a comparative weakling.)

Many of these legendary trout have been credited with superhuman genius and brain power and there is scarcely a brook or stream that does not harbor an "Old Ragged Fin" or "Rudolph." It is always a fish of gigantic proportions, usually living in a hole or under a bridge. No matter how many anglers try, their efforts go by for naught. These attributed qualities of perception and brain power on the part of the trout are to my mind wonderful bits of anglers' philosophy, designed to excuse an empty creel. Actually, the trout has few secrets.

As we have learned today and yesterday and will tomorrow and tomorrow, the trout has but three prime worries in life: filling his stomach, keeping out of danger, and carrying on the race. To accomplish these three duties, he has been endowed by nature with excellent eyesight, the ability to move fast, and the power to swim long distances. Biologists say that the trout—in fact, any fish—has but a one-track mind, so it would seem that catching him would be a very simple matter. But, fortunately for the trout, man's mind is very complicated, or at least man has the ability to complicate even the simplest of problems. Man, since he has been largely disconnected with his natural environment, has lost the ability to feel and sense, and has, instead, developed his mind, logic, and thinking. Upon these faculties he has to find his sometimes involved solution to the simple problem at hand.

Water, like this stretch, is very innocent-looking. The fishing ways are unlimited and many are obvious. But if you were to sit here and watch the parade of anglers and the manner in which they go about casting, and especially where and how they wade, you'd be thankful that man is so complicated and in most instances unrelated to the scene.

That's fine. That means more chances for us to connect.

Figure 32. Split Riffle.

CHAPTER 10

Split Riffle

CURRENT

SINCE we have fished together on a shelving riffle in Chapter 6, the problems on the split riffle become somewhat easier solved by our well-practiced techniques. There are some subtleties that can be explored, however, and a close look at the water before we venture from the brush to the stream edge is in order. This type of layout offers many ways of making mistakes through bad planning of casts, tricky drifts, and, above all, missed strikes.

Most of this type of water is fast, whether it be shallow or deep. One would think then that any hit would be a solid one, since the trout would have to mean business. But such is not the case, because in all but direct downstream fishing the line is usually slack on the drift, particularly in dry-fly fishing or direct upstream wet-fly fishing. Due to this slack, a light hit is experienced as a mere touch. The effect is not felt strongly enough for the rod hand and line-finger trigger to react quickly or forcefully enough. When they do, there is so much slack to take up that the delay allows the fish to reject the fly. Shown in figure 33, in both up and downstream directions, are examples of too much and just the right amount of slack to allow. Naturally, when you throw a bend of line ahead or aside from the fly, there is slack, so may I remind you of the diagram and instructions from the first chapter—that of maintaining a right angle direction of the rod against the slack line. Generally, it is better to create this horizontally rather than vertically, since there will be less tendency for the line to belly in the current. A flashing rod in the vertical position also has a tendency to scare the fish especially if the ferrule is of bright color.

We'll remind you of specific situations as we go along. Much of this "lesson" should become a matter of touch, for there will be times ahead when we will be fishing at dusk, when the light is poor—when you will

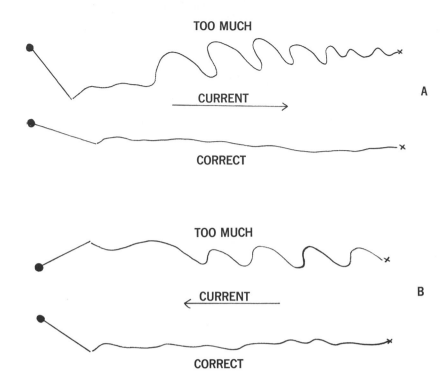

TOO MUCH

CURRENT

CORRECT

A

TOO MUCH

CURRENT

CORRECT

B

Figure 33. Control of Slack Line.

Diagram A shows the angler fishing downstream. On top, the angler is using too much slack and cannot possibly react quickly enough to a light hit—or any hit for that matter. The lower man is ready for a quick strike with a minimum of slack to absorb.

Diagram B shows the same proportion of slack line except that the angler is fishing upstream.

not be able to see your rod or the line. You'll have to become sensitive to line control without the aid of your eyes.

Let's fish this water now, in the late afternoon, and spot the places where the fish are lying during the day. Then, we'll return this evening for a bout with the trout that will be rising to one of the most interesting hatches of the season, the Light Cahill. Cahill spinners, stone flies, some caddis flies, and of course a myriad of land-bred moths, millers, and flies will be drifting on the water or skirting the surface, making the choice more complicated for the trout and quite confusing for the angler trying to discover which the trout are going for the most. Despite this array of insect menu, the trout can be highly selective, and frustrating to the angler. We'll allow some profanity, but publishing has its censored limits!

Since we have been previously fishing upstream, we approach this split riffle from below. The fast water at 3 can be very potent. The fishermen

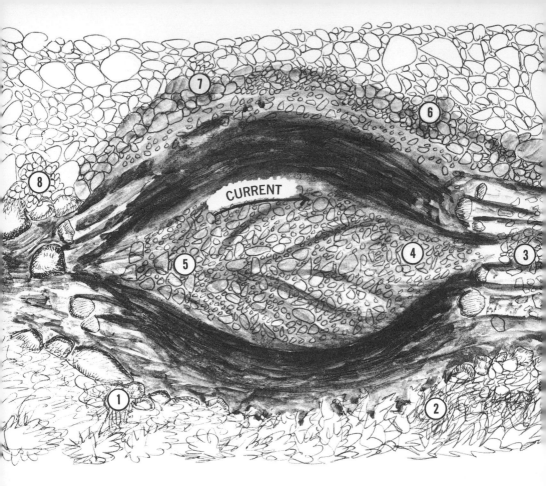

Figure 34. Split Riffle.

who have mangled the pool and runs above will have chased many of the trout down to hide in the rocks just ahead of us. Since the water is in June-low conditions (it hasn't rained in two weeks), this aerated water is a good place to start.

A couple of small wet flies? How about a small streamer or lightly dressed bucktail? A dry fly.

Okay, let's tie on a high-riding dry for this session. Since there will not be a hatch for some hours, almost any pattern will do. I tie a variable wingless dry for such occasions (see Appendix, page 327).

We'll pick a small one—size 14.

Since the water is broken with holes and holding spots between the rocks, we can approach quite near from below 3 and merely dapple the fly ahead of us. Our leader is twelve feet long, so there will be little chance to scare the trout with a slapping line if we keep our rod high.

We work the casts landing the fly in the left-hand run between 2 and

4, allowing the fly to descend by both sides of the exposed rock, into the wash. We keep the slack collected as it floats down.

Oops . . . you missed that rise from a small trout. Remember what we said about too much slack? Lucky that was not a bigger trout. Now, to rest the area, work the right side and repeat the process, but this time WATCH THAT SLACK.

It is time now to get used to the confusing currents of the riffle. Note that the water fans out from the center of the "beach" to join the main current and its obvious run. Try now and place a fly about three feet into the shallow of the left side of the rip, on the near side of 4. Note how the line gathers in coils quickly and when that line slides into the main current, the fly is the last to travel. This is absolutely wrong, as you can see.

The cure is to work the line in a right-hand bend, so that the slack never will reach the main current but will allow the fly to travel on the very edge of the drop-off. No trout will be scared away by this if you can perform it.

The other alternative is to make very short casts that can be controlled by a high rod. If the wind is constant and coming from behind you, this can be of great benefit and so extend the distance of your cast. If the wind is coming from upstream, forget it.

Now, the advantages of the split riffle can be worked thoroughly. This is not only potent water but fun to work, since you will be wading very slowly and quietly up the center of the run from 4 to 5. If you are quiet, and keep that rod tip down from now on, you'll not scare the fish.

Earlier in the season the water was too deep and fast to wade, but now it is about up to your knees at the deepest points along the "beach," over the ankles in the center. Even in the bright light of day there is enough distance between you and the deep runs where the trout hang behind rocks so that they will not be easily disturbed. It is better to work from the bottom up rather than from the top down, due to the fact that the trout always head upstream.

From your direct upstream approach, alternate casting from right to left, resting the area between casts. Enjoy this luxury and make every throw count.

To your left, note that mud bank and its enticing overhang of brambles, brush, and grass; spots where insects of all sorts hang out. When the breeze comes by, it brushes some of them into the water. Let's try that run first. Remember now, it is not as easy as it looks. Your line is going to get caught in the fast current if you are not careful. Since you are casting from quite a distance and wish the fly to drift in under the brush, you'll not be able to hold your rod high enough for the line to skip over the current. Your alternative is the upstream curve cast and a quick additional mend so that the fly will not be pulled out from its desired course. Shoot your first cast about midway between 1 and 2. There. Let it bounce along the deep water right under the brambles. Quick. Throw another bend before the line gets caught.

Didn't we say that there was a good trout in there that was hungry? I guess we didn't. But now we know it's a fact! Good-sized, too.

Now, with that success in your creel, rest the area and switch to the fast deep riffle between 4 and 5. This one offers a different type of problem, that of merely allowing the fly to grace the edge of the drop-off. There is no need now to fish the shallow, gravelly beach. Tonight, however, is another question. You'll find trout feeding in there on stone flies that are hatching. There will be Cahills drifting into the shallow there also.

Shoot a right-hand bend cast to a point below 6 and let the current absorb the line as it drifts into the center of the run. Try that several times just for practice. It's similar to much of what we learned on the shelving riffle, but a good checkup on technique.

From position 5 you can now turn your back on the best water yet to come and try again for a good drift of the dry fly in a downstream manner. Work the drop-off edges first all the way down to 4 and then shoot a short cast to the top of the brush-lined undercut, mending upstream so that the line is not pulled by the main current. There should be another trout under there.

There is and you've got 'im.

Try a bucktail in this position next time you are on the stream, especially if you are fishing in the early morning. The trout will be less light-shy and you can work them well from this position, remembering that the beach side is a potent one until the sun sends hot rays toward it. Your minnow schools stay on that flat and offer a constant breadbox for the trout.

Next spring, or luckily if we get any high water during the rest of the season, work big bucktails by letting them drift almost worm-fishing style right down the middle of those two currents, zigzagging the flies right across those rocks at the bottom of the picture up from 3.

Now, from 5 we head upstream and look at that layout! The main current of the riffle flowing between boulders with their good holding water for insects, deep runs for trout to slip in and out of while they are resting or dashing for food. This type of water extends quite a way up from the picture. There are deep holes behind those rocks, fast runs between them.

Since you will not be able to cross to either shore through this fast water, you can drop cast as you wade down to a point where you can cross through the right main current easily. Obviously the shallow side

with the beach is the one to cross. Fish upstream and drift the flies with
the rod held high as you slowly walk upstream well away from the water.
From here the rocks above the picture can be cast to without too much
subtlety. As you work upstream, use the short-line technique, dropping
your flies into the holes.

Now, let's allow several hours to pass. It is now after suppertime. The
stream has cooled off suddenly with the descent of the sun, and shortly
one of the most potent hatches of the June season will be underway.
With a knowledge of the stream currents and the almost automatic use
of certain casting and line-retrieve techniques, we can see how we fare
during the Light Cahill hatch. These flies, when they hatch in any good
amount, should bring up the monster browns and rainbows for which
this stream and this type of water is reputed.

Nature has decreed that this fly does not hatch during the hot time of
the day, but rather in the twilight. From midafternoon until the sun sets,
the nymphs of this May fly leave the bottom of the stream, drifting in the
current, so the imitation of the nymphs and wet flies (see Appendix) are
called for. Generally at twilight, I use two nymphs on the end of the
leader and top the rig with a wet fly which, in large measure, is the one
which is dappled during my short casts.

Fortunately for the angler, the Light Cahill pattern imitates several
of the May flies that hatch at the same time, so perhaps this is the reason
the artificial is such a favorite in streams east of the Rockies (see Appendix, page 323).

Yes, Dan Cahill really had something when he designed this pattern,
for he offered the answer to one of the most confusing times of the fly-
fishing season. From June on, there are about ten of the little May flies
that are well imitated by it in the dun stage. The wet when fished as a
nymph also closely resembles the underwater stage and as such is a con-
sistent killer from now on through the remainder of the season.

This does not mean that the Light Cahill will take all the trout in the
stream. The fish are extremely temperamental during this hatch and this
quality in them is further aggravated by an abundance of spinners, making the proper fly pattern, especially in dries, a problem, especially when
they choose, at a second's notice, to specialize on one type of insect, much
the same as we eat the beans on our plate, having shifted from the mashed
potatoes.

The hatching nymphs are exceedingly difficult to spot during the drift,
but the presence of a few duns and the resultant underwater flashes and
frequent surface rises will tip you off to the beginning of the hatch. The
nymph is easily recognized by the cream-buff body and amber wing pads.
The dun is the same color but with whitish, sometimes pinkish hues.

When it comes time to hatch, the nymph, like the March Brown and

Gray Fox May Fly, migrates from its rocky home usually at the head of a pool or from the fast-water runs such as we have in our split riffle. The points of embarkation are the cluster of rocks at the head and tail of the pool, and the edges of the drop-off on the riffle. Also, many insects will have drifted from the fast-water holes up above and even perhaps for a pool as much as a half mile upstream.

Just to aid the mental processes, use the wet-fly pattern and catch a trout and open it. You'll find the upper gullet filled with these little insects.

If you were to scientifically collect them from the stream, you'd find them almost everywhere on our layout except the center of the rip and the brush-lined mud overhang on the right side of the stream.

So, now, from position 8, let's fish our rig with the two nymphs and the wet fly. We'll cast them into the rocks and rollcast our line over the boulders and allow them to drift into the near-side current first. There are a few rises in evidence, mere swirls of water as the trout begin to feed underwater. There's a hit, to the bottom nymph. Next cast, then, should allow the flies to drift deeper down. The hatch hasn't started yet. Another cast. Drift the flies on slack right along the edge of the rip. Now, snub the line and make them rise to the surface. Good. Now, just let them hang there and swing back and forth until the bottom nymph comes up. Whee! There you are again. A nice brownie, small, but just the trout to prove our dissertation is correct.

Take a look downstream toward the bottom half of the rip. Look at those rises. There is a feast going on down there. Minnows and trout in one big family having a gorging good time as the nymphs are drifting down to them. With a horde like that it is a wonder that any of the nymphs ever get the opportunity to hatch. Let's give the flies a break and try to eliminate one of their predators!

Rather than wade down the center, since the trout would be heading upstream, we take to the beach side, our ultimate objective being the position 3 to start upstream again when the duns are flying. Meanwhile, we want to drift our nymph and fly rig all along that lower lip, on our side.

Look at those rises! Note, too, that they are not rises to floating or even hatching flies. That will come later, so don't be in a hurry to switch to the dry fly yet. Let's cast to that big swirl, but just above it, and try to get what looks to be a big trout to hit.

It worked just fine. He's up and out, securely hooked. Keep him from going below, for you'll have the devil's own trouble following him down-stream for the netting. Ah, that's a relief, HE chose to battle out in the center current. Walk below. The area is spoiled for the moment anyway. Net him from the lip.

Now just for kicks, throw a cast directly below where you are about to walk, the area above 3. There just might be . . .

Okay, another one.

Now, I see a few of the duns on the water. They are fluttering on the surface, since this May fly does not get off to a clean start but is sloppy and awkward in its take off.

For experimental purposes and also to prove a point, let's put on a Light Cahill dun on the top tippet. Then we will have the dry, the wet, and the nymph all on the same cast. We'll watch the score just to see as the hatch progresses which ones the trout will take. It will also show us when the right time for dry-fly patterns will pay off. Premature dry-fly fishing will be good exercise only. Learning this lesson will in large part eliminate time wasted casting with the unsuitable fly type. Our power of observation will be strengthened and the results will be there to justify our deductions. We'll also catch trout!

Yes, the fluttering flies are hatching along the rip. A look upstream, even in the dim light, shows trout rising to the flies in the bubbly water. The duns are coming down from the rocks above. A glance over into the other lane of the riffle show some duns gliding quietly along the waves. These flies have evidently gone through their hatching struggles and are resting on the water as they are being carried downstream. Since there is no hatch under them, there are no rises. The trout are letting them pass by unharmed.

Now, to cast. We head upstream. Our three-fly rig is not designed for distance work, so we follow previously described techniques and work our way up through the center of the rip to position 4.

There's a rise. He took the nymph. Quickly unhook. It is a small fish. Another rise. Again the nymph. Work the flies near the surface this cast. No results. Again. Nothing. Now, sink the cast. See . . . a rise from a nice trout to the nymph.

Five minutes later, with many of the duns fluttering about your cast as it drifts down, the wet fly is hit several times but refused by the trout despite your accurate handling of the slack line. The dry fly is still untouched. Interesting?

Now, let's proceed to just below 5 and make the cast up toward the rocks. Remember that there are many duns coming down from above in addition to those fluttering in actual hatch below the rocks.

There's a savage hit to the floater. Another hit. Another!

Now the trout are actually coming up and out of the water for the emerged dun. There's a rainbow in a typical skyward leap. The head of the pool is alive with surface rises now. There goes our dry fly. Snub him. Good show! Land the fish right at your feet as it drifts down. Recast. Bang! There's another, to the dry fly again.

It's time to switch to the dry fly exclusively.

Unbeknown to us, a couple of anglers have been watching us take trout.

"Gee, you guys are sure connecting. What are you taking them on?" one asks.

"Light Cahills," I responded.

"That's funny, we've been fishing dry Cahills for the last hour and have not gotten anything but a few short hits."

I look at you and you look at me. We KNOW why they have not connected.

"Come join us," I beckon. "There's a hatchery full of trout here just waiting for you. We've had it for the night. This hatch will go on for another half hour or so. Good luck."

As we go ashore and head for the club, we've a feeling of accomplishment. We know a little more about Mother Nature and her streamside and underwater insects and trout than we did yesterday. We'll never get to know all the answers, but the time spent in trying will be the delight. A blind man has a hard time fishing. Once you learn to see and then to look and derive answers from what you have seen, then the game of trout fishing becomes less and less luck and more and more a true connection between man and the trout of the stream. Then the mysteries and the myths become easily solved and the secrets applied.

Study the illustrations in the last chapter, "Watching the Trout." Try and be aware of what's happening during the rapidly changing hours before, during, and after a hatch and choose your weapons accordingly. You'll not catch all the trout in the stream, but you'll have an INTERESTING TIME trying.

Sure, when it comes time for the general rise and all the trout are feeding on the surface dancers, anyone can catch them, even a bare beginner fishing for the first time. Even sloppy casts are of little account when the frenzy of the feeding spree is at its peak. The other times are the ones when the amateurs fail to connect, simply because they have not learned to observe and pick their techniques wisely.

If we were fish-hogs, we could return to this spot in a couple of hours. You would not see a single rise from a trout, but very shortly, working a bucktail, you'd lure some of the big trout to the fly . . . those fish that will drop down from the rock holes and those in the twin main currents that will come in to the shore to feed on minnows. But we've a big day tomorrow, so let's call it quits for the night. After a breakfast of trout we'll be up and at 'em early.

Figure 35. Head of Pool I.

CHAPTER 11

Head of Pool I

THIS is the most popular spot on any trout stream—the pool below the falls. Every Tom, Dick, and Harry works it to a froth, and some of them catch fish here. All manner of flies and lures, including spinners and worms, live bait, and even set lines, are employed to reduce the trout population here.

Lots of trout and minnows inhabit this kind of water all season long and fly hatches are numberless. The food that drifts down from above is churned by the white water along the falls line and it all dumps into the big dinner plate, floats downstream, and settles in the center of the pool.

In some streams the big rainbows harbor at the foot of the falls for time of their ascent. They hold in the currents just below where it settles into the deep flat when they are on their return to the big lake downstream.

Brown trout of prodigious size can be taken from the runs between those rocks. They hide out there most of the time unless they find refuge in the unwadable and deep water well below the falls line. Great schools of minnows harbor in among the rocks and particularly in the washes behind the falls rocks and along both shores, especially on the beach side where a back-current whirlpool offers them still water and lots of feed.

If bass are found in the river at all, that is where you'll find them; big walleyes and perhaps a few crappie, also.

Early spring, when the water is high and the whole pool pictured has become one white-water rapid due to the excess of heavy water; mid-season, as you see it now; and late season—at all times there are trout to be had whether you fish before sun-up, in the bright light of a cloudless summer sky, at twilight, or long after dark when sensible trout and trout fishermen have gone to bed.

94

But you can also get beaten here. Such a seemingly simple problem as fishing the head of the pool can become an obsession, given three or four times at it with absolutely no success. I've been frustrated in this very spot more times than I care to relate; that's why I have pictured "my" pool as the example to study, and fish.

While there appears to be nothing new in casting and presentation problems here, we are going to concentrate on one particular aspect of trout fishing that is so important on any bit of water, but especially the big pool, be it at the head, in the middle, or at the tail.

We have mentioned so far that wading should be done quietly and as unobtrusively as possible. Wading is just as important an art as the actual casting and lure presentation. If you goof at wading and scare the fish, or fall in for a wetting or, worse, acquire a sprained ankle, then the day can not only be fishless, but painful.

Speaking here as a graduate of the class of fall-ins, I have long ago discovered how important good wading strategy is and how care and caution will make for more pleasurable angling. Most anglers try to wade the water the way they walk a path in the woods. They wade too fast and try to step and walk. They also can wade into deep holes or out on the end of shelves where they cannot escape back to the shallows and suddenly find themselves marooned. They seldom measure the strength of the current as they go, and when wading downstream neglect to measure the pressures they will have to beat if they must return upstream and back to the bank against the current.

The first essential, as we will learn while wading and fishing this pool, is to take it easy and look first where we are going. If you are a beginner it is best to keep to the shallows, advancing into the deeper and harder water with caution. When wading a sandy or gravelly shore such as the area near 4, the dangers of falling in or tripping are negligible, but keep an eye out for underwater snags and deep holes. Don't venture too near the outer rim of that whirlpool. The drop-off is almost vertical.

If you were to enter at 1 without knowing how deep and fast the innocent-looking pocket of water is there, you'd take a spill before you even got settled for a cast. Entering below 2 and wading out into the break between the bubbles and the flat pool water, you can fall into holes. Proceed slowly if you take this route. Make it a practice to place one foot ahead of the other, keeping the weight on the back or "solid" foot until the front or "leading" foot is planted securely. If this rule were followed to the letter of the law, falling in or stumbling would be largely, if not almost entirely, eliminated. A fall usually occurs because the angler steps or attempts to walk from rock to rock. This is a deadly course to follow, particularly when you are almost hip deep and the margin to the top of your waders is slight. You will find that the rocks at the heads of

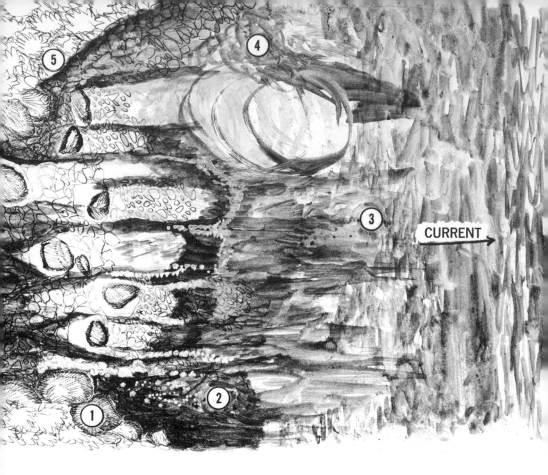

Figure 36. Head of Pool I.

pools are seldom secure, as they are constantly being shifted, under-mined, and pushed around by the changing currents and variance in water speed. Generally they are also smooth-surfaced, which adds to the skidding potential. From mid-season on, they are usually covered with a thin film of slime, which, like an icy road in winter, bodes caution.

Don't move from one foot to the other unless you are secure. Maintain a constant balance of weight or don't proceed further, especially if it is obvious that you are going in deeper and into fast water such as the entire stretch across the pool from 2 to the edge of 4. When your balance is constant, a slip or sliding motion will help you find a firm footing be-fore placing your weight on that foot. It is better to slip into a solid position than to try to step into it and hope that the rock upon which you put your foot will not turn over.

You'll note that here, at the top of this pool, the water is broken and wavy, an indication of underwater rocks that cannot be seen if the shore-line reflections blot out water vision. Stay in the semi-broken stretches,

96

for here the water is inclined to be more shallow and thus easier to wade. When the currents as shown at the head of the pool are fast, stay away from the broken water and select a course where the surface is smooth and not too deep. Such a path might be the dark edge of water just below 2 extending to a few feet above 3. Behind you it is too fast and the rocks are sharp with holes hidden by the froth.

Don't be in a hurry. The slower you go, the surer you'll be and the less you will disturb the trout that are lying in peace all about you. I have waded the water described and have seen the trout feeding right under my rod tip. They were not even aware of my presence.

So, advance slowly. There are no prizes given out for fast wading and fast fishing with resultant empty creels, broken bones, or wet clothes. Learn to feel your way "crablike" and "see" the bottom with your feet. You'll develop those eyes in time, for in water of hip depth you can't see much anyway, even if the water is clear. If reflections are a bother, you will be forced to use your boot eyes anyway. It is all good practice for night fishing when you start out blind and spend the entire night that way.

Equipped with even the best of chest-high waders, the crotch is not designed for mountain climbing or ballet dancing. Make it a practice, then, to refrain from stretching your legs to the limit in order to step or climb over a rock or stream obstacle. In addition, it is difficult if not impossible to maintain balance in this position. With one foot planted on a rolling stone you'll soon be in the freezer.

When wading downstream, say from position 2, 3, or 4, it is easy to be literally carried away, for the current may be faster than you think. So always make it a point to keep an eye peeled toward the shore for an

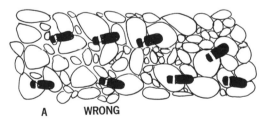 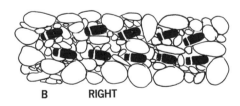

A   WRONG   B   RIGHT

Figure 37. How to Wade.

A. *Wrong. Don't take long steps and never step on rocks that will roll with your weight. This is a common mistake.*

B. *Right. Move slowly and take small "mousy" steps between the rocks, often touching their edges with your heel or toe. If you follow this technique, wading is nothing but slippering along the rug of the stream.*

exit route if the going gets too tough. More than once in this very pool I've been saved an arduous trip upstream by reserving a simple way out of a situation similar to the one described in the next chapter. Flip the pages a minute and you can see the trap at the end of the pear-shape fall-off as it enters the main body of the pool. I couldn't get back because the stream current was too fast. Ahead of me downstream it was obviously over my head.

Nice fix.

Luckily I was able to negotiate an up-and-across-stream path rather than wait there a month for the water to go down.

In downstream wading it is often advisable to wade facing sideways to the current (see figure 38)—that is, with one foot "upcurrent." I learned this lesson years ago, but I seldom see anglers doing it, even the so-called pros. Those anglers who fish the big waters of the West for steelheads or the northern waters for Atlantic salmon know what I'm referring to

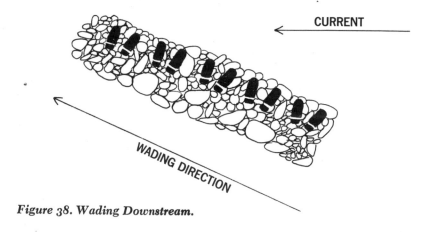

CURRENT

WADING DIRECTION

Figure 38. Wading Downstream.

We'll discuss and try our feet at crossing a section of stream when we come to Chapter 12, "Tail of Pool I," and, as we go along fishing this water, we'll refer to our wading in specific problems.

Right now, we can try for a trout in this bubbly water just as it comes down from the breaking falls.

Our season is July. The water is warm, which means that the white water or the deep holes and the deep center of the river will be where the trout are holding out. The day is bright and cloudless. There's a slight breeze coming from downstream.

Let's enter the arena from the beach between 4 and 5, armed with a stout wet-fly rod, a fairly heavy line, and two size 10 dace bucktails. We use two, a mighty unorthodox setup because fishing in this heat is tiring and if we are to get our money's worth, we might as well go at it with a brace of flies. There are no merit badges from the hierarchy of angling that say that only one fly of this type must be used. If you can handle two, use them. Sure, you'll probably hang up the rig a few times by backcasting too sharply. Try and take it easy and allow the line to make a generous curve in the air. Tie on your tippets with a pound-test considerably less than the basic leader end. Say your leader is tapered to 3X, use a 4X tippet for both flies, just in case you get hung up on a rock or underwater log and have to cut loose. There are spots out there where you cannot wade to if you do get snagged.

It's all good water and very likely, since the pool was worked over by a lot of fishermen this season and even this morning, the fish will be settled deep within the protection of the bubbles and deep runs between the boulders. The flash of our two bucktails will be about the only medicine short of a stick of dynamite that will dislodge them. A hit from anything of any size will be a real belting one, so be prepared.

Just to get the feel of the two flies on the leader, we'll cast directly upstream from 4 to the inside of the rock off 5 and, with the rod held high, skitter the flies over the surface to see how they swim in the current. We'll walk upstream a few feet and cast to the rocks above 5 and let the two of them swim down directly until they reach the top of the whirlpool and then retrieve them for a recast. Try that a few more times to get the hang of the flies and their action in the water.

Now, how about a spot cast to the near side of the big rock so that the flies will cross over into its wake and, with the aid of a slight roll of extra line, go below on the far wake line and down either side of the rock immediately below it. What a spot for a good one! Careful, even though you are throwing slack, keep in touch with the line by a sensitive handling of the rod tip and remember to place it at right angles to the line as it leaves the rod tip.

Strike! That was a real rush. Looked as big as a striped bass.

What's the matter? Buck fever? Begin your retrieve. Wham. There he comes again. This time you were saved by the current taking away your slack. The fish struck just as the current was about to whisk it away.

Yes, luck does play a part once in a while.

Fight him below. Try and save that upper area from disturbance.

Feel bold?

Well, you COULD try to wade around the big rock slightly up from 5 and, if it is not too deep, reach the rock line in the center of the run. It's worth a try, but, again, to our wading hints. Make sure that you don't venture into water from which you cannot return. There are no helicopters for rescuing anglers.

From this point you have the best of the pool at your disposal.

Don't cast too often in the same place. Try one run and then switch to another. From where you are, you are looking right into the eyes of trout that are lying between 2 and 3. Drop cast your flies to a point just below the white water. Throw one short bend of slack and let it absorb. When it tightens, throw another little one and let the flies sink down and drift a bit below. Now, raise them up in short jerks and when they reach the surface zigzag them across the current as much as you can from your upstream position.

Now, from your location in the center of the stream above the rapids, which way are you going? Return or cross the stream? Look upstream. It's too deep to wade, and is the current too fast for you? I've been that route and I can tell you that it is possible to wade across if you are careful and work slowly. I'll stay over here and watch you. Just remember that crossing the stream is a tiring proposition and you had better wade diagonally upstream rather than straight across or even down in this case, for you might get yourself in a vise.

Nice going. You made it.

Now, for a fresh bit of water and an entirely different set of problems. Let's walk downstream. I'll meet you there. The sun is going down and most of the stretch of water will be in shadow; a good time of the day for this section. It offers some of the greatest dry-fly fishing for one of America's best-loved flies, the Green Drake, hatching as it does at this time of year, and today if we have the luck gods with us.

Tonight we'll try the head of the pool again, but we won't make the attack until about ten o'clock. It'll be your initiation to the angling magic of the dark.

CHAPTER 12

Tail of Pool I

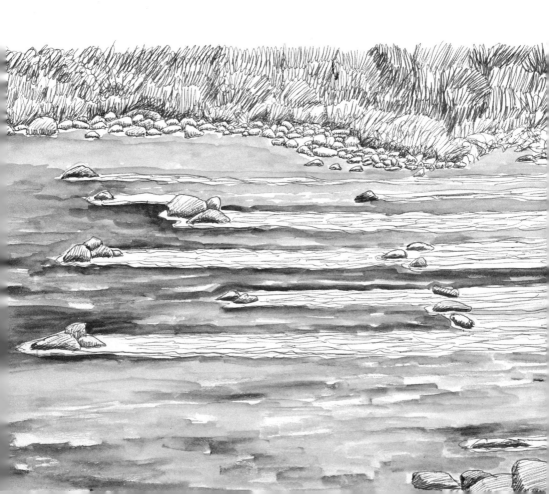

YOU'LL find less anglers working the tails of pools than the heads. That's good. They think all the trout are up there when there are really just as many down here—harder to catch, maybe, but they are there, especially if you fish the lower reaches at the right time. Sure, the water is shallow, and in the clear-water, low-level times it looks as though no trout in his right mind would stay there for very long except to feed.

Where streams are fished heavily, many of the trout are driven down as well as up by the waders and casters. Trout, being migraters—especially the rainbows—will often rest in the tail end after finning through difficult rapids along their route. Also, some of the biggest trout in any pool reside in the slower, deeper stretch just above the point where the pool begins to shallow out. Quite often you will find them dropping down to feed on caddis larvae. When conditions are quiet, they will be seen "tailing"—that is, feeding on the bottom with their tails flapping in the air, since the runs are shallow (see Chapter 35, "Watching the Trout").

So, your potential here can be realized under any of these conditions, or even under a combination of many of them at the same time. It is generally better to scan this water when you arrive at the pool rather than just dive in. Pick as high a lookout as you can find with the sun preferably at your back, so that every run and hole will be easily seen. Trout are fairly visible then, or at least you can find them by watching for their shadow instead of their body.

One of the best times to fish this water is on a summer evening. The stone flies will be hatching and the trout will slide up on the rocks and along the beach areas driving them against the shore to school them up for the kill.

Since there is more sediment and mud in the lower reaches of the pool,

this is the home of the burrowing class of May-fly nymph. The Green
Drake is the best known of this variety and we are going to fish the
Green Drake hatch this afternoon, after a general round of the section
just to get to know it first.

If we have been fishing the head of this pool (not unlike our experience in the preceding chapter), we would be dropping down to position 1.

Since the light is bright at our noon hour, I'd suggest using very small
dry flies on a long leader tapered to 5X. Our casting will have to be very
well executed and we'll not be allowed any sloppy work or unnecessary
line movement. A look at the water between 1 and 8 shows the end of
the deep. We can cast up and out of the picture for a long drift down
the center until the fly reaches a point directly across stream. You'll not
likely bring up any monsters; in this light, you'll be lucky to snare even
a brash little brownie; but the point of the cast is to get used to the slow
flow of the water and to perfect your line handling.

Your next casts will be directed to a point directly across stream although on this pool you'll just about reach the center comfortably. The
gentle current will slide the fly to the cluster of underwater rocks immediately upstream from the two large boulders. The runs between them
harbor trout and a well-placed drift can bring a rise.

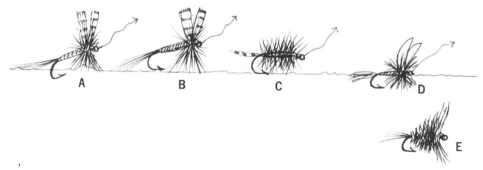

Figure 39. Five Types of Dry Flies.

*Note that each dressing gives the fly a different height from the water and
varied angles.*

*A. The conventional hackle size allows a generous angle and a medium
height off the water; the most general type tied by professionals for all-purpose
use.*

*B. The high-rider type where the fly is almost all out of the water. Note
the stiff tails that help keep the barb just in the surface film.*

*C. The Palmer-type fly with the hook riding well out of the water but
parallel to it.*

*D. The sleazy English type with soft, webby hackles. This fly floats like a
bug on the water, in the surface film, and is most effective when used during*

a hatch or on broken water where the silhouette of the fly should be obvious to the trout.

E. *The wingless all-hackle bivisible. A few turns of white hackle are used in front for better vision in bad light. The fly generally rides high due to the closely packed hackle.*

At this point I'd like to show you the various types of dry flies that I and a few professionals tie for our own use. We have discovered that not just any old dry fly will do even if it is tied to a specific dressing. A is dressed with a conventional-length hackle. B is the high-rider type of fly for fast-water fishing. C is the Palmer type with the hook riding parallel to the water, again for fast, broken water; and D, my favorite for this type of fishing situation, is the low rider that gives a buggy kind of impression since most of the fly is sitting on the water. It could represent a stream-bed fly such as the May fly or caddis, but it could also represent any kind of a blow-in that summer could produce from the woods and fields along the water course.

It may be a small point to bear upon, but I've seen the times when the mere change of the angle of the fly and its relationship to the current made the difference between no hits or light hits and solid-taking rises.

So, to humor me, and give you something to challenge, we'll use a Light Cahill of the D style and go forth. Since the nearest water is worked first, how about a downstream stop cast to the underwater rocks below your position with an allowed drift to the first exposed rocks out from 2. That's a good run. There's a small trout. He dashed out from behind a rock but lost his courage. In the evening he will become much bolder. Fishing down "dry" is often good!

Walking down to 2, we can now work upstream and across to the center boulders and rock clusters around 5 with a drift to 4, all in the same casts if we remember to mend upstream and keep our rod high.

The water looks barren of fish, you think, as I read your mind.

Have you ever fished a small stream, or at least a smaller one than this? If so, you've seen a great deal of water as shallow and as bare looking that has contained some mighty good trout. True, right now, the trout that are there are settled under the rocks to avoid sunburn, but they can be pulled up if you talk to them with the right medicine.

Later on, in the afternoon, our Green Drake will be busting out all over this water, so let's proceed to fish the runs, just to get to know them for future reference.

From 3 the up-and-across casts are obvious and you can flip the flies and skitter them from rock to rock, letting them slither down the little washes between the rocks. From 4 you can cast directly upstream in conventional upstream work, remembering our lesson of the first chapter where we used the right- and left-hand curved casts. Before crossing to 4 we can fish the lip of the section between the end of the rock washes and the fall-off into the broken pebbly deeper section below. Drop your fly to the lip of this.

There you go . . . nice fish too, and he's going below. See you later.

That's good enough for both of us for lunch with a big hamburger as the side dish!

Back to the stream again. The sun is at a slightly lower angle now and shadows are beginning to build up in the holes and around the rocks. Let's go out a few feet and look for some nymphs.

The May-fly nymph lives a year or more in the underwater or nymphal stage, but after reaching the dun and spinner stage the insect exists for but a few days, usually one or two and at most a week. Much has been written for the dry-fly angler about the flying state of these insects, but little fishing or scientific data have been available recently about this

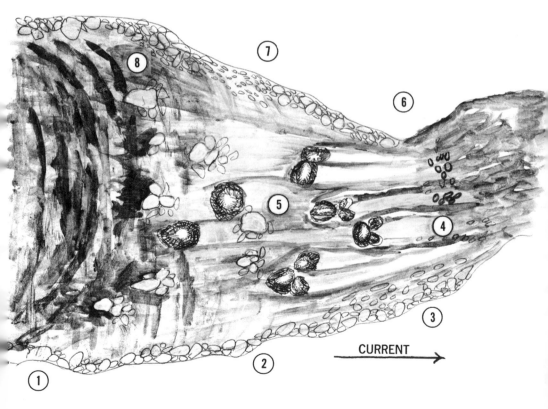

Figure 40. Tail of Pool I.

most interesting phase, the nymphal underwater period. Some anglers who are also aquatic biologists and serious students of the elements in their sport have done exhaustive research as it applies to angling. There have been some notable books written on these insects over the years, many of which have gone out of print because of such small circulation.

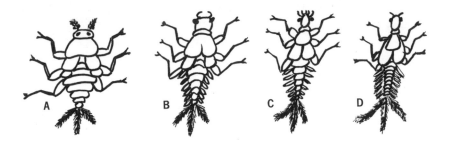

Figure 41. Four Types of Nymphs.

  A. *Clinger (Quill Gordon).*
  B. *Clamberer (Hendrickson type).*
  C. *Burrower (Green Drake type).*
  D. *Swimming (Leadwing Coachman type).*

As our illustration shows, there are four types of nymphs as grouped by scientists according to the insect's physical characteristics. Each, therefore, has definite peculiarities as to habitat, hatching activity, and life cycle. All of this in its interrelationship to the trout affects the trout's feeding habits, too, and consequently the angler's approach and presentation of his flies and lures.

Our Green Drake, a burrower, does just that: it burrows into the soft mud and silt of the stream bed, in the muck between the rocks and in the back eddies behind big rocks. Let's look for a sample in that lazy stretch between 1 and 2, where the current has left silt and ooze in the snags and along the sloping edge of the stream bank. See those small mining marks, similar to worm holes or mole tunnels, under the water and along the shore mud bank near the grass? Look, there's the tail of one of the nymphs. Let's pull him out gently. Watch him, he'll burrow in again to safety. He and his brothers will be hatching this afternoon and for a couple of weeks while this hatch is in its peak. They are the largest of the May-fly nymphs, ranging from one to one and a half inches in length. They are hairy and fuzzy-looking, semi-oval rather than flat like the nymphs of the fast water. Their only active means of locomotion is by kicking or flipping upwards as the current carries them along.

From the angler's point of view, the nymphs at this stage are of little importance except when a rain or sudden squall washes them into the stream and down into the mouths of hungry trout. They are extremely important, however, when it comes time for them to rise up from the bottom in an effort to reach the surface and hatch. Look out there about ten feet from us. There are two of them riding and kicking in the current. Let's watch and see them hatch as they drift downstream. Oops. Sorry, a trout saw them first, and he was a nice one. Came out from nowhere and disappeared into the same. No trout out here, eh?

In about half an hour this place will look like Grand Central Station at commuting hour. You'll see trout rising to the dry fly that you wouldn't believe existed.

At hatching time, usually mid or late afternoon, depending on the temperature and water height and Mother Nature's mood, the nymph rises to cast off its outer shuck or shell in transformation to the winged state or dun. It is now at its prime from the standpoint of food value to the trout. The nymph becomes very active and must cast off the armor-like suit quickly, for it is now vulnerable to attack from fish and birds. Nature puts it in motion during this period with full steam ahead. It's antics—there's another one drifting by now—at the surface while casting its shuck and working out its wings and the ultimate take off into the air cause much surface disturbance.

This is a big insect in relation to most of the others. The trout know all about this story, for they have been following the nymphs or awaiting them in the feed lanes.

For us to be successful, we must accurately imitate the hatching insect's movements, for if the trout were ever highly selective, they are on this hatch from its beginning until the final hours when the duns transform into spinners. Once they become "hooked" on this flavor, nothing short of a miracle will switch them to something else.

Once transformed to the dun, the insect will never feed again, but must live on the energy stored within until its final act of mating in the spinner stage.

So, let's join the nature sequence from the point of view of our imitation. Fishing the Green Drake nymph in the late afternoon in quiet water such as our lower section of this pool is one of the most interesting and productive forms of nymph fishing. It is quiet water presentation demanding most of all a very careful and wake-free approach. We must learn to wade like a heron. And if we work it right we can fish both sides of the stream right up to the head of the pool, if mud and ooze is present. Remember, too, that if there is any amount of mud bank or overhanging undercut banks upstream, many of the nymphs will drift down from there and follow along the shore of our pool.

Let's take a position upstream from 8 and work that section down to

7 and 6. We'll throw a fairly long line, say forty feet—nine-foot leader included—placing the nymph in the moving water, and we'll guide it slowly into the pockets or still sections in front of and behind submerged or exposed rocks. Fish it very slowly, almost as if you were dangling a worm. Rollcast your pickup to make a minimum of disturbance for the recast. When fishing the deeper section, such as the tail of the pool between 1 and 8, you can allow the nymph to sink and then imitate the action as you saw one struggling to the surface when the trout hit it.

Now, look out there in the current. There are nymphs preparing to hatch—moving up to the surface, kicking along and trying to swim. Some hatch in the still water; others will make it where they can, often in the wash behind midstream rocks where the wash holds them in and whirls them around in the confines of the rips. This sort of action is what tantalizes the most wary trout. Look over there in the wash behind that midstream rock. See that nymph? It's reached the surface and is casting its shuck. It'll soon be airborne.

Oh, no it won't. It's in a trout's stomach. A very gentle and hardly noticeable rise, yet did you note the size of that trout? Cast over to him and give him a taste of the fraud.

Now, look closely at the twin rock cluster just below us between 7 and 6. Several nymphs have crawled out and . . . congratulations, there's the first Green Drake of the day—on this section of water that is. The hatch has begun. Here come some floating down from the waters above.

Pretty little thing, isn't it? There's one that just flitted onto your rod tip. Note the tannish-green and silvery color of the wings and the pepper-spotted cream body. There's one right at your feet at the water's edge—on that small rock. He's hatching. Let's watch. See him flex his body back and forth? He's breaking open the nymphal shuck. He just split the shell down the back and is squirming out of it. Watch him unfold the wings from those small pads. It's quite a trick. There they come. Now, he'll flex them a bit to flatten them out. Now with the wings upright he can further undress down to his actual toes and the very tips of the thin hairy tails.

There's a slight breeze and, with the wings together in an upright position, he rocks a few times. Ah, away he goes, like a tiny helicopter to the safety of the woods.

Look up now. Your stream is having a snowstorm of Green Drakes.

Quite a sight, isn't it?

And that stretch of water you thought didn't contain any trout. Look at it boil now.

Hurry. Switch to your big Green Drake dry fly and to work!

Here come the swallows, the kingbirds, the phoebes, the flycatchers. The whole world of the trout stream is alive to the feast. You are a witness to one of the most beautiful and fruitful hatches of the entire cycle of the season on Eastern trout streams. You'll see millions of this insect species in the lakes, too. The Great Lakes region is no exception. I've seen hatches along the lake shore that were so heavy that the great amount of the flies cause the roads to become so slippery that cars stalled. The flies roll up in the lake surf like clods of seaweed.

Before you go at those trout like Grant taking Richmond, note one thing. A theoretical proposition first: If the hatch occurs here and the insects drift downstream each time they hatch, wouldn't the stream run out of the insects in a very few years? Sure it would. But it hasn't. They have been hatching here, perhaps for thousands of years. How come?

Use your eyes. Where and in what direction are those flies flying, other than toward shore?

And remember the caddis hatch? Same situation here.

Look closely again. See, they are all flying upstream despite the wind that is coming down the valley. If you recall, every time you have seen a hatch the insects always fly upstream.

Somebody must have told them to do it to survive in future generations.

I wonder who it could've been. Mother Nature?

Now, with three big trout in your creel, let's cross the stream, work the other side, and shoot a few casts into the head of the pool and then go in for supper. Looks easy, taking trout on that big floater. From 2 let's make a few casts up and out.

Wham, there's a rise. Right next to your fly. There was a dun there. Three flies are drifting by yours. There goes one of them. It disappeared into thin air. Watch closely. See that big old brown. He's not letting anyone know he's there—just sucking in those flies one by one, without any surface fuss. Smart old buzzard.

Pick up your fly and send it upstream of him. That's fine. Now, when it drifts over his position, twitch slightly. That's it. Bingo. He'll go fifteen inches, if you land him.

Let's quit while we are ahead and return for the spinner flight and some streamer fishing at dusk.

We'll use a sparsely dressed Coffin Fly (see Appendix) in a size 10. After the flight and the mating dance is over and the stream dark and somber, we'll work those lower flats, fishing right across them with some small streamer flies—streamers rather than bucktails because they seem to have a more wavy motion and can be jigged up and down more enticingly in such shallow water. We'll take a good trout or two this way from that stretch of water that has been feeding you all day.

Don't underestimate the tail of the pools. Leave the heads to the amateurs.

Figure 42. Head of a Typical Meadow Pool.

CHAPTER 13

Head of Pool II

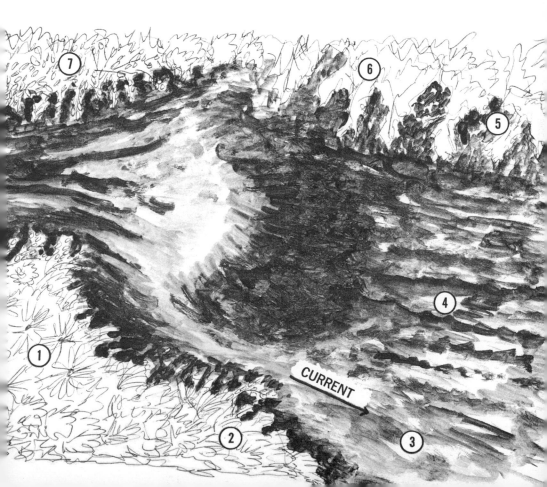

CURRENT

THIS is a typical meadow pool. Few if any rocks, lots of overhanging foilage, undercut banks that are exposed in the late season, and an obvious path of advance both downstream and up for your wading and fishing. The subtlety here is quiet approach and accurate and scare-free line handling.

Let's rehearse it once, since there's not a fly on the water. The day is sultry; no wind, nothing happening. Perhaps, before we are through, we'll wind up with a decent fish in the creel.

In the early spring when the water is high right in under those bushes, the fish congregate in the roots and branches to feed, seldom holding out in the stream center. The force of the water at that period is strong and there are no rocks to hide behind. The stream is all but impossible to wade. The worm fisherman have a grand time dunking their charges from the bank as they walk along.

But now it is summer. As we come upon this stretch we leave the brush at 2 and survey the runs and the deep hole, looking for the routine to follow and also for the fish that might be lying out there in the gin-clear. This is a good pool for downstream and across-stream wet-fly fishing. In early morning and late evening it is excellent water for the bucktail or a set of smaller streamer twins. Dry-fly fishing, even though there may not be a hatch, can almost always bring up at least a keeper trout until a hatch brings the big ones out from their stream-edge cover or up the hole in the center of the run.

Care is needed, as mentioned, for one false move and all the fish in the center will race for the cover of the overhangs. Those already there, with their noses pointed upstream, will simply back in under cover and sink down deep until you quit exercising.

So, watch it.

Yes, I see you looking upstream and there is a glint in your eye. But remember to fish the nearest water first; don't go spoiling all that water by a cast upstream from this position. Roll one from the bank, since there is no room for a backcast. Point it downstream to 3, let it drift for a couple of feet. Keep the leader high and the line off the water altogether.

What fly to use? Almost anything. A wet will do, so will a small bucktail. Why not a bucktail? It's easy to manage while we learn the currents and the drifts.

Now, mend that cast and flip it upstream between 3 and 4 and fish that broken water. It's deep under there and a likely place for a trout. No?

Okay, then, now try one up toward the shallow at the head of the pool and just as soon as the fly lands and drifts about a foot or two, roll it forward into the center, and let it drift back down to 4. Then begin your surface-dappling retrieve. That's the ticket for this water under the circumstances. It is easy to manage this from high on the bank.

Still no action? Let's go below the picture and wade in so that we can fish upstream to 3 and 4. We'll introduce you to the spider fly since there is a slight breeze to help it become active and enticing on the water. Surely we'll get a response from it, even if it is only an undersized hatchery fish. We've got the two undercut banks to work from our downstream position as we wade ever so carefully upstream.

The spider fly is meant to imitate almost any big fly that might land on the surface of such water. In many cases, the spider imitates the spin-

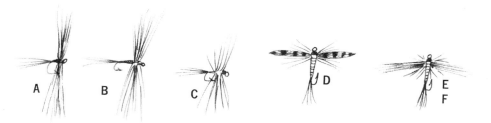

Figure 43. Spiders and Spentwings.

A. *Conventional-size spider fly with long tail, short shank hook, turned-up eye hook.*

B. *Spider on long shank, turned-down eye hook.*

C. *Modified fuller-hackle spider with enormous tail on conventional light dry-fly hook.*

D. *Spentwing fly, hackle-point wings, and spiral hackle (example: Adams pattern).*

E *and* F. *Spentwing made from feather fibers (hackle).*

ners of the May flies and is quite effective on smooth water at the time the spinners return to lay their eggs during the evening rise. It also imitates the crane fly and many of the land bred-insects, including the daddy longlegs spider. Strangely enough, it also imitates a plain old spider walking high on the water, as they are often seen performing. Trout like spiders, both real and artificial!

We enter the stream below the stretch illustrated, down from 3. The water is fast, the bottom gravelly and sandy and about up to the knees at the deepest place. If we wade quietly, placing one foot ahead of the other softly so as not to rattle the stones or make any wake that would telegraph our presence upstream, we can wade right over the good currents that hold trout. I can remember many times fishing this pool when I have had fish actually following me and my wake. They seem to like to ride in the currents and slower water that curls behind the legs. Perhaps you'll see a couple after you have stood in one place without moving for a few minutes.

Here you have the choice of fishing the undercut first or trying a few casts directly upstream. To get used to the spider, a size 12 with a span of about an inch in diameter, make a few casts to see how it handles in the breeze and during the false casts. On a light leader such as we have offered, tapered to 5X, the fly will tend to spin and hold back in the air, so a little extra power and more acute direction will have to be used to land the fly where you want it to light on the water. The slight breeze from up the creek will also tend to halt it in the air before it reaches the the water. This should make it land very softly and naturally.

Better stick to the open water for a few casts. Then you can shoot a few under the brambles. The first cast goes to 4 and lights nicely on a bouncing bit of current. Note how the fly cocks. Keep your rod high now. Gather in the slack, roll it forward again over the same run. You won't scare any fish because only the leader is on the water. Repeat this a few times, flipping the fly upstream farther and farther from your position. Now, do the same thing, only work over to your left toward the bank. The fly is now just at the lip of the deepest part of the center of the pool. Any trout hanging low in the hole will see that fly on your next casts, as they will be heading upstream. Nice cast right over the deep. Your fly settles down into the cocked or upright position. Twitch it a couple of times before slack develops. That's it. STRIKE!

See that? A nice trout came up from the hole and made a quick pass at the fly. Throw another cast farther to the left, right beside that white water stretch. Bingo! Another rise, but he failed to take. The sun must be a little too bright for him. Try again. Move up another few paces, for it is better to fish with a short line if you can wade carefully without disturbing the water. This whole pool can be fished without the line touching the surface. If necessary, use a longer rod and a longer leader.

Stopping now at 3, make your cast to the top of the hole with a right-hand bend. Let the fly bounce on the waves until it curls around. Raise your rod high when it reaches a point above 4 and skitter it right to your rod tip.

Take in the slack! Any fish that will strike it now will do so suddenly, as you have seen. Work your fly in toward you now. That's it, right under the rod tip.

Spray in your face? You bet! That trout came to within seven feet of you; he must have thought you were a stump in the water or something. See how you can wade tight in the good water and still not disturb the fish?

Now it is a matter of which bank to work. Before you make the choice, look at the direction of the sun. Which bank has the most shade at the moment? The far one, of course. That's the one to work. But don't stampede it over there. Move a foot at a time, casting as you go along. Place one right at the break at the head of the pool directly above you, then one about halfway to the bank. Now move over to 4. Careful, the water is deeper there and shelves off still deeper until it dives right into the undercut. There must be an armload of trout in under there. What a spot!

You'll cast right to the far corner, just where the shallow empties into the deep run along the overhang. Roll an upstream left-hand bend in the line so that the fly will descend first. If it does not reach in under the brambles on the first try, you can cast again. Try the first cast so that it will skirt the edge, just to see what the currents do to it. Good drift. Now skitter your retrieve with the rod high and the slack collected. False cast for the next throw and this time send it a little farther and follow it up with a generous bend of line before it has drifted at all. That's it . . . Now it will drift by under the brambles. Mend upstream. Don't let that current belly the line and pull the fly out from that good path. Retrieve again and this time be a little bolder with the extra mend. That will put the fly way in under. If you get snagged, so what? Flies are expendable.

Now risk life and live dangerously. Place that fly right into the wedge between the brambles just up from 6. Mend your line upstream as usual. This is the payoff shot. Now, let the fly drift down freely. Don't mend or you'll get hung up. Boy, that fly is really searching out the darkness under there. There must be a lunker . . .

There is, or was. What a take! Looked as if he fell in rather than rose out to take the fly. Hit hard, didn't he? Nice fish. Now pray that you can keep him from the snags.

Don't hold your rod back too far. No, you're too low. Split the difference. You must learn the right position for playing a fish with such delicate tackle under such tough conditions. Get your rod down, off the vertical. Play that fish from the horizontal position so that your line will help you in the battle and will not become snagged in the overhang if the fish decides to go in for a safety push.

He did it. He's under the worst of the snags. Pray hard, but keep that line as tight as possible against him.

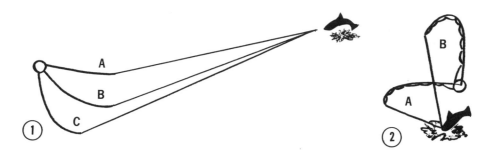

Figure 44. Playing the Fish.

In sketch I the angler is playing the fish. A is too straight a line from the rod to the fish. No chance of a cushion from the rod tip in case the fish jumps or makes a sudden burst of speed. No control here to aid the line hand. B is just right . . . It is a right angle to the line with just enough cushion from the rod. In C the rod is too far back and a sudden jerk from the fish will snap or overstrain the leader unless your line hand is extremely sensitive. The layout shows the rod in the horizontal position, not the vertical.

In sketch II we show A—preferred in almost all cases. B—the vertical is good for the photographer and the theorist but is not preferred.

Now he's body-rolling. You've stopped him and he's drifting down. Out he comes and up to the surface.

It's a big brookie. What a beautiful sight! Hold him. Wade below now and over near the brush. Let him lead out into the center. It will be good if you can get below him, or get him above you—same thing. That is the best position for the netting. Watch your slack. Keep that rod parallel to the water, not angled up.

Ah, safe in the net. Nice one, eh?

You should be congratulated. You have waded properly, casted well, and drifted your fly in one of the most difficult situations in trout fishing. You've reacted to the hit, hooked a good one, and played it correctly. There are not ten out of a hundred anglers who would perform that well. I've seen some pretty sad times at this type of problem, or, worse still, I've seen the whole situation passed up because the angler was not bold enough to really try to get his fly way in there where it would count. The proof that I'm right is the trout in your creel. That is a nice fish, and he had been there for some time. There are no hook marks in his jaw.

That one will look mighty nice on tonight's platter.

Let's leave the stretch alone for a while. What do you say we try fishing the bucktail upstream, for without moving a foot we can shoot a fly well up into the beginning of the current fan out and jitter that fly on its descent, particularly into that corner that was your previous target. We'll go back to dries when the Coffin Flies, Green Drake spinners are flying.

Sure, you could sail your spider up there, but let's go down deep and see what we can conjure up.

Shorten your leader. Take off the tippet from the basic tapered leader. You are now down to 3X, which is about right for a lightly dressed size 12 long shank. We'll try a black and white bucktail, one that I tied with the rear-end hairs just short of the hook bend. Those long streaming flies look good on the counter or stuck in your hat. I like my flies tied short so that the trout don't nip them and escape the hook.

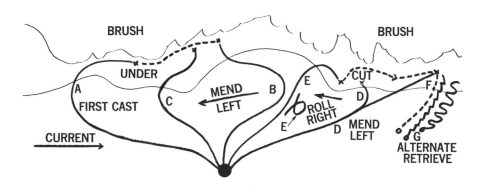

Figure 45. Fishing the Undercut Bank.

A typical delivery of the fly to the undercut bank way in under those pesky overhangs of branches and brambles. The trout in there are coolly settled behind the rocks, but with their noses pointed outwards and upwards as they keep a sharp eye and look out for passing food or dropping insects from the storehouse above their heads.

In A the cast goes out in a left-hand curve. Line drifts to B and begins to drag. It is rolled back to C with slack. The rod isn't placed at right angles, to offset the slack and in preparation for a strike. Line drifts to E and begins to drag again at D. Feed some slack line as it drifts to F, and as it swings at G, begin your retrieve to pickup point O.

Away you go. That's it, dead center, now mend to the right; quickly, raise your rod high. Step on your toes if necessary!

The fly went right into that corner. Skitter it out in a short jerk.

What a smash! He missed, but he'll try again on your next cast. He looked hungry.

Drift in to the edge of the overhang and . . . okay, now zigzag the fly back to you for the pickup and return it to the hot spot and do exactly what you just did before. You'll hook him this time.

Nice. Dead center. He should take. Good drift. Well, the teacher isn't always right. Maybe we'll take him tonight. Leave him be for now.

That left bank? We haven't touched it yet. That should be easy. Just reverse your mends. While you try in there, I'm going ashore to have a smoke and clean that brookie. I want to see what he's been eating lately.

Figure 46. Tail of Pool II.

CHAPTER 14

Tail of Pool II

THIS is big water, fast water, tough water to fish no matter what the season. It is holding water for big fish in the early spring, a haven for large fish needing cool runs and lots of oxygen in the summer. Even in low water the deep spots can care for many big fish.

Let's go back to the date of our first venture together when we fished the big central rock. That day was cold and forbidding, remember?

Our stream is a fast mountain stream falling down the high hills into the valley where city people cram the woods during their summer vacations. Below this stretch, about a mile of similar water tumbles down until it quiets in a big reservoir. Twenty-inch rainbows ascend this river from the big deep in droves as soon as the ice is out in March. April finds the large redsides ascending to spawn and descending after they have done their duty. Add to this migrant population big resident brown trout, some weighing as much as ten pounds, and you have the potential of the finest stream in the Western Hemisphere, yet a well-pounded water not more than a hundred or so miles from New York City.

In this early season, the water is cold, sometimes less than 40 degrees. I've often fished it under flurries of snow. Many times it has been impossible to cast the line through frozen rod guides. Yet this is the time to work such water for the big fish. Now you are not fooling around hoping for something to rise to your cast. You are literally hunting for the big ones. While many of these fish will be taken from the heads of the pools, many more are taken from the broken water and tails of pools by the anglers who know how to fish such water.

Wading here is hard work and, because of the temperature of the water, dangerous if you should fall in. Bring along a stout wading staff. You'll need it, if you choose to go out there in the rocks.

Big bucktails are in order. If no one is looking, use a spinner of the Colorado type, perhaps with a worm attached. Personally, I like to use the minnow imitations, bright-colored ones. The water sometimes has a chalky color or clay tinge. Much of this stream flows through the mountain passes where the banks have been eroded. Exposed clay banks are washed in every year.

The live minnow talent and the spin fishermen who know how to fish this water can score a barrelful of these rainbows. I know one poacher who for many years used to fill a tub with these fish and freeze them for his meals all summer long.

They never caught him at his exercise, but I did several times and learned some of his tricks. He used to tell me that he could catch as many of the 'bows on my flies as he could on his bait. Several times, when I met him on the stream he'd perform and taken rainbows right under my eyes as if he were picking up meat at the supermarket.

Here's how he did it. First of all, he went forth armed with a veritable

Figure 47. Tail of Pool II.

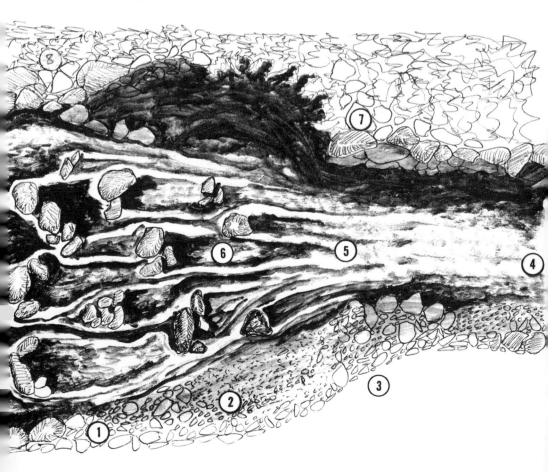

salmon rod. It was nine feet long, almost bass-bug action—stiff and power-ful. His line was a GAF taper. The butt of his leader tested fifteen pounds and he tapered the nine-foot strand down to only 2X. He didn't fool with any light stuff, not for fishing in this fast and deep water after three- or sometimes five-pound fish that hit like a thrown brick.

"Let the experts use that thin stuff. They are the conservationists who drive up here from the city for exercise, not for trout."

He'd start at almost any part of the run, and, incidentally, one day I saw him take six rainbows, none under twenty inches, from this very water, so pay attention!

For the sake of example, let him enter across the stream from us and our grandstand seat. Put him at 8. Out goes a short cast down into the first white-water run at his feet. He'd tumble the fly as it went down in the froth, jerking it up, rolling it forward to sink and bringing it up in quick and almost drastic motions. If he did not provoke a rise on the first cast, he'd swing the cast over into the deadwater near the bank in short jerks between long pauses, rollcast down again in the same run, and repeat the process about ten times before moving into another lane.

He worked fast, covering the heads of the rocks to the very left of the picture, not letting the fly drift between them yet. He'd skirt that fly right on the surface despite the fact of the deep water under it.

Then, before he left his pose on the shore, he'd shoot a very long cast that would land in the water just above the corner at 7, let it sink down, rollcast a partial pickup to lift it again to the surface, and allow it to sink again. What a commotion—and it usually netted him at least one or two good hits. He seldom missed a strike as there was little if any slack line due to his constant manipulation of the fly.

He'd shoot one more, an even longer throw to 7, and drift the fly right into the deep run and, by vibrating the rod tip in combination with line-hand snapping, zigzag the fly right back to his feet. That usually pro-duced at least one good trout, brown or rainbow.

By this time he usually had a group of anglers gathered around him to watch the show. The beginners in their smart new fishing togs would stand there transfixed and glassy-eyed at the size and frequency of his catches. Then he'd attack the deep holes behind each rock. One by one he'd spat the fly, flash it once or twice, and snap it out to recast into the same hole again. He seemed to know just which spot contained a trout that would take his fly on the bounce. He'd work that hole until the trout took the fly from annoyance if for no other reason.

He was smart as well as fast and hard. He wouldn't reach out too far, any farther than he could control. The big rod obviously gave him a mar-gin over the light-tackle boys and he took full advantage of it.

So far, he hasn't even wet his boot bottoms.

He'd march down to 7, lighting a big cigar on his way. He'd never stop to light it, but apply the torch en route. From 7 he'd land at least three fish rollcasting slightly upstream into the pockets in and around 6, letting the fly drift right down through 5. I remember one fish that must have followed the fly right to his feet. It struck just as he was fingering the end of the leader to uncoil a loop. The shock almost knocked him into the water!

Then he'd go home, carrying more than his limit of big trout, taken in less than an hour. The clan would disperse, probably go to the nearest bar and decide to give up trout fishing altogether. They had seen how easy it was and the frustration of the scene would likely send them to card playing and reading fishing books.

Now, that's how HE does it, and I suggest, rather than visiting the bar just yet, that you try the same tricks that he used. Go get yourself a whopper.

Starting out from the beach at 3, throw a good one to 5. But before you do, let's put a fly on the leader. This makes it a bit better game. Here's a setup I use for such water. Take my rod, a big strapping nine-footer with a good heavy line and heavy butted leader. See how I've rigged the leader and the flies?

Now, to keep that rig from fouling up in the air on the back and forward cast, you'll have to learn to throw a high, wide bow. This calls for a slightly longer and slower rod action to let the flies bow up high so

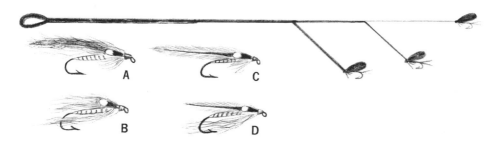

Figure 48. Tapered Leader and Flies.

Shown at the top is the nine-foot leader of poacher origin. Three feet of fifteen-pound test, three feet of ten-pound. The tippets are ten pounds to avoid coiling with the main line, which is lighter, tapered to five pounds and then to four pounds for the last fly.

    A. *Typical store-bought bucktail with long wings.*
    B. *My version, so trout will not hit and miss.*
    C. *Typical and pretty streamer.*
    D. *My shorter version, dressed sparsely, only two main feathers but long hackles on the underside. I prefer silver bodies on all minnow imitations.*

that they will not drop down on the line (see Appendix, page 302). Remember, you won't be false casting at all. Rollcasting this rig will demand the same slower yet more powerful action from your wrist and line hand, like making a rollcast in the double-haul technique.

With that rig and its handling under control, go stir up those rainbows. When I meet you for coffee, I expect to see you lugging at least three good trout.

Now some month and a half later, we are back on the same stretch of water under vastly different conditions. A few of the rainbows will still be in the stretch, but the biggest percentage of them have returned to the depths of the reservoir. There is always a good chance of finding an odd one, however. Certainly there will be some of the medium-sized ones and, of course, many good brown trout.

The Quill Gordons, Hendricksons, and March Browns have already hatched. For the past few days we've been experiencing very heavy caddis hatches of the Dark Cahill variety (see Appendix).

We are fishing now at late twilight. It has been a hot day, with little breeze and less activity than was experienced in the earlier hatches. Even the songbirds and swallows are quiet, waiting for the return of the caddis for their evening flight over the water when they will be depositing their eggs in order to continue their species. Since it rained for the past two evenings, restricting the return flight, there should be a great invasion from the skies tonight.

The caddis does not transform like the May fly to a spinner stage but is a completely developed adult the moment it emerges from the water and leaves behind it a life underwater as larva.

In this evening flight, the female is adorned with the egg sac, generally of olive-green color but sometimes bright yellow, depending on the species. Catch one of the insects in flight and the eggs will drop off in your hand. As usual, the insects are all directed by some mysterious power to fly upstream regardless of wind direction. When the wind is coming down the stream, especially in gusts, many of the insects are knocked into the water to struggle on the surface, drifting as they go right over the holes and into the feed lanes where the trout are waiting for them. This can produce an underwater show of submarines rivaling the exercises of the big powers. I've seen this water and stretches like it come alive all of a sudden. It makes you wonder where all those trout come from. They cannot be seen before the action starts, since there is no nymphal or larvae to drift toward the surface and bring the fish up.

The females rarely deposit their eggs in the main stream, but generally crawl into the water, usually down a rock.

Look at those midstream rocks. Here come the flies from the bushes and forest. Some will come from a distance of half a mile. They are landing on the rocks. Some, of course, slip or are blown into the runs and eddies, and wet-fly fishing using the skittering technique is in order. If you prefer, tie on a bulky, low-riding dry fly, such as the March Brown, in a size 12 or, better, a 14. Almost immediately, the eggs are laid and the insect merely floats downstream dead. Great quantities of these drifting flies are congregated by the current in the backwater and undercut between 7 and 8 and a hot spot where the flies are funneled down is the stretch of good current and deep holding water along the sharp bank of rocks below 7. A few of the flies will drift into the beach area, feeding the minnows, and quite often the big trout, seeing them rise, will come in and knock the school into the air. Many times I have watched big browns scow up the water of that beach and drive the minnows right onto the bare rocks. Once a big brownie jumped so hard and high that he landed on the dry rocks two feet from the shallow. I tried to get to him before he slithered back, but he was lucky.

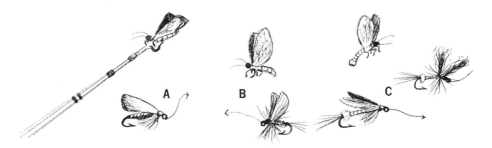

Figure 49. Caddis Return Flight.

A. *Adult caddis that has just hatched, resting on your rod tip. Note that the insect is fuzzy and soft, not clean and slick like the May fly. It is well imitated by this type of wet fly in several patterns such as the March Brown and Beaverkill.*

B. *The flying adult, though seldom found on the water, is well imitated by the duck wing, split-wing English-style dry-fly patterns.*

C. *The female carrying her egg sac is imitated by the hackle-point wing patterns dressed sparsely. The dry fly in the Wulff style tied very small and sparse is good when the flies are drifting in the fast water. Use the white wings at night; they're easier to see in the dark.*

About a week from now, you'll see nymph cases of the stone flies all over these rocks along the shore and in midstream. These are the shucks of the species shed the night before during their hatch. They wait until dark to crawl out on the rocks. They are slow flies and clumsy on their flight into the air. The slightest night wind will knock them down. Big trout like big flies—at night—but that's another situation we'll tackle soon.

Figure 50. Head of Pool III.

CHAPTER 15

Head of Pool III

TODAY we are going to break a rule. We are arbitrarily going to fish dry fly, whether or not the conditions call for it. This pool is just made for floating a fly and, let's face it, the art of delivery and the mere joy of watching the artificial come down toward us is fun, even if only chubs go for it.

Also, we'll indulge ourselves in the use of our favorite dry-fly rod, a slight but stiff seven-foot two-piece rod, made of bamboo of course. Glass just simply cannot duplicate the action and the feeling of a good bamboo rod. The tip action of this one is fast and I enjoy the whispy crack of the line and leader as it sings in the back-and-forth casts. A look over the shoulder on the backcast shows a flat, fast loop as the tiny fly zings past the air above my head and straightens out high above the water behind only to zoom forward well up from the water and then flutter down easily and lightly to the surface.

Once you get yourself a dry-fly rod that suits your needs and your feelings you'll be lucky. It took me about twenty years of constant investment and trading to find the one I like best. I would part with my wife before I'd part with that rod. (Don't quote me!)

I also believe in good rods of specific action for other kinds and types of fishing. I like a limber-tip soft-action bamboo for wet-fly fishing. It will throw a wide, deep bow. I slow down the push of the cast to bring out its best delivery. Then I like a stiff hard-tipped rod for use with big bucktails. Three rods, then, will suffice, although I must confess I own many more than that (see Appendix, page 291).

But, back now to that pet dry-fly rod. I'm armed with a ten-foot leader tapered to 5X, for I intend to use some hook size 16 dry flies. They are different than the usual store-bought 16's. They are overtied in a size 14, and so ride high on the water (see figure 51). I also tie a bivisible for this kind of water for bad light conditions.

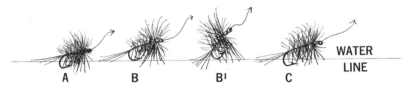

Figure 51. Dry Flies.

A. *Conventional-size hackle in proportion to the hook size.*
B. *An oversized hackle on a 14 hook.* B¹. *Still-longer hackle.*
C. *An oversized bivisible for puffball dry-fly fishing. This one is also good for fast and broken water.*

You'll note we haven't diagrammed this pool. We'll just fish it together. There are fish here to be caught and chances are if we show them enough good casts they will come up to investigate.

One of the reasons why I pick a high-riding fly for this comparatively easy flowing water is that the trout will not get too good a look at the fly and so reason to reject it before he hits. Chances are that if the fly gives the illusion of a beefsteak dinner he'll jump to his conclusion.

We enter the shallow at the tail of the pool. Foot after foot we inch our way slowly so as not to send a telltale wake upstream to warn the inhabitants. We'll cast from left to right, drifting our flies down from our right- or left-hand mends as we have shown in previous chapters. That instruction has now become second nature, hasn't it?

Watch most of the anglers you meet on the stream. Hardly one out of ten will ever use that technique. They'll throw the upstream cast directly over the area the fly will be drifting down upon and then they'll wonder why the trout are shy. Your use of the mend cast and the habit of holding the rod high is now going to be put to the test here. If you can enjoy this fishing, with the effort to learn and deliver your flies according to past directions, the day can be a real vacation. Also, it is a good chance for testing, for we will be fishing the smallest and then the largest flies in the book in this pool later this evening. We'll be midge fishing with dainty size 20's and then, when we return from our evening card game, about eleven o'clock, we'll tie on some big flies and choose the big fly rod that we use for bucktail fishing.

Nice flow to this water. It is traveling rather fast but is not broken by rocks, even underwater. The whole mass is one moving carpet as it flows down creamily from the break-up above.

It's really a hot day. Let's wade up a bit. We'll be up to our belts and be able to cool off a bit while we fish.

Here, try my rod, my little fast-tipped one. False cast with a zip. Don't be dainty with it. Now cast to the left, then to the right, then up the center, and finally begin to extend your casts until you reach the rocks on either side of the pool. You know what to do then. Mend the drift and let the cast go below you undisturbed by the pull of the current on the line. Delightful, isn't it?—even if a fish doesn't agree with you.

Just the pleasure of performance is sufficient reason to be astream.

For a change of pace, now, turn around and face downstream and stop cast your flies at your feet and work those runs as they develop below. You'll be fishing that water in the next chapter, so there is nothing like a sneak preview.

A small trout, that one, and glad he missed. Rest the area a minute and try upstream again with another pattern.

There's a breeze, I can hear it coming down the valley. Leaves fall into the air from above and some insects will be with them, dropping down just below the falls. There's a rise, and that means there is one trout up there that might be interested in almost any pattern. I'm going to try my old standby, the Royal Coachman. I bet I can bring him up again. There's another rise on your side, so we both have a target.

Nice throw to that rise. Now, let's see if I can work that wind-resistant fanwing up in that corner. Ah, there it goes. Now for a breeze to kick it about. Look at that thing flutter.

Smash! He's on. Nice rise to yours too. All we need now is for your trout to fight in my corner and mine to take off over to yours.

Since there are no hatches on the water let's see what these fish have been feeding on. Perhaps we can determine from their gullets what to expect for this evening's fishing.

Mine's got a gullet full of little black larvae. How about yours? No wonder they are not rising. They are feeding well down in the current where no one can see them. Ah, tonight, we'll fish midges, for there will probably be a good hatch according to this record.

When cleaning fresh-caught trout ever wonder about those tiny little black wormlike flies in their stomachs and how hungry the trout seem to be for them? Ever try to figure out the tiny dimpling rings made by trout noses during the times these insects are hatching in veritable droves in the evening twilight?

Ever think of trying to imitate these flies and learn to fish them effectively?

The midge fly in its many variations does a good job provided you use the fly at the right time and place and are able to present it properly to the trout. This pool is a perfect layout for fishing this fly, as we will see.

Most logic is against the use of such small flies for trout except, maybe, in very small streams. But, in nature, man's logic seldom gets him anywhere. Sure, a lure this small is difficult to see while fishing in darkened water. One also wonders how in the world a trout could see it among all the other bits of stuff floating down and tempting him; also, why he should consider a tiny bite when a big hunk of food might be floating right beside it. And, even if a trout were to get hooked on such a tiny barb, the chances of landing it would be about ten to one, conservatively. Despite all this logic, midge fishing is effective and perhaps the most exciting, under the right conditions.

While there are many heavy hatches, a most continual supply of these flies is available. The most prevalent, of course, is the black fly—the pesky biter that drives anglers and vacationers crazy. This scourge of the woods generally hatches in the peak of the best fly-fishing season: late April and into May in the central belt, and into July and even August in the more northern climes. When it hatches, it does so in actual clouds. Every trout you catch will be filled with them, especially if the fish is caught in the afternoon or twilight, the most potent time to use the black midge pattern, which imitates the black fly very well.

I can recall many times when I've all but been driven off the stream by the invasion of these pests. They may give us serious trouble tonight, so we'll arm ourselves with some repellent. We'll need to smear it on just as the fish begin to rise and dimple all over the water. You'll see lots of tiny rings, some made by chubs barely two inches long, and rings of the same size made by four-pound brownies. You can never tell which will

Figure 52. Midges.

These little larvae, usually of the black fly or mosquito, constitute a big portion of the trout's diet, especially when they are hatching. Size 18 or, better, 20 or 22 hooks are needed and the flies are tied in black and brown colors, very sparse—usually only two turns of tiny hackle over a ribbed body.

A. The actual insects in various positions in or near the surface film.

B. The artificial fly acting in the same manner. Fine leaders, 6X and 7X, are needed; also a dead-drift, drag-free delivery.

take your fly, so be prepared for the worst. Between swatting, spraying, and scratching, we'll be able to weather the onslaught and, if temper and steadiness continue, we'll connect with some good rises from chubs as well as lunkers.

As I look out over this pool, I can recall one evening in upper Maine that was a real stunner. All day long, the river had been free of black flies and the casting and photo-taking was a delight, even though we did not get a rise from other than fallfish and chubs. But once the cool air crept over the runs and pools, drifting out from the shaded side under the old spruces, the blacks took to the air in a vengeance.

Out came the fly dope. Then came the tying on of the tiny hooks.

The stream that for hours had not offered anything but drinking deer and circling hawks suddenly was transformed into an aquacade. Dimples, tail walks, jumps for joy (by the trout) were the order of the scene.

I threw my flies out in utter abandon and took trout with almost every cast. I was using three flies and believe me, you can get quite a come-uppance when three big fat wilderness brookies take hold all at once. They are a lot different fish from their hatchery brothers.

I was fishing with two other anglers in our party. They didn't take a trout until I yelled for them to put on some midges. Since they didn't have such a thing, I had to wade down to them. All in all, three of us hooked and released over forty fish that night. We kept the big ones, all over fifteen inches, which is quite a mark for Eastern brook trout.

Also, just in case you don't have such flies with you during one of these hatches, just tie on a bare hook, as small as you've got, wrap a bit of black thread on it and cast it out. Chances are it will work. It has at times for me.

I usually tie on three of these flies, so let's do it right now, since the sun has fallen and I've been bitten three times by blacks already. Select a nine-foot leader taped to 4X. Tie on 7X tippets about a foot apart, the highest, three feet from the end. Now tie on a 7X on the bottom. Keep them short, not longer than three inches, so that the cast will not tangle in the air or on the water. Dope the entire leader so it will float.

Now, see those rings ahead of you in the reflection. Can't tell what's under them, but we'll soon find out.

If the water were warmer than it is tonight, I'd fish the pockets behind boulders or at least the streak runs and deep runs of the bottom of the pool below us. There's a good one right above us. Cast your flies now, lightly. Merely let them drift down. Never mind worrying about the line. Trout are not skittish when they are feeding on midges in this kind of water and, particularly, in this darkened area.

Rise! Feel it? No, and you seldom will unless the trout hooks himself. Don't try to react to the strike. You have to depend on their hooking themselves in this act. You can't do it without disturbing the water. Besides, if you were to strike, you'd pull the hook out of the fish anyway!

There, another strike, but he missed. You can see that they like your fare. Just a matter of percentage now. Whoops, there you are, snub him gently and remember you are only powered by 7X and you don't yet know which fly he has taken.

That's the art of midge fishing. There's really nothing to it. It's the easiest casting, and before long if you don't have to pause to tie on a new one, you'll have landed a dozen fish, minnows, fallfish, trout, and perhaps even a good-sized brownie.

Possibly the best times of the year for midging are in the peak during April and May, and again in the late-August or early-September low-water period. Also, trout seldom move around much during the day and are touchy when it comes to any disturbance when they are about to feed. They'll rise to midges over the flats and just below the bubbly rapids before they'll react to bigger flies.

Work the heads of pools such as this one. Cast into the shallows earlier in the day, particularly if there is a shadowed portion in under some big old trees.

Let's quit now. I'm being eaten alive. Between the no-seeums, mosquitoes, and those black flies, I feel the need of refreshment behind the copper curtain of a screened-in bar. When all those pests but the mosquitoes go to sleep, we'll return to this pool and the stretches of water at its tail for a go at night fishing. About a month will pass at that bar and we'll likely hit into a good hatch of stone flies, the main fare of the big trout that only come out at night.

Let's flip to see who buys. We'll discuss the prospects and the story of the stone fly over a cool drink. In actual practice you'll find out more about wading and feeling the stream with your feet and inner eyes and inner ears than you ever thought possible.

The stone fly, a clamberer-crawler type of insect, is known in its most prevalent form as the water cricket (see Appendix, page 326). There are a great many species of this fly, generally distributed, that hatch at various times of the season. As their cast-off shucks will disclose, several species may hatch during the same night. All of the stone-fly nymphs are an ever-constant food supply to the trout, as they are largely bottom crawlers. With the exception of the giant species, they are quick of movement and well designed to hold on to their perch in the fast water as well as scamper off on strong feet to safety. Quite often slim wet flies and sparse and small bucktails imitate them very well. Stone flies depend on their ability to move quickly when aroused. They are generally found in and around big midstream or near-the-current rock clusters and in the trash of backwaters. Their bodies are somewhat flattened and range in size from three eighths to one and three quarter inches. They seldom venture far from the darker sections and are almost never found near the top of the water in the company of many of the May-fly nymphs. In imitating them the angler learns to fish near the bottom, especially in the early spring in order to interest the trout in his fly.

During the spring washouts some of these insects become temporarily dislodged and are whisked away in the current, yet they are far from helpless, as in the case of most May-fly nymphs. These stone flies can readily return to the safety of the bottom or at least grab hold of a rock and then look for safe quarters.

In sharp contrast to many of the other insects, the emergence of the stone fly is relatively unimportant to the angler, for the majority of the stone flies transform at night, and, as their name implies, they hatch on the stones along the stream edge (as pictured in figure 52) or on large midstream rocks. The empty shucks are a common sight on all trout streams, so study them for use later in tying your imitations or selecting the proper-sized wet or dry fly.

Figure 53. Stone-Fly Nymph and Adult.

The flashlight shone on the rocks by the edge of the stream reveals the stone-fly nymph and its hatched adult with wings folded but about to take off into the air. Tomorrow the rocks along the stream will be covered by the empty shucks of this specie of fly, telling you the story of what went on the night before.

The fully developed adults then dry their wings in utter safety and fly away to the trees, bushes, or rocks nearby. Only when they choose a low-level rise out over the water will the trout jump for them. A sudden gust of wind will knock them down and then the trout will come up in a fierce rise and tear the surface of the water to pieces in order to catch their succulent morsel.

The adult winged stone fly has four equally long, smooth, shiny wings that it folds flat over the back when at rest, not in the vertical position similar to the caddis fly.

Figure 54. Night-Fishing Flies.

A. *Standard duck-wing Leadwing Coachman in size 10.*

B. *A March Brown in size 10 or 8 is a good night fly for fishing the stone-fly hatch.*

C. *The author's imitation of the stone-fly nymph. This can be weighted or unweighted (see Appendix).*

The return flight occurs the night after hatching and at dusk or after dark, which points up the reason why we will shortly partake of excellent night fishing. There is no real necessity for actual nymph imitations, despite the fact that there are many on the tackle counters. Any large and dark wet fly will do when properly presented in the rips, along the shelving riffles, behind the midstream rock washes at the heads and tails of pools.

Before we go forth, one more bit of refreshment while I discuss some "musts" that will help you in your wading and casting. You won't have any light out there.

Night-fishing success requires that you know the particular stretch of stream that you will fish. That's why I picked one with no holes, jagged rocks, or sudden bursts of strong currents. Never attempt strange water in the black of night or you are liable to break an ankle or fall into a hole. It is also better to use the skin divers' "buddy system." Don't go alone unless you advise the innkeeper or your wife where you are going. Sounds scary, but it doesn't have to be if you use some sense. Also, when the water and terrain under it is known by day, a course can easily be plotted that will lessen the chance of accidents and will, in addition, lead to fishing the water properly with the final objective of taking some really big trout, fish that don't show themselves to the daytime vacationer.

The best night fishing is reserved by nature for summer and late-season angling when the days are hot and the water low and clear. It is then that the trout hide under rocks, ledges, or in deep holes.

The largest trout generally sleep out the day in a semi-dormant state and, following the adage of "mad dogs and Englishmen," stay well hidden from the sun and light and wait for the coming of darkness before foraging for food. Their hiding ability is amazing, for during these bright days, every nook and cranny, every inch of the stream bottom is blatantly visible.

Lest there be any doubt about the sporting aspect of night fishing, I'll go on record saying that this method of taking trout is no less sporting than any other. Method does not take fish from the stream—it is the angler. There is no law against returning hooked fish to the water. There is a law against night fishing in certain states at certain times, so check the books before you put this chapter and part of the next one into practice.

Now, let's go.

As we leave the car and head down the path through the woods, we'll use the flashlight only sparingly to get used to the darkness. When we arrive near the stream we turn it off for good, smoke a last cigarette, for absolutely no light can be used from now on. We also note that it is the dark of the moon, a better time than when the moon is high and shining brightly.

Now here we are at the stream edge. Note how quiet it is. Take a few steps over the rocks and gravel. Notice how noisy you are? That can't go on, especially underwater, for that vibration will put any fish down that are feeding or about to go on feed.

We'll enter the stream near the top. Down ahead in the path is the silhouette of the two old dead trees. Out in the brush we'll just stand here a minute, get used to the darkness, accustom our eyes to the water and our ears to the sound of the falls. Peaceful and quiet, isn't it? Only an owl breaks the rhythmic din of the water rolling on over the rocks.

As our eyes clear, we begin to see the movement of the water as it flows below. A bat flies by; a good sign. There's another fluttering about near the falls.

Hear that? Listen.

Hear that rise? There's another about ten feet down from the falls.

Wow, there's another farther down in the center. He flapped his tail at something. Our trout are on the feed.

Come through the brush quietly. Remember, now, you have no backcast room so you'll have to roll. Pick your target carefully, for you will only have a few casts before scaring down that rise and you'll have to wait until the trout come back and go on feed again. With luck the slight breeze will send some of the stone flies onto the surface.

Try a cast now, carefully, before you enter into the water.

That's it, right across the center. Now just allow slack to feed from your line hand; don't mend the cast. Keep a trigger finger on guard and hold your rod high but not too far back, for if you get a strike you'll want to react instantly. It will not be a hard smack, but rather a tug. If you were to see your trout in his feeding position, he'd be slightly angled up with his nose in the surface film. He doesn't usually see the fly, but senses it near him, or feels it rub by through touch. He then merely opens his mouth.

There. You were caught off guard on that tug. He bumped the fly and a slight tug on it gently flipped your rod tip. Don't retrieve, let your fly drift down. There he goes again and this time he's on for good.

Haven't felt a fish like that recently, have you? There he goes, straight down the center of the pool. Snub him a bit, turn that rod to right angles to the line and flat to the water.

Wow, what a splash! That must be a monster.

Now, since the pool is pretty well disrupted, it will be some time before things settle down. Come with me toward the tail of the pool. You haven't been there yet, so I'll guide you by the hand, since there are some deep runs there that you could fall into.

The first deep run on our side begins after the quiet water. You can feel it begin to tug at your waders as we go downstream. That black stretch straight down is a good run. This time you merely drop the fly under your rod tip and feed out line at it pulls. Get to know that feel.

I hear another trout feeding. He's in the center of the middle run, so rollcast a mend to your left with a generous push and about four feet of line. There. That's it. Let it drift down now and also allow it to swing as the line tightens. Just about the time you feel the current act on it you'll likely get a touch. There's the splash again just below where the fly should be.

You're on! He took that one for certain and is tail-walking to throw the barb. Snub him a bit. Swoosh, there he goes under. Lucky you have such a deep bit of water to fight him in. Now that he's in the net, we can turn the flashlight on him.

Beautiful fish, isn't it? Bigger than your first. Make you hungry for more night fishing? Limit yourself to three fish a night; don't get too hungry. Release as many as you like, and save them for another time.

Listen. Hear that rise? Right behind you upstream. It's an easy cast.

Just turn around. Throw one upstream and hold your rod high. If he hits, he'll explode in your face.

That's calling the shots! Not as big a fish as you took last time but it will°have to be bent to put it in the creel with the others.

That's a sample of night fishing. I put you into an easy pool to fish and we were lucky to find the fish feeding right off the bat. Usually I have to wait for half an hour before I hear a rise. There is not much sense in casting until you can spot a feeding fish by locating the general vicinity of this activity. Too much casting could put down any trout that might be just about to take up their feeding position.

The main thing to remember is to wade ever so softly. Because of the darkness and quiet, you'll become aware of your feet and the noise your boots make as they crunch, crunch on the rocks. Hold that noise down to a minimum. The experience is a good one to have now, because it also gives you some idea of how much underwater noise wrong wading can make even during the day, for there is no difference between day and night underwater. You can then begin to realize just how many trout are put down or scared away long before you have the opportunity to spook them with wrong or badly directed casts. You can deduct correctly that ninety per cent of the reasons why anglers fail to raise trout is because of the noise of their wading.

Tomorrow morning, if we haven't tired you with this midnight fare, you can go to the stream—to this very pool and fish with the same big wet flies and repeat this process of wading carefully and casting more deliberately. You'll get the entire picture then. There will still be some stone flies about and, of course, millers and moths. There will be fish rising at least until the first rays of the direct sun pierce the water from atop the hill. By that time you'll be needing ham and eggs and good strong coffee.

Figure 55. Tail of Pool III.

CHAPTER 1 6

Tail of Pool III

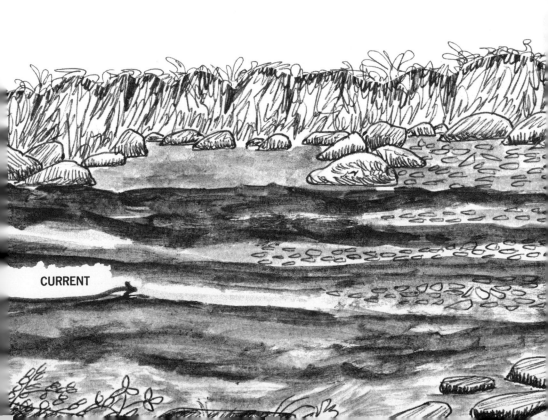

CURRENT

A full day can be spent on this type of water provided no other anglers upset it for you. The whole gamut of flies and techniques can be brought into play from early morning until late evening, especially during May and June, the prime hatching months when the principal species of flies are constantly emerging.

In the early spring, the runs are not so well defined. Late in the year when the water is clear and low, they are even more defined than shown in figure 55.

On a nice May afternoon when, perhaps, nothing is happening, we could start with the wet flies, say a Dark Cahill and a Light Cahill, and from 1 drift the flies beginning right from the downstream-pointed rod. Feed out the line by hand-feeding it to the rod and tip-flipping it out, to fish the entire run almost to 3 and pickup in the shallows. To rest the area, throw a cast smartly in the direction of 10 and let the flies drift over the edge of the deep and down perhaps into the shallow below 8. A longer cast could encompass position 9 and the drift to 8 with a swing into the run just above 3.

If nothing rose to any of these casts, we could then move to 2 and fish both up and down. Quite often the mere change of direction of casts and consequent line flow due to a fresh rod angle will sometimes bring a strike from water that has been previously worked to no avail.

Since we are experimenting and "hunting" for fish at this hour, we might add a bobber dry fly of a puffy tapered hackle type rather than the conventional dressing. This will pop and flutter on the water enticingly. This technique works particularly well during the March Brown and Gray Fox hatches, the two insects that sometimes overlap at this time. And since this is the period when a hatch of this species could come off at any moment, let me tell you about this favorite.

Through the winter the March Brown nymph, in company with the Quill Gordon and other clinging-type nymphs, has been clinging to the undersides of rocks and gravel found in the fast water of the stream. If this were March, before trout season, we could easily turn over some of the rocks around 2, 3, 4, and 6. We'd find that through the dark, bleak weather, when to all intents and purposes our stream has been asleep, he has been living his precarious underwater life. Spring freshets threatened to dislodge him. Other nymphs of the carnivorous type, such as the stone flies, lie in wait for him. Minnows also hiding in the backwaters behind the rocks like to feed on him when he shows himself vulnerable. Hungry trout are ever-present and ready to take him when he is off guard. During his growing period he sheds eleven shucks before hatching from the last one into the dun stage.

In this month of May the stream receives more light from the higher sun and there are warms spells when the current becomes more equitable to the developing insect. The wing cases on the nymph's shoulder have begun to develop and turn from a rust to a deep, dark brown in preparation for the wings-to-be in its future adult life. Comes the time of emergence, the nymph releases himself from his rocky home along with

Figure 56. Tail of Pool III.

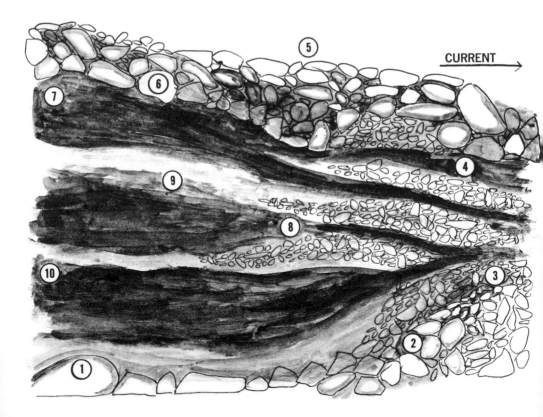

countless others of his clan and begins to drift helplessly in the bottom currents and side waters of the stream. The layout in front of us is excellent water for such a condition to be seen.

Look out there in the middle current. See those trout beginning to flash. They are not feeding on the bottom caddis like you've seen them do many times, but are taking drifting nymphs, March Browns, and it is time we worked our way back up to 10 to cross over into the head of that run. From there we can work all three stretches successfully with our March Brown nymphs. Later as we work downstream we'll turn around, and when the hatch is beginning to get started we'll switch to the dry fly. In the space of less than two hours we have theoretically fished from the bottom to the very top of the water, killing the old theory that nymph fishing is for early spring, wet fly for in between, and dry fly for the crest of the season to its end.

Those nymphs, as you can see if you look down into the water as it passes your waders, kick and squirm. They do not drift as the Hendricksons do in a lifeless manner.

There's a trout right beside you. Did you see him flash and take a nymph from under your nose? You can catch trout now by duplicating the action of those nymphs in the water just below you. Tie on my suggested March Brown nymph (see Appendix) and go to work. I'd weight the leader with one bit of wrap-around lead so that it can be removed easily once the flies begin to pierce the surface film. Work all three lanes, starting with a short drop cast and letting the current pull the flies down into the lanes, bouncing them on the bottom. Pull them toward the surface as we have shown before to let them drop again. Study the nymphs that are drifting by you.

Hit? Sure it was, but your slack line was too generous. Try keeping it a little tighter. There. A nice fish, that one . . . a brownie.

Open him up. See what he's been feeding on? March Brown nymphs.

Cast over to 7 and let the flies sink deep in that run. I just saw a good fish feeding about halfway down. He's on. Now, keep your tension steady or you'll lose him!

Some of the insects are approaching the surface. Note the trout action. See, they are breaking the surface in follow-through leaps up to the surface film. That's the action that fools the dry-fly fisherman. Sure, if he were to cast a floater over the action area he might get a trout, but he'd stand a better chance of drifting the nymphs, now unweighted, right under the surface film, skittering them and allowing them to swing in the current just before the pickup.

Try that action down your center run. Three fish just bulged down below you. Good drift. A take? No, he missed. Try again. There, he's on.

Now it's time to get rid of that leader with the tippets and switch to the March Brown dry fly. Wade downstream quietly as you rerig. I see a few of the duns already on the water fluttering in the currents in the center of the pool above the illustration. They have hatched from the head of the pool, or perhaps even from the rocky ledges above it. Anyhow, they're here. There's a rise to the dun. There's another. Quickly now, cast while this wave of insects is fluttering on the surface trying to shed their nymphal skins and take off into the air. Quite a sight, isn't it?

Now, take a fish on your floaters!

The March Brown dun is one of the easiest of all the species of May fly to identify. It is the largest of the flies in the cycle of the season so far, the Green Drake being the largest. Note that the wings, usually held in an upright position by most species, are slanted back about halfway down over the body (see figure 56). The insects are generally a cream and rust-brown mottled coloration with grayish mottled wings and speckled legs.

HENDRICKSON   MARCH BROWN

Figure 57. Hendrickson and March Brown Duns.

A. *Hendrickson example with wings held erect.*
B. *March Brown and Gray Fox with wings "bent" down.*

Like all the May-fly group, the insect has one more stage of development similar to that described in previous chapters in this book, that of shedding the dun skin and emerging again at nightfall in the adult or spinner stage. If we bear in mind this life story, the fishing technique becomes readily apparent.

This is the season when most of the wild flowers are in full bloom and the air and bushes are alive with all species of sparrows, warblers, finches, verios, phoebes, and wrens, to mention the most common. It is apt to be a changeable time of the year, weatherwise, since the weatherman is confused as to whether it is late spring or early summer. On many a May afternoon I've found myself suddenly running for cover just in time to avoid a cloudburst. Other times, the day has started out warm and sultry, almost humid, and by lunchtime clouds have gathered suddenly and the temperature has dropped to near freezing by night. All these changes affect the fish as well as their insect menu and watching these changes can help to show the way to cope with them when it comes time to choose the right fly and its presentation.

Any true angler and lover of the out-of-doors cannot help but enjoy watching the emergence of the March Brown or the other insects, especially when acquainted with their basic life story. It is also comforting to know that the countless species of flies are going to be developing the whole season long. Every day the drama goes on, each week of the season another cast of characters and an overlap of species.

Sometimes overlapping the March Brown, the Gray Fox is every bit as important to our angling. The nymphal habits and life cycle of this fly is very similar to the March Brown, though the nymph is a shade smaller. Fish a size 12 and you will approximate it (see Appendix, page 322).

The nymphal and wet-fly imitations are so similar that either pattern will suffice. Their colorations vary somewhat. For instance, the light phase of the March Brown is difficult to distinguish from the dark phase of the Gray Fox, so here again some experimentation is in order if exact imitation is called for.

Think I'm splitting hairs? Well, when I first started studying the stream insects years ago, I'd make copies of them from the insects I had captured and secured in liquid plastic that hardened into slabs for studying the various light rays that approximated their natural surroundings. I'd go forth with artificials tied exactly the same BUT WITH VERY MINUTE DIFFERENCES IN COLOR. The fish at times would take only one pattern consistently.

As far as the dry-fly patterns for the floating duns of either species are concerned, I have seldom had experience that would definitely point favorably to one or the other. Generally, a good rule to follow on any hatch is to fish a dark pattern on a dark day and a light one on a bright day.

Tonight let's fish this water upstream first with the dry flies. We'll keep our eyes peeled for a midge hatch and the telltale dimples from rising trout. Just before dark, if we see the trout scrambling around in the shallows at the very tail of the pool, we'll drift some small dace imitations right to their noses. There is also the possibility of a stone-fly hatch, which if it comes off will lure us into fishing until the moon comes up.

Nice bit of water. We'll remember it clearly, from our experiences. We'll plan to work it over well, perhaps on Opening Day next season when we'll sink our wet flies or nymphs and course through the runs with heavy bucktails.

It will feel good to be on the trout stream again after so many months of dreaming about fishing, tying flies and pondering over our missed fish, reveling in the memory of big ones hooked and landed on such water. In our vision we will remember many streams of our travels and the similarities of the problems that are basic to all trout streams, be they East or West, large or small.

We'll find this stretch because it lies at the tail of a wondrous pool that we can work well, even if the water is high and roily. We've seen it when gin-clear and lower. We know its bottom contours; the places where the fish will be hiding and feeding until the water drops later in the season.

We'll likely stand ashore and drift wet flies deep. We'll try our green caddis larva imitation, weighted. It will drift down along the near side and along the currents. When we arrive at about the head of the lower section of the pool, we'll probably find the urge to tie on a bucktail and work the surface water in the fast zigzag to scout out a big 'bow. We'll look forward to the Quill Gordon hatch, for it is usually a big one on this pool. Later will come the Hendricksons, March Browns, the first caddis, and then the May flies, the Light Cahill, and of course the big stone flies.

This is the water that we can really become part of, not remain just a passing stranger trying to pick off a trout. It becomes a friend that will gladly give us rewards for our efforts.

The head and tail of this pool have figured in a great deal of my fishing experience over a period of many years. I can recall, when, during the war, gasoline was rationed and I fished the river only as far as I was willing to walk from my bed and the local diner. Conditions forced me to fish the same waters over and over again. That's about the only thing I can thank the war for. Had I brought the big-city drive to accomplish and cover the whole stream in a day as so many anglers do, I'd never gotten to meet it and become intimate with it.

Discover your trout stream. Hold hands: in the early morning when the fog is still shrouding the pools, in the hot midday when you are about to parboil in your waders, in the cool of evening, and, of course, in the freezing days of April.

Figure 58. Ledge Pool.

CHAPTER 17

Ledge Pool

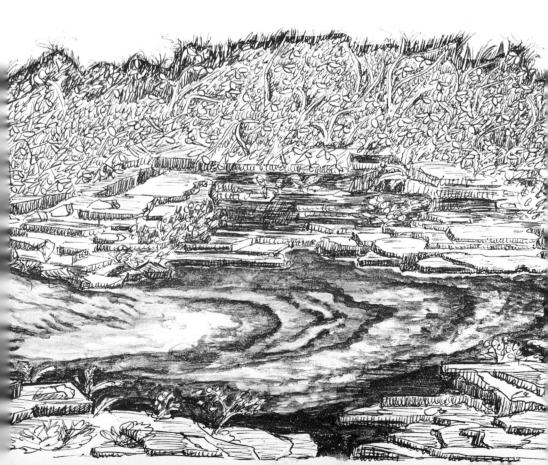

THIS is the replica of the most delightful spot I've ever fished. From our vantage point under the hemlocks, we glance across the stream to the almost bricklike slab rock so characteristic of Pennsylvania and New York State. Laurel and rhododendron, ferns, and lichens decorate the almost man-made appearance of the steps. It's a perfect place for a picnic, nice spot to wait for an angling partner who is habitually late to arrive. I've sat on these rocks and read books, tied flies, and watched the insects. A pleasant occupation is just sitting here, drinking in the quiet and restfulness of it all. Watching for trout is also an interesting occupation, for when they are sitting on the bottom there is no action. But when some reason develops, they seem to come out from nowhere and begin to play and feed on the surface.

This particular layout is a very narrow strip of what is above and below the pool, a very large and fast-flowing stream—or small river, I guess you'd call it. As a consequence, there is always a good supply of water bulging over the drop-off and into the pool. The water in the center is quite deep, perhaps ten or even fifteen feet. One year when the stream had all but dried up, I fished this pool at night and the center stretch was still far from wadable. This means that trout, big ones, can take up residence here, and if no one knows how to catch them, they just grow and grow until they die of old age.

Crawl down cautiously to the very lip of those steps and peer down into the greenish-bluish water. Shade your eyes or, better still, bring along a piece of cardboard to kill the light and the surface glare. Curl it and submerge the wide edge of the circular cone into the water; place your eye in the small hole and what do you see?

A deep-shaded ledge and below you trout as big as reservoir carp. These are the kind of fish that will feed on 12-inch trout, and they'll eat

148

perhaps a couple of them every day. What a spot to fish live bait! Just dangle worms over the brink well weighted. It would be just like fishing for catfish, or flounders. All you'd have to do would be to sit and wait.

Well, if this were so, there would be no monsters in that deep. And remember, you've seen only a few feet of that tantalizing bottom.

I spoke of this pool with one of my skin-diving pals and he gave me several lessons in diving, so that we could explore the pool together and I would then be able to do a little subsurface research into the lives of trout.

Going down in that deep required a rope, due to the fast current. The bottom and underslabbed edges of that pool was like a huge room, with endless shelves, nooks, and crannies, places for insects to live, fish to rest and feed. The bottom was made up of broken slab rock, and smooth gravel and rounded rocks that had been tumbled down from the stream bed above.

There were trout, big, small, and medium-sized, everywhere.

But how to fish for them?

About the only way I knew was to await their rise to insects on the surface. With all the bottom food available to them every minute of the day or night, who could tell when if ever they would go to the trouble of swimming to the surface to feed. There were schools of minnows all over the bottom. Caddis and other aquatic insects were everywhere. Upstream under the flash of the white water was a quiet area where the fish could stack themselves sometimes four deep, just sitting there as if they were living in the city aquarium. Down near the tail of the pool, the shelves are wider, offering deeper undersides that are generously shaded most of the day. The pool finally spills out into a run over fine gravel. In the late spring, its path curls and ribbons through two high walls of rhododendron and mountain laurel, topped by cooling hemlock, spruce, and pine.

How to fish this water?

Well, the first and most obvious lure to employ would be a big, buxom streamer or bucktail, weighted, of course. You'd work from the top of the pool, casting from the protection of the laurel right into the foam, allowing the lure to sink down into it to the quiet water under the shelf of foam. From there it would search out its prey. Several casts can be made from here, including the side at the bottom of the illustration. Obviously, you'd work your way down as far as you could cast keeping a maximum of line off the water. The speed retrieve, described earlier, is excellent treatment for the big fish early in the spring.

An even better way, in a deep pool of this kind, is to work the bucktail from below, throwing bends of line upstream of it to aid in the sinking; the problem here is to keep enough slack line while the whole thing drifts down toward you. When fishing deep like this you do not need to try to manipulate the fly; its natural drift in the current is enough.

Nymphs can be handled in the same way.

But there is one secret which I hesitated to bare here, one that has taken trout for me here and elsewhere on the streams and situations of of this book. That concerns the actual live caddis-fly larva and its stick or sand case. Using a weighted leader, I attach three hooks on tippets in standard arrangement, and hook on the cases in almost any manner— the best ways I've found are pictured in figure 58.

Let them sink and drag the bottom. Best time to do this of course is when you can spot the fish flashing on the bottom on this feeding activity. The caddis drifted or dropped into the dark crevasses is another tempter that usually gets a fish or two if you have the patience to dunk, wormfishing style.

Figure 59. Various Ways of Hooking on the Caddis Case and Larva.

But this pool is not always devoid of surface action. The Quill Gordons, Hendricksons, caddis, March Browns, and even Green Drakes from above filter downstream from hatches above. It is surprising how those little miniature sailboats survive the ride down the rapids and falls to drift like a flotilla on a Sunday race right down the circular bends of the current. The trout go wild at that time, be the hatch in the bright time of day or in the darkened hours of sunset. Situated as it is in the deep woods, this pool becomes cool and shaded long before the more open stretches have had their glare taken away.

Dry-fly fishing, then, is a good prospect when conditions warrant. One of these is in the summer when a good breeze knocks periodic waves of insects from the high trees and foliage and wisps them onto the surface. At this point almost any fly will take trout. At the same time, I have found that even though the meal is diversified I seldom find the pattern that they will treat with equal abandon. I've seen butterflies, moth, bugs, flies, inchworms, and spiders on the water and the fish were having a ball.

You'd think that even a nondescript but enticing spider fly would produce rises and good takes. More often than not, the fish will rise to the fly and even take and quickly reject unless they become hooked by themselves. Many times I've had my fly nosed and actually bumped into the air in much the manner of a circus seal playing with a ball. Light hits by the score, and from big fish; but few real "takes."

One day, I used the bait technique that I learned from my poacher friend. In the early morning when the dew was still on the grass, I collected a bottle of grasshoppers. Taking his advice to counsel, I began throwing them into the head of the pool one by one until I created an artificial "hatch." Then, like the sneaky guy I can be, I just happened to sink the hook into the collar of one of them. The brown I took that day still adorns my study wall, but I usually don't tell just how I got him.

About the only fly that I can count on in this situation, unless I am matching a definite hatch, is the Fanwing Royal Coachman. Those trout must have known Mary Orvis Marbury! The big fanwing patterns and the large Wulff flies, particularly when the water is in shade, usually bring rises; though again, they are usually short. When a big fish does really connect, you can tell it to your friends, for it is really news. Postmortem investigation reveals the "why." They are so plumb full of everything that I believe they just like to shop for tasties, like women looking in store windows, be they with absolutely no intention of actually buying.

Figure 60. Standard Leadwing Patterns.

    A. *Leadwing Coachman wet-fly standard version.*
    B. *Leadwing nymph.*
    C. *Leadwing dry fly with Wulff-type wings rather than conventional split duck wings. Wings are gray color or can be white. The white is better for evening visibility.*

There is one hatch on this river and particularly on this pool, which is a delight, and that is the Brown Drake or Leadwing Coachman. During this hatch the trout really hit, and if you are fortunate enough to be there at the right time, you'll come home with legend trout.

The nymph is of the swimming or free-ranging type, a little over a half inch in length, dark rusty brown with darker wing pads when near the time of the hatch. The imitation (see Appendix) is tied on a long-shank size 12 heavy hook. Standard leadwing patterns also suffice (see figure 59).

It is the most active type of all the May-fly nymphs, and as such can call for zigzag motion even when the imitation is drifted on the bottom, in the midcurrent, or on the surface, depending on the period of the actual hatch; during the two or three hours that the real thing is performing its first stages of transformation into the dun stage.

June is its most active period and if you hit it right, you'll see them swimming in the quieter stretches beside the fast quick runs along the edge of the shelves.

But these nymphs, unlike most of the other types, do not drift far in the current but swim to a nearby rock, climb up, and undress in public

Figure 61. Hatching of the Leadwing.

For some reason known only to the lead leadwing fly, the insects seem to congregate on one rock—a whole tribe of them. The adjacent rocks will find none of the insects. They swim to the rock, climb up as quickly as possible trying to establish a rockhead in the face of danger from birds and fish. There they shed their nymphal shuck, flex their wings, and fly upstream. Later the same evening or the next evening they will return, in typical May-fly style, to dance, mate, and deposit their eggs. The return spinner hatch of this fly is very popular with the trout.

as shown in the illustration. They are quite a sight to see as they select a particular rock and climb up, sometimes in groups of twenty or more. The adjacent rocks will be completely devoid of them, for the "leader" has evidently led the flock to one stage for the act.

At this point, the trout go crazy. They leap and slash in the collar of water that usually curls around the base of the rock. The nymphs cling there all lined up like cordwood until they get their strength to climb up the precarious footing on the "cliff." Once on secure land they immediately begin to shed their shucks. Quite often the trout, seeing or at least knowing of this activity, will deliberately leap up out of the water and flop down on them, throwing a handful back into the current. Those that survive continue their disrobing until they are able to fly away. They point in the characteristic upstream direction, flex their wings to make sure, much in the same way pilots race their engines before take-off— and away they go to the trees. Many are bounced down by the breeze, or actually fly back to the surface to drift downstream a bit before finally taking off. They can get into the air much quicker than the March Browns or Light Cahills, due to their more agile makeup.

Throw a Leadwing Coachman wet fly into the situation, or even the nymph, right on the surface and usually the trout will gobble it up without so much as a teasing touch. They mean business now, and your imitation even if it is not a close copy will bring them to rise to it.

It seems almost needless to say that this pool is perfect for late-night fishing. You need not wade at all, but quietly stand back, well away from the edge; wait for the trout to begin to feed on the stone flies and big moths and other blow-ins that adorn the night winds.

Quite often, if there is no rise, nor has there been for a half hour of waiting, a Marabou streamer, solid black, can be cast sparingly toward the head of the pool and allowed to drift. Do not impart any action to it.

Come back to this spot during the year, right up until the last day or evening of the season, and if you keep your eyes sharp, your actions limited and well directed . . . you'll take trout, big ones, and in a veritable Garden of Eden.

CHAPTER 18

S-Shaped Pool

THIS is a tricky one, but not an uncommon bit of water on any medium-sized trout stream that flows fairly heavy down from the hills or mountains. It is almost two pools in one, yet can be considered as one water, since the problems and approaches overlap and should be considered together when the approach, presentation, and seasonal aspects are combined in the mind in order to ascertain just how to fish it.

Flowing as it does down a quick falls or rapids, it breaks loose after passing through the gates of boulders that render the fast current into froth. The current rapidly stops for a curved swing in under the bank at 2, but curves around the point between 7 and 8 to break again in mid-pool by another set of rocks that are well covered in the early spring. Then is a good time to work the bucktails, for right below the rock break will be deadwaters where big fish will hold on their upstream migration, or, in the case of brown trout, they will nurse the lower lip and sit it out until food is dropped down to them from a spring freshet.

The pool then begins a reverse bend, sliding by the shallow below 7 that is also covered by about a foot of water in the spring. All sorts of driftwood and flotsam collect here and it is a good spot to pick up a brookie. Then the pool breaks in a last dash in white and fluffy water as it grooves its speedway down to the boulders, and away downstream it goes tumbling later into a larger river where small-mouth bass are found in company with shad, crappie, and once in a while a good-sized walleye.

In midseason it produces a good hatch of caddis flies, for the bottom is covered with these insects. Many times I have walked to the pool through the brush to look into the water and seen a dozen or so fish, flashing the bottom, nosing up the larvae. I've found it a pretty problem

156

to sink artificials down close enough to the bottom in the current to put them practically in their mouths. I usually try this from the bushes behind 1, rollcasting the rig into the tail of the rapids to let the weighted flies sink down on slack line. Gradually the current pulls the rig downstream while I keep the line off the water and from dragging the frauds away from my intent for them. After catching a nice little fish and maybe a couple of breakfast-sized ones, I'll switch to the bucktail and cast to 8, whisking the fly right through the boulders, down to 1. By an upstream mend, I'll put the fly into position for the drift right under me in the hollowed-out undercut. Only my rod is sticking out from over the bank. All I can do is to watch the rod tip. When it jumps, I hit back and a nice brookie will body-roll in under there and make noises like a football player taking a shower. He'll work his way out into the center and then I'll slither down the brambles and gradually work him upstream to the net.

Then, I'll change tactics again, after working the rest of the overhang, and tie on a big Wulff dry fly and work the tail of the rapids above.

Why the Wulff fly? I dunno. I like to see it bounce on the water. Usu-

Figure 62. S-Shaped Pool.

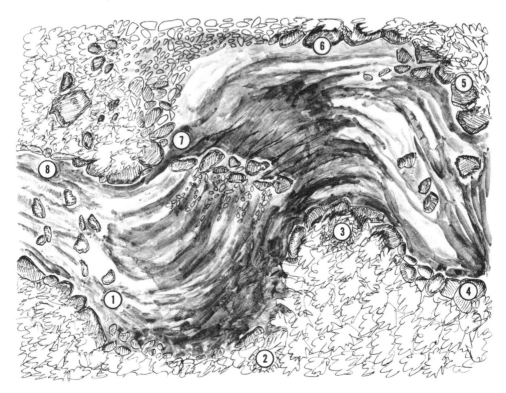

ally it doesn't get a rise from a trout, but the chubs and dace like it. That fly will produce later in the season, so this is just a rehearsal.

From 7 to 3 and the water above and in the rocks is perhaps the best part of the pool. Trout drift down to the rocks and hang, as we said earlier, with their noses right in the fence of boulders. With this type of concentration I am bound to bring up a good trout if I cast with care and never allow the line to belly over the hot spots. Small wet flies, size 16 of varied patterns, are aways good here, not because they imitate anything specific, but because the trout seem to like the varied fare. Almost any fly delivered into this hotbed will provoke a rise, even if it be only a small trout.

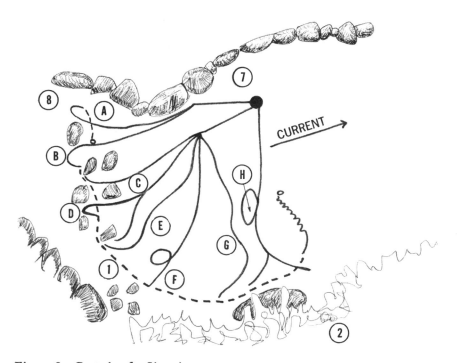

Figure 63. Casts for the Situation.

Standing near 7 the cast is made to 8 with an upstream bend. It drifts down and is recast with another upstream bend at A but without lifting the fly from the water. This is repeated at B and drifts to C and needs another upstream bend to D. Fly drifts to E and begins to belly again, is rolled spare line at F, drifts to G, rolled once more, and allowed to drift to I and then skittered on the retrieve to pickup point.

What a spot this is in the early morning and late evening. Then it is another story, and unless there is a hatch going on I adhere to the dogma of big fly, big fish, and usually prove it to be so. Big wet flies, three of them, slopped down on the water well up from the rocks and allowed to drift down, finding their own way, will take trout. If they drift by the rocks without a strike I can depend on some monster coming up from the deep edge right below to take a look, perhaps make a pass, and, possibly, get himself hooked.

I love this pool!

If I do connect, the water below is disturbed for the while, so I tie on a long dry-fly leader and again head myself upstream for some fancy line handling, as I attempt to allow the dries to drift naturally on the upstream curve. Handling the line in this water to avoid drag is a pesky problem.

Let's say I stand near 7 and wish to work the fly from below 8, across under 1, with a drift in under the brush ending the cast at 2. That's asking a lot of one cast but it can be done. Since it is a typical trick to be mastered for other similar conditions, here's my routine and method.

Now, let's try the same business from a position standing just below the current rock off the point from 3. The first drift will take in the far side of the upstream section of the stream and the second will drift under the overhanging brush by 2.

When you have mastered trick situations like that, you can quit reading fishing books!

Your next is another hard one. From that same position, you need to cast right to 7, work the water across the lower edge of the midstream rock line. Now, to work the far shallow, cast again at 7, throw a mend of extra line upstream, and the fly will head for 6. Retrieve it back across the pool and pick up by the roll method when it reaches the center. Next cast goes to 6, drifts across that cluster of rocks, drops down into the white water and, wham, a big rainbow takes you for a long walk downstream.

For a change back up at 4 you upstream a bucktail, retrieving it quickly over the frothy surface and, again, a redsides carries you down to the water below. He'll jump ten times, probably, before you net him; so watch it. When it comes to the business of those jumping trout, I've a few ideas that may help you in holding onto them, but we'll deal with this problem in another chapter.

While I've been taking you over the course, you've probably been seeing other possibilities in this water. You are right. A whole book could be written about the potentials of this pool. As a matter of fact, it is the water where I spent many seasons studying the nymphs and larvae while preparing my first trout-fishing book published by Little, Brown and Company, titled *How to Take Trout on Wet Flies and Nymphs*. The pool is located on the Neversink River in the heart of the Catskill

Mountains of central New York State. Ed Sens, a trout-fishing saint, spent his youth on those waters. He gave me the benefit of his guiding hand in teaching me the great principle of the relationship of all living things in the trout stream to one another. He shared the secrets of matching nature in the artificial flies and their presentation in order to understand how trout are to be caught.

Crossing the stream below, a walk to 5 will instantly call for a wet-fly or bucktail cast toward 3, dropping the fly right on the corner, mending the line upstream quickly, bouncing it over the rocks, and allowing the fly to fish its way to a trout that will take at 4. (One always does, except when someone else is fishing with me.)

Dry flies look good from here and a rollcast can put them right in the

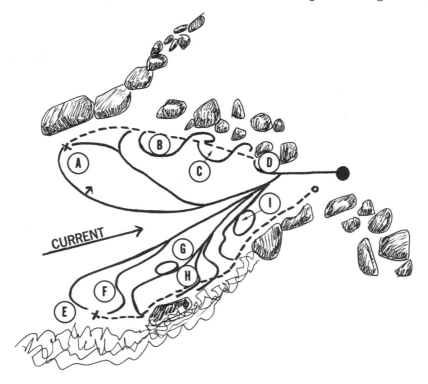

Figure 64. Casting the Situation.

Standing below the current rocks off the point from 3. The first drift will take in the far side of the stream from 7, beginning from an upstream bend cast at A, a drift to upstream mend B, the drift down and upmend again D, and then to retrieve.

The second cast will be up toward the bushes above 2 at the point E with a right-hand curve cast and slack for drift. The line bellies at F, is rolled up at G, bellies to H, rolled again at I and then allowed to drift to retrieve point right under your rod tip.

middle of the deep section of the pool. A right-hand curve cast puts them in a position to drift near 6 and down through those rocks.

From 6 you can call the camera crew in for the shot of a big one that will take a high-riding Wulff dry fly at near dusk as it drifts down a foot and not much more from 7. Wading above 7, you can cast to the break in the white water and, after spacing several casts across with the curved drift down, a good one is thrown to 1 and allowed to drift right under the bushes.

Finally, from 8 you have the whole gamut of the upper stretch to work bucktails, nymphs, wet flies, and dry flies cast stop-fashion and allowed to drift at will in the current. There are enough trout in there with enough possibilities to keep you busy for centuries.

One of my favorite hatches on this river and particularly on this pool is the Dark Hendrickson. It usually starts between April 25 and tapers off around May 9. The flies hatch in the afternoon, early if the weather has been cold and windy, later if the past few days have been hot and dry. The water is usually at the height as shown in the picture and the water as clear as crystal.

The Dark Hendrickson nymph is one of the most common of the May flies and lives in much the same type of broken water as the Hendrickson, described in an earlier chapter (see Appendix). Fish the nymph in the shallows beside the fast riffs, such as the section between 7 and 6 or along the overhang between 1 and 2.

The duns emerge to the side of the fast water in more or less the same locations as the Hendricksons select. They are often seen hatching at the same time as the Hendrickson, or, in the case of a stream where the Hendrickson is not found, they are the prime actors.

I recall a red-letter day on this water. It was evident that I was not the first angler to arrive, as there were a number of cars parked along the road and many fresh boot prints on the shore. After tying on one of my best black-brown wet flies I began to cast dry-fly fashion upstream from the midstream rock cluster slightly across the current directly below 1, which allowed the nymphs to travel along the edge of the bank at 2. After covering the water thoroughly I was rewarded with a couple of small hits but failed to connect. I was content to enjoy the twittering of the birds and the sight of the brave green leaves poking their tiny heads into the spring sunshine. As is often the case, my mind drifted off to these streamside distractions, so I was hardly prepared for the rude awakening as a fifteen-inch trout hit the fly and securely hooked himself. Upon later examination I found him to be crammed to the very gills with small black-brown nymphs similar to the fly on which I had taken him.

A new year I fished the same water again in April and identified the insect as *Blasturus* and enjoyed nice fishing with one big seventeen-inch brown in the basket taken on the nymph. I missed his bigger brother that afternoon when he chose to plummet up and over a dry fly of the Hendrickson pattern.

Pools similar to this one are found on almost any trout stream. Get to know this kind of water at all times of the year and learn its moods during all types of weather and water conditions. It will fare you well and offer many hours of excellent fishing. You'll learn just how to spot your casts so that the water is disturbed to the minimum. When you can calm down and fish slowly enough, you'll get into the habit of turning on your inner and outer radar for the signs that will help you make the right decisions as to fly selection, presentation, and delivery.

Even late in the season, when the stream is almost dry, you'll appreciate the rise of even a small trout to a tiny floater. Night fishing, too, will be on the books. You'll have gotten to know every rock in the stream and the places to wade as well as the places not to; where the big fish feed when they come out under the deep of night. Big browns are here for you, but not for everybody. Night fishing demands a relationship, one that can be fostered over the years.

Figure 65. Bridge Pool I.

Bridge Pool I

THIS is a familiar scene in the more rural set-
tings of our backcountry. Commercially minded contractors and busy
politicians have "improved" most of the bridges in the townships and
counties and, as a result, the wider roads and more modern structures
have ruined the trout fishing in many such good old holes.

This bridge and this stretch of water on this particular stream was
located in Maine. This is the way it was when I was a boy. Today, a four-
lane double-track highway has cut through the area and the old stream
is relegated to being a drainage ditch. Progress has made it possible for
anglers to speed along at seventy miles per hour so that they can get to
the wilderness waters a couple of hundred miles up the state, which
makes a lot of sense for a while—that is, until too many anglers and
new towns spring up along the route. Then we have to go still farther
over the old roads that lie beyond the progress and small trout to the
lack of progress and the big trout.

But there are streams like this near our centers of population where
the citizens have discovered that they have lost their birthright to progress and have bent all backs to restoring the wild conditions of the
streams and are stocking them with trout. They are fighting pollution.
So the cycle of progress goes on.

There's a stream not fifty miles from New York City where there is
such a bridge and just such a stretch of water. I fish it quite often in the
early season, and usually return to it for a final go in September just
before the season closes. The stream always has a good flow of water in
it since it is now the connecting link between two of the reservoirs of
the great system that feeds New York's millions.

There are trout in it at all times of the year, either stocked fish that are

164

introduced in March before the season starts, in May after the initial
wormers have had their go, and by migrants from the reservoirs.

I've taken bright rainbows fresh in from the reservoir that would go
three pounds. I've also been skunked here and all along its course. It is
a perplexing bit of water.

It is full of green caddis larvae in the spring, and as a matter of record
is the first stream where I had my introduction to this insect. There are
continuous hatches of very small insects, which argues for the use of
small flies. That's one reason why I like to fish it. The whole water spreads
a congenial atmosphere, a closeness and friendliness that bigger waters
with their wide-open valleys and barren shores cannot possess. I always
feel at home while fishing here. I've made friends with the hardest wading spots and have become acquainted with all the overhangs that lie
in wait for badly cast flies. I've met many anglers on the stream, many
of whom are members of the local conservation association and the local
rod and gun club. All such associations add to the pleasures on a trout
stream and that includes the feeling of brotherhood, a relationship that
the world powers could imitate with benefits all around. Yes, I've taken
the world's troubles, my office, my personal fortunes and misfortunes to
this water, and it has cleansed me of them.

Most of all I love the stretch above and below the bridge. It has yielded
many good fish, not whoppers of magazine-writing qualifications, for
catching the biggest fish in this brook would not qualify for a yarn in any
sporting magazine.

I usually fish it upstream. I'm always armed with the same rod, a light-
action, seven-foot split bamboo, older than myself. My father gave me
the rod after he had used it for ten years before my birth. I've dressed it
several times in the past thirty years and it still is as straight as the pro-
verbial arrow and just as supple as the day it was bought by him in a
London tackle shop. It's not a fast-action stick like so many of the modern dry-fly rods, nor will it cast a baker's mile. It's good for about thirty
feet without a strain, just enough for this little water, when I use a nine-
foot leader tapered to 5X, or at the most when I'm using small bucktails,
3X. As you can see, there's not much room for long casts and certainly
less for backcasts unless I gauge the direction accurately and fish directly
upstream with a straight delivery. I prefer the shorter cast so that I can
work my way through the overhangs and drop a brace of wets or
weighted nymphs or my littlest bucktail (see Appendix, page 326, and
also figure 66).

This is spot casting all the way, and quite often only the last two feet
of the leader are in the water, guiding the flies daintily into and around
rocks and snags, into runs and eddies, over gravel bars and deep holes.

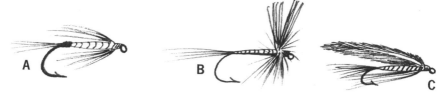

Figure 66. Sparsely Dressed Flies.

All in size 14, the very sparsely dressed wet fly, split wing with hackle points to the side of the body. The dry fly, exceptionally sparse, hardly enough dressing to float it. The streamer or bucktail, also on a size 14 hook, tied in proportion, and similar to a half- or three-quarter-inch dace minnow. All good for small-stream work.

I work my way up the river slowly, noting the bird species that seem to flit by in front and in back of me as if I did not exist or had not intruded at all. I've seen fox drinking under the brush, raccoons along the muddy shore after frogs, mink swimming across ahead of me, deer coming through the timber for a drink on a humid summer's day.

With all its delights, this brook requires a certain brand of patience. Quite naturally, one who returns to such water season after season knows what he is in for. There is no easy casting or wading here, no open stretches to display casting skill and fishing prowess. It's almost like dunking rather than fly fishing; yet it is possible when you get the focus for the short casts and short drifts to deftly handle a dry fly so that it bounces just right over the rocks. Most of the time you use less than twenty feet of line and leader, whether fishing wet or dry.

I hurry a bit when I see the bridge, for I know that during the summer especially there is at least one trout in there that others haven't hooked and there might be a cruiser working his way between the reservoirs. I secretly hope I tangle with him, even though he will get away scot free!

If no trout takes in the bridge shadow, I know that I've a good chance about a foot or two upstream just where the water stops tumbling down from the drop.

I cast the dry fly with a horizontal flip rather than the usual vertical delivery, and it sails up in under the bridge, disturbs the nesting phoebes, and lights square in the lip of current. The fly cocks and drifts about an inch. A puff of spray, a dark snout, the flash of a tail; the line pulls on the delicate rod tip and I'm fast to a nice one. A thrill begins to jump around my nerve ends. Funny, the biggest trout of Labrador or Argentina never caused that feeling.

A nice plump rainbow fights his way against the current and then drops down to me rolling defiantly and jumps three times before finally drop-

Figure 67. Bridge Pool I.

ing down to be netted. He's set free and scoots away under the bushes to the safety of quiet and cool waters where no one will get at him very soon.

Now, for contrast, my smallest bucktail. I turn, facing downstream, pick a miniature dace, tied on a size 14 dry-fly hook (see Appendix), and drop it at my feet, to watch its course as it drops down over the golden pebbles and rocks of the stream bed. A shadow comes after it, turns, another shadow glides in and misses the fly. I retrieve it in short jerks. Two shadows come and one gets hooked. A smart-aleck little brookie. This water has never been stocked with brook trout—at least to my knowledge. Here's a real native and I salute.

You're probably expecting me to become technical and step-by-stepish in this example of a trout-fishing problem. But how can one get formal and "thinky" about such a pretty bit of water? This water "learns you," as the woodsman says. You bring only your gear, your patience, and your frustrations to it. Your gear receives its exercise, your patience its reward and your frustrations disappear. No need to know all about hatches, fly patterns, temperatures, and the rest. This is a vacation spot. You become like a little boy who doesn't know it is difficult to catch trout and you go right ahead and do it.

Look at it carefully. How would you fish it?

Figure 68. Large Bridge Pool.

CHAPTER 20

Bridge Pool II

I intentionally put an old cow-barn cover on this bridge, mainly for those who like to remember their Americana before the busy contractors began to cover the countryside with "improvements." As a youngster growing up I remember "riding in the tunnel," as Grandpa used to call it, as we rattled through the shade of that roof, cooling and refreshing as it was on a hot summer day. The charm of those old bridges remains on but a few rivers in the United States. Canada still has a few also. The other reason for placing the cover over the span was to serve as an example to your grandchildren who, if they grow up to have trout streams and want to go fishing, will ask, "Daddy, what's that box house over the stream?" You can then give them a short history lesson.

In the days when this particular bridge was built, roads were narrow and traffic little. The creation of the span was not in any way injurious to the stream. Poisonous concrete wash and constant oil and chemical wastes did not flow into the river from the accumulation from passing automobiles. The bridge just sort of stood there, not out of place in the countryside.

Another thing I used to love about such bridges was the way in which I could lie on the boards out of range of buggies and cars and peer down through the cracks in the boards and watch the water below. Naturally, this gave me an eagle's-eye view of the pool under the bridge and a look at the trout lying there waiting for me to try and tempt into a strike. I learned much about trout this way. When I grew up high enough I could tiptoe and look out of the rough-cut windows. I can recall looking up and down the river and, finding maybe one or two anglers, becoming discouraged for the day because the stream was crowded. Now during the first weeks of the season, the road is jammed with hastily and badly parked cars. Anglers from many states converge on this stream and the first place they fish is the water immediately adjacent to the bridge. The braver ones and those used to at least a short walk will work up and down the stream for a hundred yards or so. They'll arrive in the early morning, cast the dickens out of the water, and scare the trout into the bushes and holes where even the smartest anglers would refuse to throw their flies. They'd hardly ever catch anything, but it gave the trout good exercise. After the weekend *débâcle*, I'd return on a Monday morning, fish at leisure after the trout had returned to their normal runs, and catch a mess for supper. Yes, it was on a long lunch hour during school, or I'd duck afternoon exercise for the pleasures of angling.

In recent years I've become one of that army of weekend fishermen, having tied myself down to worldly responsibilities, and due to the march of progress, it is now possible for me to leave my castle in the big city, drive half a day and all night and, with luck, arrive to the stream at dawn. It's doing it the hard way, but that's progress.

My tackle has been refined by modern genius and I've read a lot of fishing books since those early days and written a few too. But, you know, I fish that water just as I did as a boy, despite the rod and gear in hand that allows much more refined and "expert-type" tackle handling.

With one exception—that of the shaded area under the bridge—there isn't much difference in this water from the stretches above it or below it. As a matter of fact, I've taken better and more fish from pools and runs a half a mile up or down. Yet the bridge pool has its magical and mythical appeal to the angler. Also, there are always trout that can be SEEN lying there, and the opportunity seldom comes when an angler can view his water so well as he does from the bridge or even from the roadside. Knowing that big fish are there somehow makes the game more exciting than SUPPOSING the trout are in the stream.

I've always been thankful for bridge pools such as this one. Yet, I've been a constant irritant to road and bridge builders while in the working press, since I've been on the side of the conservationists who try, usually with absolutely no hope, to kill bills that would permit the widening of roads and building of bridges. The claims of the conservationists are simple. Such goings-on will kill the river for fishing forever. But, funny thing, give that river five years, or in some cases, even less, and you'll find the bridge pool more crowded with the local sportsmen than the waters up or down from it. Somehow or other Mother Nature seems to be able to heal any wounds and, in fact, she helps the brush grow over the scars, utilizes the big boulders in the new stream bottom for home building by insects and trout. The shade of the bridge is an added plus, particularly in summertime when most of the stream is devoid of a shadow of any kind. Many insects live in the shade and drop in to feed the trout. Songbirds build their nests nearby and phoebes and perhaps swallows take up their real-estate claims quite soon after the span is dedicated.

As you look at the picture of the bridge pool here, you're seeing it from the south side. The morning sun is glancing off the weathered timbers and a warm sultry breeze is rippling the foliage along both banks. It's June and the birds are announcing it with all kinds of calls and songs —sounds like fifty radios all going at once. A few flies hatch intermittently and blow-ins pop into the water, making slight rings as they land.

We've parked the car about a hundred yards from the bridge. We edged it into the side of an old lumber tote road, and hope that no one parks in front of us.

Going back to a childhood day, we walk along the planks in the deep shadow until we find an old rotted one with enough space to look down. Below is the golden-colored water, oily, slithering its way over the deep holes and over the jagged rocks left there when the span was built. At first we don't see much, but as soon as our eyes are accustomed to the problem, we begin to spot signs of life. There's a trout's snout just poking out from behind one boulder. There's another. In a deep run, there are three trout, each as long as your arm. We look through the boards at various intervals along the bridge and see a handful of trout basking in the shade of the right embankment under the span. None of those trout are small, so none of them have been planted this year in the annual spring stocking program. Some of those fish have been there for some years, despite the trials and errors of an army of fishermen, particularly the local boys who prefer to feed the trout hamburgers, worms, and hot dogs, and then sink a hook into a piece of the meat. Despite all this, those trout are still there—waiting.

It isn't easy water to fish, as you will see.

So before we casually wade into the water, we survey the layout and decide where to enter and how to fish the bridge pool properly. At first we'll concentrate on this area only, as the water above and below is no stranger to us since it is similar to many of the other problem layouts we've fished so far in this book. Ordinarily, fishing this pool as a stranger approaching it from above or below, our tactics would be slightly different. We'll handle that proposition later. For now, let's try and dislodge one of those "pet" fish from its hiding place under the bridge.

Remember, it's summertime. It's a hot day, the water is clear, nothing happening in the way of a hatch. No anglers about. Most of them have taken up lake fishing, golf, or boating with the family. We've the stream to ourselves, other than an occasional rumbling of a car or farm wagon as it crosses the bridge.

We have the choice of entering at one of four spots: 2, which would put us on the shady side upstream on the left side of the stream; 7, the

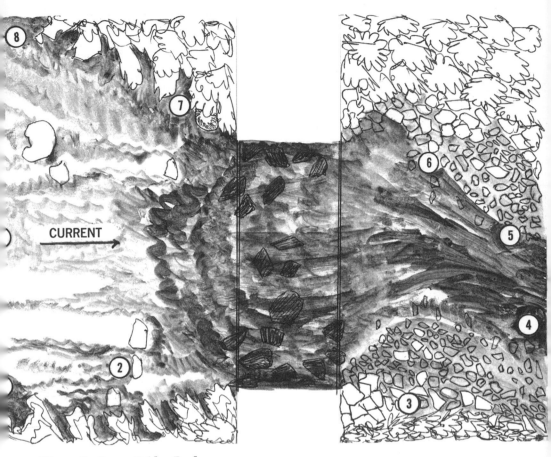

Figure 69. Large Bridge Pool.

same general position on the right side; 3, on the downside, and 6, right across the stream. Any one of the four would put us in a position to place a lure in under there, where it should count.

As indicated by the number, I'd start out to fish the under-bridge water from 1 since it is high up from the hot spot, and a good casting position presents itself for downstream delivery of the fly, be it a dry, wet, nymph, or streamer bucktail. Following our habit pattern, we will make our first cast to the nearby water. Before casting, we'll put on a searching type of bucktail, a Mickey Finn, which resembles no living species of minnow. About the only fish close to it is a goldfish, but I doubt if there are any in this brook. The attraction, of course, is the brightness, and I follow the theory of bright day, bright fly. I dunno if it's a rule to religiously follow, but let's start out with it anyway.

Since it is not yet known whether we should sink the fly or fish it on the surface, let's split the difference and feel our way along. The first cast to 9 swings and we retrieve the fly just as it circles down just above the deep-water drop-off. We don't let it go down into the black, since we might be able to tempt a fish to rise out of there to hit the fly. We try this a couple of times. Only result is a small trout, which we throw back. It's a sign of life, anyway.

Now on our next cast we begin to allow the fly to drift under the surface and as it swims down into the deep, we roll an extra mend of line for it to absorb as it goes deeper and downstream. Now, under the bridge we can begin our retrieve. We have been holding our rod high, as usual, so that the line would not be taken by the current, but we lower it to the lateral now and zigzag the fly through the current in a slightly upstream direction as it swings toward our side. It passes just over the first hidden rocks that reside about four feet below the surface.

No rise. No action.

This time we extend our cast to a point between 9 and 7. The fly goes its customary way and swings in under the bridge sweeping the middle of the shadowed area.

Another rise. Another small trout, but fortunately he missed the hook. But it's still some action. What do we do about those lunkers down there under the little fish?

Let's try an oldie on them.

We'll leave the Mickey Finn on the end, but we'll tie on a very small minnow imitation to a tippet just a very few inches above it (see illustration). Note that the distance is much shorter than the conventional rig when tippets are tied in for wet flies and the usual two- or three-bucktail rig for the open and fast water. This should imitate one fish chasing another! It's worked before, so it may work again.

We'll cast it to the rock outside from 7. There it goes downcurrent; sinks, and begins its work. To keep it in a course along the far side of the bridge wall, we throw a mend of line ahead of it, flex the rod to adjust the line bend in an upstream direction and await developments.

They aren't long in coming. A shadow of a big fish rises to the drifting flies and just as he is about to make a final dash, we trip the rod tip a bit to raise the flies in an escaping-form-of-life movement; and that does it. We don't see the hit, but the leader and line straightens out with a zing and the rod tells us that a big one's on.

It's quite a battle under that bridge and noisy. A whopper brown like that does not usually jump, nor does it usually work to the surface in an effort to shake the hook. The big boys usually sound to the bottom and fight it out there.

Not this guy!

He's up and out like a rainbow, tail-walking; thrashing on the surface.

Now a body-roll and another and another. Without notice he heads straight down at the moment we have shown him a bit of slack. I hope he won't find an old saw, bear trap, or scythe to cut that leader on.

We drop down below 2 and hope that we can get the fish above us for the netting. If we have to go below, under the bridge, we'll disturb that side of the deep for future reference.

Fortunately, he tires by holding in the current and comes in easily . . . a nice dark-brown trout. Notice his long underjaw. That's a cranky old male. I also note some hook marks. He's been tempted before and evidently was able to break his way to freedom.

Well, the bridge pool has netted us three trout, one a good specimen; not bad for our beginning, and we haven't even begun to experiment with the other possibilities.

If we had not taken a trout of disturbing size there, we'd have fished the water from 2 in much the same fashion. I introduced the two-fly technique just with the hope of a lucky break.

So, to vary the approach and learn the vagaries of the bridge, let's fish it, dry-fly upstream, from a position below the bridge. We'll work our way gradually up to 4. Remember, the sun is shining brightly into the lower end of the pool and the shadow line offers a contrast that is quite noticeable to the trout as well as to us. Since the fish will be heading upstream, the chances are that few if any will be hanging in the current at the very lower bulge of the pool. Just to prove that I'm wrong, we'll fish the dry upstream anyway and approach with caution. Our first meaningful cast will land to the right, about halfway in under the bridge. We'll put it there by a left-hand curve cast, so that the line will not fall back into the path of the descending fly. Let's tie on a small Dark Cahill of the soft, deep-riding type, not a light-colored one that rides on high hackles. Since there is no hatch, we are not imitating anything, so the fly could be any sort of insect, such as a blow-in that came from the overhang upstream.

The cast drifts down nicely and bobs along in the current. Once outside the shadow it is easier seen by us. It is also seen by a small trout and we pull it up before he can take it. Action again, so we can't exactly kick.

This is a good pool during the March Brown hatch and, a bit later, the Light Cahill fly is a common sight for about a month. It is also a great pool to fish at night.

Another small trout and we release it. I'd hoped for a decent-sized one that we could open and inspect for its dinner record.

Let's try a big spider fly. That just might turn one of those dark rock sophisticates. Up it goes, dead center. No need to be tricky here. We'll pop that fly a couple of times, and when it begins to drift down, we'll roll the retrieve and flip it upstream again for about four or five repeats. That should do it.

Overconfident? Maybe. Sometimes we need to be.

There. Strike! A light touch that was barely felt. We flip the fly up again without retrieving. There! That's better. It's more than a keeper . . . another good black-spotted fish from Darkland has grabbed the summons. Down he comes thrashing and mad at the outside world.

Note that two out of four tries have been made with slightly unorthodox patterns and setups. This kind of a situation calls for a broad mind.

I can remember fishing this "hole" in the early spring. The water was a foot higher, cold and murky. It was perfect for out-and-out worming or live-bait fishing. But being a fly man by nature and always of a mind to give the wormers a battle (that's the ego thing that sometimes possesses us) I try two big bucktails and use the technique I have shown you for taking those big whopper reservoir rainbows. Work the fly fast either upstream or down, but always across and skipping on the surface, dropping the flies in under the bridge shadows.

Another day when the wind was blowing a gale and casting was all but impossible, I took up a position upstream from the bridge and merely dropped a weighted leader and three of the green caddis nymphs for their dredging operation. It was deadly on those hatchery trout that had been dumped in there two weeks earlier. I released the lot of them, and I noted that they drifted downstream to take up residence in the waters below, making it harder for the city anglers with their worms and spinning gear to snag them out easily.

Study this pool for a while. Sit back and relax, now that you and I have had our taste of action. Think how you'd fish the stream on Opening Day; during a hatch; on a hot humid afternoon in August when no fish, no insect—nor any being, for that matter—should be doing anything but lying in bed. Take a peek at those trout first from a crack in the bridge. If modern times have taken away the old barn on your bridge, there will be no cracks to peek through. It's too bad, but that's progress. You'll just have to try and see in there with the modern approach. Take along a good casting rod and don't wade too close. You'll chuck and chance it many times before you connect. That's the general approach for such waters, until you get to know them.

I like this pool at twilight, during the early days of July. Midges hatch after boiling in the waters above, and when they settle into the flat surface film under the bridge, all sizes of trout have a time with them. If you can hit the pool when this hatch is on, you'll see those great big fish that ought to be playing a bigger game taking those little larvae with the gentleness of a lamb eating grass. An easy cast, with three of the black pattern on a gossamer-thin leader, is placed just right—in the very center of the pool. There will be a dimpling rise. It may be a chub, an under-sized trout, or a big brownie with spots almost as big as a penny. What-ever, you have fun with trout there.

In these days of crowded conditions on the more popular trout streams, it is unfortunate and, as we propose, unnecessary for anglers to become annoyed with each other's presence. Dry-fly anglers, spin fishermen, and bait dunkers sometimes find it difficult to live together on the same water at the same time. Often their dislike at the mere sight of one another causes a withdrawal into disapproving silence. Seldom will they even say, "Hello," if it means that the other fishermen might encroach on "their" water where they are fishing. It is impossible to suggest boundaries, and when unorthodox actions cause overlaps of territory, harsh feelings are exposed. None of this need be.

Nor is this condition in keeping with the "Brotherhood of the Angle," a mystical group of men and sometimes women who claim an inner friendship based on a common bond of outdoor enjoyment. The excep-tions and, therefore, the true brothers are those who have learned that it is fun and profitable to fish together, sometimes in planned concert, or at least be friendly enough to live and let live; greet each other with a smile; ask, "Any luck?"; and even net each other's fish, or share a lure, or a tip.

This inner circle is most fortunate. They may be good friends off the stream as well as on, or they might be total strangers who meet at the head of a pool, somewhat in the way I met an angler one afternoon on an Eastern trout stream. Since that day, Henry and I have not only be-come very good friends, but actually, since the meeting on the water, have become partners in business and in trouting during our days off from office toils.

As is our custom this last season, we approached the stream at the covered bridge near where we had parked the car. Henry walked down-stream for about half a mile, planning to fish up to the bridge with the dry flies. I followed the trail upstream for about the same distance plan-ning to work the broken waters with the wet flies and small bucktails. We would meet in about an hour at the bridge to compare notes, take a few minutes off to enjoy coffee, fruit juice, and a sandwich before getting set for the evening rise, and its frequently active period.

It was fun fishing with Henry, even though we had never actually fished side by side. That moment was yet to come.

This particular day I had reached the bridge pool first, since I had not had a single rise. I'd spotted a big old brown trout feeding gently to floating insects that were bobbing along an old log snag in the darkened water beneath the bridge. In terms of the usual trout to be seen in this stream, this one was big, fat, and full of energy. I'd tried three wet flies drifted drag-free to him on the surface. This combo was later changed to two small bucktails which I zigzagged in front of the old log where the floating insects and bits of foam collect momentarily until the current sweeps them down. The trout was in an advantageous spot for his casual feed, but it was a touchy problem to cast to him, near enough for him to see the flies. It was difficult for me to reach out and drift the flies without becoming snagged in the rusty nails that protruded from the old log.

As I was about to draw in my line after an unsuccessful drift, Henry showed up about fifty yards below the bridge, casting his dry flies into the tail of the deep pool that extended down from the bridge. He had taken three nice trout, which he did not hesitate to display. I had nothing to show after an hour's efforts, but told him of the trout at hand, though yet to be captured.

"There's a big fat old brown up here, Henry. He's on the feed, though in a lazy sort of way. I've tried wets and bucktails, but can't seem to bug him into a strike."

"Stick to it, old boy," he answered. "Perseverance pays off, and all that sort of rubbish."

"I'm game, Henry, but suppose you join in for the pay-off. Come up here, carefully, and see if your cast from below can entice him. He's been feeding on insects that drift along the edge of the log. Perhaps you can interest him with a couple of your floaters."

"Oh, I don't want to barge in on your trout, Ray. If I caught him, I'd never hear the last of it."

"Cut the nonsense, Henry. Look! See that splash? That was just his tail. Make a cast up here and I'll watch it as it drifts down. The reflection angle allows me to see right into the water from where I'm standing."

"Okay, if you say so."

"Cast so that the fly lands up here at the head of the log. Throw a curve cast so that the fly will drop down ahead of the leader and line and then rollcast a bend upstream just as the leader begins to drag on the fly. That should drift your fly right between his eyes."

Henry's rod went into action; fast, snappy false casts to dry the lure and to gain an accurate direction for the drop-down. The fly lit and cocked upright, just as planned, above the log; drifted down, bouncing its way just like the other insects that touched the foam flecks and rough contour of the log. Just as his fly skirted the end of the log, I pitched my small bucktails to the upstream end of the snag so that they would drift down in the same path flipping them just under the surface film to offer the trout a slightly different fare. When the flies had reached the center of the log, I gave them a slight twitch, preparatory to making another cast. The water spilled up into droplets as the big tail of the trout again slapped and swished on the surface. He had risen, but did not connect.

By now, Henry was ready for another cast. He had seen the rise of the trout.

"Cast again, Henry," I said.

"No, he rose to your bucktails. You try for him."

"No, Henry, it's your turn. Try again while he's interested."

Henry's cast went out as well and as directed before, and the fly bounced off the log into the foam line. A quick smashing rise from the trout shot up from right under the fly and I saw the feathers pitched into the air as the trout again missed his mark.

"Now, that was close. Now it is your turn, Ray."

Once again, I tried the little bucktails in a dead drift. I held the rod high, the line up off the water so that the leader would keep the flies close to the surface.

No results.

Henry tried again. Nothing.

Maybe we had put the trout down and off his feed.

"Let's rest him for a while," was the consensus of opinion.

While we withdrew to the bank, we kept an eye on the log, hoping to see the old boy commence feeding again. We figured that once he began to rise once more we would try our wares, perhaps from a different angle. Henry went up on the bridge with the hope of finding an open spot between the boards where he could look down on the situation. I just stood by the bank and watched.

"Boy, that's some trout, Ray," the voice boomed from the echo chamber of the bridge.

"Well, you can't catch him from up there, that's for sure."

"Let's try for him from the upper side of the stretch under the bridge. We can both cast from the same spot and alternately drift dry flies to him. That should do it."

Taking a position slightly upstream from the log, just far enough away for an easy reach and drift with more freedom to cast the line without hitting the frames of the bridgework above our heads, we marched our dries along the log in quick succession and the effect made the flies appear like a natural hatch of insects coming down. As soon as one fly reached the end of the log, the other was cast and floated in its wake. Several times we were accurate enough to place the flies merely inches apart so they could dance downcurrent and drift close together, like twins.

Several casts went by unnoticed apparently by the trout but our team-work is improving. Then, on one of our best drifts he again rose, this time showing his magnificent snout. He took a natural fly that was riding the foam just between our artificials. Here was a trout that seemed smarter than both of us, or at least very particular in his choice of food. We withdrew our casts and switched to smaller size flies to try and fool him.

When the new setup was in action along the log, close together on the drift, he rose with a splash that had the feeling of solidarity and finality about it. One of the flies disappeared for a split second and at that moment, neither of us knew which one he had taken. We both shared in the instant. Henry's rod bent, and I quickly withdrew my fly and leader to get it out of the way, fast. A few minutes later, I assisted with the net from a downstream position, since the water where the fish had been hooked and played was far too deep to wade. Had Henry been alone and the fish had gone below as he had in this instance, I cannot imagine how he could have landed it, since, from his position it was impossible to wade through to the shallower water, below. I had to go ashore—up over the road and down again into the water below the bridge in order to be in a position to net the fish.

Since that day, Henry and I and several others of our acquaintances have been buddy-fishing addicts. We are so in the habit of fishing together and working the water in combo, that we would rather team up than fish alone any more.

Figure 70. Stream Snag I.

CHAPTER 21

Stream Snags I and II

THESE are the spots which hold the romance of trout fishing. Most stories of the big ones that got away find their drama stage under some tricky overhang like the one pictured here on our water for today. There are many such trees and bushes all along this stream, or big brook, as you might call it. These are the spots that try men's patience, fortitude, and tackle. Look at that windfall in the very dry season and you'll see clusters of bait hooks, bobbers, sinkers, spinning lures—enough gear to start a store.

Yet, it is a place like this that harbors an old trout, either a big brookie or smart old brown, until he dies of old age. Funnily enough, many fish are taken from such obvious snares to your tackle. But the percentage of loss to the tackle box is usually high. I'm not even going to guarantee that we won't add to that grand old tree's collection of loot. After all, to see the show you must pay the price.

This is a quiet stream that flows through forest in New England. It is good grouse country in the fall and many a deer has had to be dragged across it on its way to camp, for one of my favorite game trails starts just above the light foliage toward the right-hand side of the picture.

In the early spring the water is well into the bushes and willows along both banks. The conservation club got together with the state and the local boys' club and planted the stream with willow shoots some years ago. As a result, the bank has held out against the ravages of sudden flash floods, spring washouts when the mountain above dumps its melting snow into the course.

The fishing is great then. Regardless of how many books I've read or written, I like to fish this stream with a worm. It is too cold and high to wade, and dangerous. I prefer to work the worm from wherever I can get near the edge. I know that the trout will be nosing in and around those willows, looking for worms and grubs that hang in the leaves that are caught there in the high water. Very seldom have I ever taken a trout in this stretch from the midstream runs.

Then I come to that snag. Like everyone else, I see it from afar and build up a desire to throw a succulent worm just upcurrent and let it drift down into the snag branches that try to hold back the snow-water. At that season, they are jammed with twigs, leaves, and grass, making the whole scene a perfect hiding place and dinner table for the trout.

It doesn't take a genius to see how this should be fished. It doesn't take a genius to get caught at it by those twigs, either. Of course, you do the obvious. If you are working or fishing with a dead minnow, you work the same as you would with a brace of nymphs: weight the leader heavily and heave the rig out in the current directly above the snag—say about twenty feet—and let the menu bounce along the bottom. It won't be long before you are snagged to a branch or charged by a trout. You play the percentages and don't expect to break the bank. If you did, there would never be enough trout under there to make any effort worthwhile.

It looks fishy. There MUST be a trout in there—I was going to say, as long as your arm, but I've used that one earlier. You measure it.

So, to get the drift of the current well in mind, I like to start above those stream rocks well up from the snag. I'll get to know the extent of the bottom, the speed of the stream flow and the general feel of the water against my boots. Previous trips have shown me that there are no deep holes to fall into, nor does the current, even in high early-spring conditions, become too severe.

We'll tie on a couple of succulent stone-fly nymphs. This stream, again, from previous observation, has good hatches and a bottom loaded with these creatures. So, even in early spring, especially when the fast currents are whisking by, they dislodge the insects that skip about in the current until they come to the snag. There they hold on to a branch, unless a trout is hungry and gobbles them up first.

Two weighted nymphs are tied on extra-heavy size 10 hooks (see Appendix). The leader is weighted by two split shot in conventional sequence. The flies are tied on much lighter leader than the main stem, so that if one becomes snagged it can easily be broken off. If a big trout hits, we have to remember this pound test is light and thus handle the fish with as much care as possible. Previous successes have seen the trout make a wild dash for the midcurrent and downstream in a run. This time it may be different. It depends on their mood. We have to be prepared for any action, including that of the trout tangling quickly right after he sees that he's caught on a hook. That usually doesn't take very long.

So, it's do or die.

The cast goes out. It's short and immediately below us in direct line with the snag. The weights are felt bouncing on the bottom. We lower the rod tip to the horizontal, ready our spare-line hand with slack, and quicken our pulse in the rod hand. Just as the flies are judged to be about to the snag, we tighten the rod tip, snub the line gently, and the flies rise to the surface and swing back and forth. Let them drop down to within inches of the topmost snag.

No hit. Retrieve.

We try again; same routine. This time we were working the outside where the trunk of the tree enters the water. Now, let's try the drift to spot the snag at about mid-distance from shore.

Still no hit.

So, we work the shore, dropping the flies and angling the rod tip so that the line, flowing as it does, will force the rig to slither its way in toward the rocks along the shore. That should be the hot spot.

Bum! A hit! Another, before we can strike. Another. Somebody down there is curious but not anxious. I secretly wish I had a worm. I'd attach it to the hook on the bottom nymph and drift it down to him.

Another try, but before we cast it this time, I'm going to put a brown and black bucktail with a silver body on the end of the leader. That just might turn the trick.

The cast goes down and the drift is perfect. I begin to tighten. I can visualize the minnow imitation beginning to rise and wave in the currents. The trout sees it, although I cannot know this.

Zoom! What a strike. Where is he? The rod's bending and the line is tight. He's struggling in the snags.

I relax the line. Soon the fish swims out upcurrent from the snags. When he has gone far enough away, I tighten again and the battle is on. I can hold him now, and when I see slack, I mend it out toward the center of the stream. This action brings him out there with it and the battle from then on is easy.

It isn't the romantic big old trout of wide repute, but it's fat and well colored. Open him up? Yes, certainly.

He's been feeding on stone flies, dragonflies, and other bottom insects. Well down in his gullet, probably from the early-morning hours, are caddis larvae and their stone and sand cases. He's got a stomach full of gravel, poor guy. I wonder what trout take for cathartics?

We could tell tales of big fish and awesome snags for hours. I bet you could probably top me with yarns.

To fish this kind of situation, one doesn't need to be cagy or tricky or even smart. One has to be lucky.

The picture is from the memory of a northern stream where there is lots of driftwood and snags. While most of our streams in Pennsylvania, lower New York and Jersey have few of these obstructions due to washed-out stream beds, northern streams in their setting of wilderness forests and more wood to find its way into the water, obviously have more snags.

In and around these snags, particularly on a bend, pockets of foam gather—sometimes a great expanse of it, all puffed up in a broad sheet. In calm weather when sudden rain is not common, these pockets may accumulate as much as a month's supply of the foam. In shaded areas where it does not evaporate, or where there is much foam coming down from a falls or rapids, the pocket becomes quite extensive.

Right under it you will find trout. Here they have a curtain from the sun. Foam collects here; so do the drifting insects—a perfect serve-yourself supermarket of all that comes down the stream from above.

There is not an angler alive who fails to throw at least one cast into this pocket. The trout underneath are on the alert and will strike at anything unless they are so full of feed that they cannot open their mouths. On wilderness streams, one can hook into a real fish here, since any big

Figure 71. Stream Snag II.

trout will chase any other contender away. On the contrary, this same condition of foam on a heavily fished water will likely contain only normal-size fish, since there is a continual arrival of new fish to take the place of the ones snaked out.

Fish this one with me, first on a wilderness stream in the lumberlands of Maine. No one has been by here, perhaps, this spring. The ice has been out of the lakes for only three weeks. Landlocked salmon and brook trout use this stream as a go-between the lakes. We are gliding downstream in a canoe, quietly being polled by the guide. Here's the spot for the lunker. It should happen just like in a movie. You make the first cast. Your brace of wet flies, a White-Winged Coachman and a Parmachene Belle—two typical Maine flies—go out to the gap between the two rocks at the right of the illustrated area, to drift down into the lip of the white foam. A short hit from a little trout.

Fortunately, you jerked the fly away before he disturbed the pool.

Rest the area, and throw one to the rocks on the very right-hand side of the pool. Don't go in the foam again until it settles down.

That's the usual mistake, particularly on much-fished waters. The angler usually persists and thus scares the trout.

You can take as good a trout from that left-hand rock as you might from the foam, so why not try it anyway. The flies go out again and liquidly flex and flash along the outside rock wash. There's a glimmer of action from underwater. A fish, perhaps a landlock, whisks by, makes his pass, and drops down again. We'll remember that.

But, now, back to the foam. This cast might go the limit to the left of the rock to be drifted right along that old lumbered spruce.

Out you go. The current pulls it into a position behind the rock; therefore, mend the line so it lays right on the rock and gently dribbles over to the right side and into the water. Throw out a foot or two of extra line. The flies are now under and stuck in the foam. No action.

Flip out a bit more line to dislodge the top fly from the foam. That's it. That'll put 'em in position for a strike.

Still no action.

Okay, we have a trick for that trout—but wait a minute. We want to try our wets on that far-left rock again. Out goes the cast—same spot, right at the head of the wash. Again a shadow of something big, but he doesn't take.

Okay. Light a cigarette. Just let the flies dangle in the current.

The guide, seeing this, knows what to do. Gently he moves the bow in the direction of the rock. The flies hang in the current unnoticed. You fumble around for the matches.

Whammo (sorry to use that one, but it expresses what happens).

A nice big, fat, luscious brookie. Look at those pink fins and those sky-blue spots. Boy he'll taste good . . . if you land him. It took real talent to hook that one.

Now it is time to work the trick on the foam.

The switch is to a big Wulff dry fly. We'll spot that big fluffer right into the middle of the foam, let it set there a minute, and then jiggle it enticingly. The trout won't be able to see it, but he'll get the idea that SOMETHING is up there above him.

That does it. He can't resist. Now all we have to do is to keep him from the snags, from wrapping us around that rock, hanging us on the bottom snags that we imagine must compose that hideout. Boy, what a thumping he is giving us.

The guide moves the canoe downstream almost to the rock. We gather in slack and try and hold on as the brookie goes into his typical fight of the twisting body-roll. If it were a rainbow of this size, he'd have long ago broken us off.

So, you think it's all over now and we can go in for tea?

The best is yet to come. You've hardly noticed the big old tree and it's sunken boughs a bit down below right at the bend of the stream and alongside the wash from the rock. What a perfect triangle. It's a good spot to hang into a landlocked salmon. Good holding water there. Since landlocks seldom take trout flies, but trout take landlocked salmon flies, we'll tie on a typical Maine Gray Ghost streamer fly and tease the hell out of the snag and the water immediately below it.

As if to know our minds, the guide drifts us down on our canoe carpet and we fish away. At lunch on the shore just out of sight below, we lay our fish on the rocks, wet them, and burn film.

That same type of water on heavily fished streams? Work the foam of course, but remember that most of the fish will be taken from it due to their instant action. There will remain good fish in the rock wash, ahead of both rocks, especially planted rainbows and browns, and you'll find that anglers, heading for the foam, will forget all about these mentioned places and so skip by them in their desire to fish the cream puff. Bless them!

CHAPTER 22

Shallow Flat Water

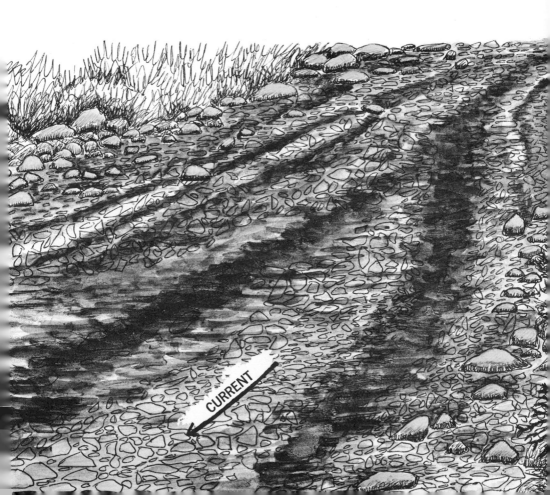

"BEAUTIFUL dry-fly water." That's the usual comment. Sure, it is flat, lazy, with slight ripples, with no problem midstream rocks, deep snakelike runs, or tricky currents. All one needs to do is cover the water with the floaters and sooner or later something will come up.

That's all rubbish.

But that is how the usual angler fishes it. And you know what? He doesn't catch anything, except maybe a small fish by dumb luck.

I know, my neck is out a country mile. But I do know from much past trial and error how I like to fish this water and when.

As you look out over the flat you are seeing only about ten per cent of this particular run. At its head, the current narrows into a bouldered spill and then flattens out. Foam specks drift down quietly and about here they have all but dissolved. For about the same distance below you, the water remains the same. It is seemingly characterless, but on closer examination there are small valleys and gently rolling hills under there that ever so slightly affect the surface currents. These are difficult to represent on the drawing, for I was more interested in showing the contour of the bottom from shallow-light to deeper-dark than to show the currents, since what happens up above is virtually dictated by what you see here, as it is pictured in late May or possibly in June. The level is normal, the water clear and cool. When the light is right you'll see trout nudging and nosing the bottom for caddis larvae in the morning and afternoon, since both times offer a bit of shade from even the flattest of rocks. There is no holding water here for big fish, so for the most part it is inhabited by the littler of the clan. Only when the feeding sprees are being enjoyed do the bigger trout enter this flat parklike arena for the bout with the flies.

But it is pretty dry-fly water. I enjoy fishing the fly over it, just to see the fly and the action of my leader and line. It offers a good schoolroom for the beginning angler. The noisy wader will seldom see the trout dart ahead of him, sometimes having been spooked from fifty feet below. Any trout that might be there to grab a fly would have long since left the area due to faulty wading.

You are not allowed any sloppy casting even if you are interested in hooking the smallest trout. Midday trouting here is mere exercise. Hole up in the nearest bar or go find some fast white water to spat your bucktails in.

But, comes the twilight hour and hatches are in order (that includes any time from mid-April until late July) and the whole scene takes on different proportions.

But, where do the trout come from? Both banks are bare of shadow or snag or hole. Obviously, there are no trout hiding out there where everybody can see them. I've never been able to answer that question. But I can recall wading along quietly and seeing trout lying just half hidden by a shelf rock that had to be dislodged by the rod tip being poked at them. That's how stubborn and perhaps sleepy they were. Of course, there are many trout that will come up to or drop down to the pool when the twilight hour approaches, for they seem to know that there will be insects hatching. They also can drop down at any time of the day and, as we can see now, feed on caddis larvae to their hearts' content.

But how do we catch them?

We discard the floating-fly routine. The sun is just too bright. It is difficult to drift a sunken nymph from the downstream angle, so we start in at the top of the run. Since there are at least ten good fish nosing the water as far as we can see, we'll try a very unorthodox way of catching those trout.

You won't find this one in many fishing books. I've only seen it done three times in my life before I latched on to it as the medicine for such a moment.

On a fifteen-foot slightly weighted leader, we place three drab wet flies of about size 12. They can be March Browns, Dark Hendricksons; it doesn't make too much difference. The way we handle them is going to make or break the bank.

Now, from a position near the top of the glassy run, we cast the rig as far as we can across and downstream on a good angle for a drift. If the leader is weighted too heavily it will snag, so we'll try to go light, but heavy enough to sink the flies and still let them drift in the soft current. We are going to attempt to drift those flies deep down, somewhere between one and two feet under the surface, which will put them inches above the bottom of the deep lanes.

By line manipulation and mending once in a while to the left or right, the rig will wend its way slowly just where we want it to go, right to the eyes of those trout. By some luck they will possibly grab one of the flies, thinking it is a dislodged caddis case.

You'll make only about one cast in fifteen minutes. But you may catch a trout. It is going to be tough, trying to figure out just where the flies are and where the trout are in regard to them. When, and if a trout hits, it will be a gentle bump, not a thrilling rise or even like a quick pass at a nondescript dry fly. They'll simply mouthe the fly and if they don't feel the steel or the barb, they might swallow it until they do. If you are able to tighten the line soon enough you'll likely snag the fish before he can open his mouth and reject it. If not, he'll spit out your creation with disdain and you'll be none the wiser. But it's worth a try, for, believe me, there is no other way designed for this situation at this season on this kind of hot day that will take even a brash little chub.

See your line move? That wasn't the current. That was a bump from a fish. Who cares if it was a chub or a trout. It was a hit. If someone were on the shore below watching this performance he could tip you off as to the position and action of the trout. But, for now, you'll have to do your own scouting.

Keep feeding out the line. Don't let it tighten and so lift the flies up off the bottom. Be careful, though, not to let too much line go slack or the rig will sink, or, as we said, with so much slack you'll never feel the hit. Get the balance of the game and play it as if you were winning.

There. There, see your line move? Strike! Strike hard. You've that whole rig to move before the trout will even feel it.

That's it. He's on.

Fifteen inches? Gee, I thought we agreed that no such trout would be in such a broad open space at this time of the day. You caught him in the act of feeding.

Let's see on what.

Caddis, of course. Now, look at the March Brown he took. Similar to the caddis case. (If the designer of this fly is not turning over in his grave, it'll be a wonder. That fly was painfully designed to represent one specific May fly that is prevalent in English chalk streams and here we've used it as a caddis-larva imitation, of all things.)

But that's the game of troutin', son.

The best time of all on this water is during the Green Drake hatch. The insects usually drift down to this quiet water from the mud-lined pool above where the nymphs crawl out and hatch in relative security from the trout. By the time they float down here they are well set with their wing problems and usually are sailing along peacefully, enjoying the late-day breeze and warmth—that is, until the big trout that are not supposed to be here all converge on the surface at the same time.

Late twilight or early evening when the swallows are about and the first bats begin to wing out over the water is another great time here. The spinners from miles up and down the river will be dipping to the water to deposit their eggs. Again, the big fish will come to them and to your floaters if you wade quietly, fish carefully, cast no more and no longer distances than necessary, and retrieve with the forward roll and quick air pickup. (Thought I'd throw that in for a review reminder, for without this training being followed, your chances on this kind of water are virtually nil. I've seen it absolutely murdered by amateurs to the point where it is a wonder that the trout had not all gone to a mental hospital from fear sickness.)

The other time to fish this type of water is when one or the other side of the stream is in shadow. If you work your flies from the sunny side, remember you are like a flashing Coca-Cola sign to the trout and so is your waving rod. Wading, too, must be very, VERY slow, especially if you are fishing the water across from you or particularly below. Any leg motion in that water sends out waves; and waves are the signal for the trout to take cover. An angler is coming.

Resist the long casts with the snappy new and expensive rod. Limit your casts to forty feet and taper your leader to the thinnest-possible tippet, even if you have to taper by short lengths to get down thin. Rub fish slime on the leader especially when your hands are covered with the line dressing.

April and high water? Shoot 'em a bucktail.

Figure 73. Deep Flat Water.

CHAPTER 23

Deep Flat Water

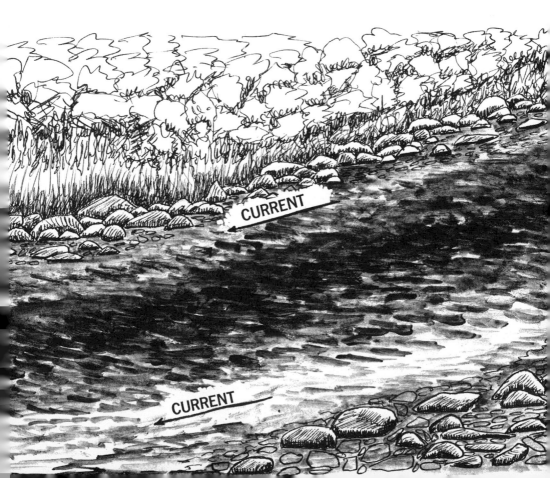

THIS is a rushing torrent in the early spring. There is nothing here to hold back the floods. Ice, trees, old tires, anything finds its way to this water, and when it reaches this stretch it skips by in alarming speed. The water is high up in behind those willows and the rocks you see now, sunburned, are just poking their heads out when the initial run-off is subsiding. At that time the pussy willows will often bear an ice cap in the early morning. When the hatchery men come to deliver trout to the stream in March, this is chocolate-brown water, or at least smoky and discolored. Only if a sudden freeze takes place here and higher up, harnessing in the banks, will the water be the least bit clear or inviting by Opening Day.

At first glance the water seems much like that of the preceding chapter, but at closer scrutiny you will see that it is far different. It is also not quite the same as the straight center current described earlier, although many of the techniques of these and other chapters are naturally applicable here.

As we approach the stream now, it is in late May or June. The run is a long one with only a portion of it shown here. On the big broad rivers of the Catskills, such as the Beaverkill, Esopus, and Delaware, there are miles of such stretches. Here the rainbows migrate through, not stopping long. The big browns usually use this for a slip-through going up or from pool to pool down. Yet, strangely enough, I've taken both species and in big sizes from this kind of water.

The center current is slow and lazy now. The water clear and deep, with a slight ripple as shown. With the exception of the run along the rocks at the bottom of the picture, the stream has no visible currents or eddies to speak of and so no definite drifting patterns for the food to follow as it comes from above.

This is easier to wade than the water of the preceding chapter. For one thing, it is deep, possibly over your waders in the middle and not shallowing out much until it almost reaches the banks. Wading, then, will be of no great problem, since there are no holes, snags, or big rocks to step around or bump into. The only care that is needed is to enter quietly making no waves that will telltale your entrance. Then, you MUST not step, but feel the bottom with your feet. Remember in our night fishing how noisy you sounded, just the feet of your waders crunching on the bottom. Take care. Wade more quietly and you'll have fish feeding all around you.

Bucktail water in the spring? Sure is, and we have detailed some typical manipulations of the bucktail that you can learn on this water, for it is easy to see the fly in motion (see figure 74). The main thing to get to know in the zigzag-motion technique is how much of the rod and line jerking that you are doing is having its effect on the fly. Study the diagrams and when you fish try a bright fly that you can see clearly and note how enticingly you can actually move the fly. Use your line hand in conjunction with your rod motion (see Appendix, page 295).

Not that I recommend only the action technique for such water. On many trips to this particular pool I've chosen the bucktail and have deliberately drifted it salmon-fishing style, dead-drift in the current, allowing the little motion of the water to undulate the feathers and fur. I like a streamer for this type of fishing rather than a bucktail simply because the soft feathers allow more action than the stiffer hairs.

It's great wet-fly water, too, when the day is overcast, particularly right after a rain. Blow-ins, hatched and drowned insects, will be floating in the surface film and it is just a matter of placing any fly in the water, since the trout are not actually engaged in feeding to a specific insect hatch.

My standby for the pinches, the Royal Coachman, particularly in the old-fashioned Fanwing, is a killer on this water, even in broad daylight when trout are not supposed to rise to artificials due to the extreme brightness that you hear anglers kicking about so generously when they return to the noon feast at the beanery—fishless and hungry.

Long-line nymphing close to the bottom is equally effective here as it was in the shallow flat. You just need more weight, that's all. When those trout are seen feeding on the bottom, put this rig to them that we have detailed and you'll likely connect.

I like this water best, perhaps, when there is a hatch on. The Quill Gordon fly hatches at the head of a run like this, and by the time the flies get their wings going well, many of them will be drifting on the surface. Because the hatch has come off well up above, the trout are not actively feeding, since they have not been engaged in taking the nymphs before they actually hatch. For this reason, the trout that come up to

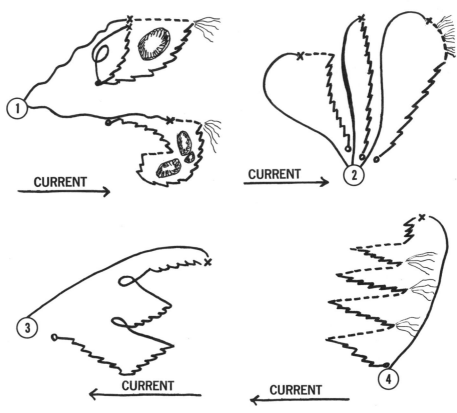

Figure 74. Four Typical Exercises in Fly Manipulation (Wets, Streamers, and Bucktails).

(Note: For the actual technique instruction of the casts made, see Appendix, page 308.)

1. *Facing downstream the angler wishes to fish the area immediately below the rock to a rock, snag, or hole. The cast to the left drifts straight down to absorb slack and sinks the fly. The rod tip is then raised and as the fly drags on the surface you execute a zigzag return made by line-hand pulls and rod-tip flipping, until the pickup well above the hot spot.*

The cast to the right is a bit more involved. Here, the fly is dropped on slack line, allowed to sink on drift to a drag point where the angler wishes it to come back up on the surface. At this point, the zigzag motion is employed in an across-stream path to be then switched in direction by a mend and then again zigzagged as it is allowed to drift down. The final action retrieve is made directly upstream as shown, to the pickup point.

2. *This across-stream position and aim is a common one and three casts of slightly different procedure are shown as examples to be used as guides. The first uses the upstream cure cast, short drift, and direct across-stream*

pickup. The second is the fast return without any drift allowed. The third allows drift until drag sets in and then the action retrieve is made back to the angler.

3. Facing now upstream, the curve cast is thrown well up with the rod held high. The fly is zigzagged by rod tip and hand pickup of slack back on the drift, rolled back upstream again for a few feet and the action repeated as many times as possible before the final pickup.

4. Now, facing across stream, the angler casts slightly upstream, throwing a modified upstream curve. This allows the drift to absorb the curve of line and then, by line manipulation with the rod tip, a sawtooth zigzag sideways and an up-and-down motion is performed either on the surface, or, with a weighted fly, a deeper run.

CODE

fly washes on surface

cast line

drift – – – –

zigzag retrieve

fly lights ✕

these floating flies do so with nowhere near the same hard-hitting impulse. They rise in a much more deliberate and planned way. This makes the game more difficult but at the same time more fun. Here we have to be careful about drag, for that leader will surely put them down, since they have plenty of time to inspect their prey. The curve cast is also a must.

Again, the Green Drake hatch is the event, and you can time this for about the second week in June in most Northeastern streams. Those big May flies look just great floating down that water in no current pattern. Sometimes they will take off, light again, and take off. At this moment, the trout really rise with abandon. I've seen as many as five big trout in the air all at the same time right in the water you are looking at now. Curve casts are in order and the usual pickups and mends that we have described in earlier chapters.

At twilight, especially when one side of the stream is in at least semi-darkness, wet flies skittered gently on the surface will pull up those trout that up to that moment have been feeding incessantly on caddis and other life on the rocky bottom. Step aside for a moment when the light is right and watch them at work. Pick your spots and drift the flies right over them, skittering them as you go. The dry-fly man working his floaters can add a bit of popping and skittering. A spider fly is good medicine then too. Drag, then, is an aid!

When you can hardly see your fly—that's the time this water can really come alive. It is unbelievable the amount of trout that will materialize out of nowhere—big ones, too. They'll slap around as if they did not have a care in the world, and, with exasperating coolness and accuracy, take the naturals drifting right next to your best imitations. I find that at this time, I do not try to imitate anything, but throw a contrast at them. I use a white-winged Wulff-type dry fly that at least *I* can see, even if they can and don't want it. Usually the white has some sort of attraction, especially when the late spinners are dipping down on the surface. Perhaps it is the white in the fur that catches the light and looks to the trout like the shine on the glassy wings of the adult May flies.

Makes good sense, even if it doesn't put many trout in the creel.

Why fish this on such an evening? Wouldn't it be better to be working the head or tail of a pool? I might agree with you, but, I still like this water, maybe because I've been skunked on it many times, but the events that I remember when big fish hit, even if they did not actually take, are etched deep in my memory.

Perhaps one reason why I like a hooked fish in this water is that I can really have fun with him. He has the whole wide water to run in and I generally let him bounce around if he is a keeper or one that I want to bring home for the roasting oven. Usually fish will dive for cover in the rocks, snags, or fight out their battle against the current and so tire too quickly. I've enjoyed the fight of a brook trout or brown for many more minutes in this kind of water. They can jump and tail-walk at their choice and I merely follow along.

Netting of a fair-sized trout in this average, not-too-fast water does not offer too much of a problem. I try and guard against bringing the fish close to the net before it is thoroughly played out and is actually turning on its side. That's the keeper. It is better, with little fish, to bring them in quickly before they become too exhausted. But when that big one comes in it doesn't take too much talent to remember to submerge the net long before he is nearby. It is better to have the fish upcurrent of you so that you can control his drift downstream into the hoop. Trying to scoop the fish up when it can lunge forward and away with the current adding to its pressure on your thin leader is a much more difficult situation.

When the fish is a big one and the conditions of netting are rough and your footing none too secure, play the fish out and do not horse it through the water toward you unless you have a heavy leader, for the weight of the fish against the current will break even a strong leader if he suddenly gets the urge for that last getaway. The best plan is to move shoreward and pick a spot where there is quieter water or even a backdraft of dead water. Remember to keep your rod in the horizontal position, not the vertical, so that the line in the water will offer an additional cushion against his sudden run. Also, you will not be aiding him into a jump this way.

Keep that slack line under the touch of your rod hand when you are actually netting the fish and don't relax it until the fish is actually in the air, having been scooped out while thrashing in the net.

When wading deep, net the fish close to your body. It's easier that way and the current is not likely to throw you off guard as it might if you were leaning way off your balance point.

Figure 75. Stream Tributary.

CHAPTER 24

Stream Tributary

CURRENT

ONE of the most provoking, yet productive spots on any trout stream is the area where a tributary stream enters the picture, bringing its colder water and entirely different signs of life to the main flow. All through the season, a different set of situations exist here to be seen, used and remembered.

In the early spring we would see the main stream swollen by high water. The tributary would be spilling additional water into it, adding to the flow. Below its entrance there are now actually two streams; one the main river, usually discolored. The tributary might be bringing clear water. By the same token, the situation might actually be the reverse; the main current might be clear and muddy water could be coming down the tributary. In either case both sluices must be fished separately with, of course, a blend of fly manipulation where the two streams parallel each other and begin to blend.

It's a great spot for bait fishing, and both local talent and the city "fellers" will give the area a good going over. In streams where there are rainbows, the holding water just ahead of the join, a foot or two upstream, is the spot to pick one up with a heavily weighted night crawler.

On that cold first day, I'd be inclined, as I have in previous years, to fish bucktails downstream as figure 76 presents. I'd enter the water above the join and wade out to a position as far from the rocks as safety and balance would permit. (There are six potent casts in the illustration starting upstream of the tributary that can be made with bucktails and the drift-and-zigzag retrieve technique [see figure 76] from above the tributary.) If these did not bring any action, I'd then switch to weighted nymphs and repeat the process. I'd not leave without working both the rocks directly downstream and those in the center of the run as shown. From these positions I would have worked over the area thoroughly with

lures of seasonal preference. With no fish in the creel I'd then wade
ashore, think for a minute, and decide to take up a position upstream in
the tributary and drift first the nymphs, then the wet flies, and finally the
streamers down into the hot-spot area, as shown.

This same procedure could be followed later in the season, particularly
in the early morning before the sun had risen, to drive the fish to the
cover of underwater shadows or into the deep currents or overhangs. I'd
also fish this water of an evening when nothing spectacular was happening in the way of hatches. Wet flies, with a bobber dry fly (see Appendix,
page 314), might bring up some of the trout of the kind that make good
stories. Note that little wading has been necessary.

During the middle of an early spring day, when there is a chance of
a Quill Gordon hatch coming down the sluiceway of the tributary or from
the big water of the main stream, a brace of tiny Gordons would make
good first tries. For this, I'd be inclined to follow the casts shown in figure
76. It would be upstream wet-fly fishing with the later possibility of a

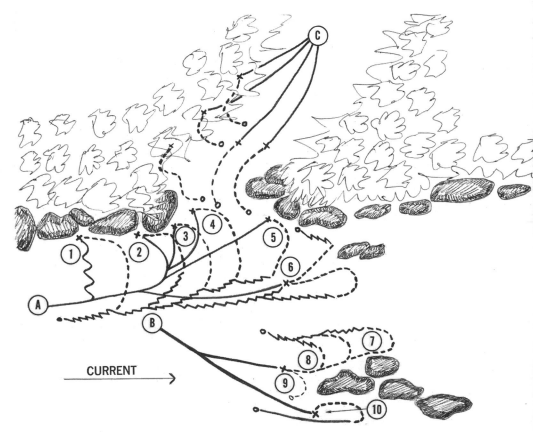

CURRENT

Figure 76. Fishing Tributary Entrance Downstream.

quick change to the dry fly. From the position of the angler as shown in the diagram, both the wash from the tributary and the rocks of the main stream can be worked successfully without moving. When the water is high this is a great advantage. Later, when the water is lower and the current less strong, wading farther out and up along those inshore rocks can be negotiated.

Standing at A, fish the near water first to 1 and the drift of the fly is quite natural. Cast 2 goes up a bit farther and with two rollcast mends, the fly is allowed to continue its drift without line drag. Cast 3 is the extension of this. That's a potent run, and without moving, and with no action as yet, I'd take the time to switch to the little but potent bucktails that represent either stone flies or very small minnows, rigged the way we have discussed before; short tippets, and perhaps, slightly weighted. I'd then work the water of 4, 5, and 6, as shown before I moved upstream. All our fishing so far has been from position A. If the water is too fast to go to B, we can cover some of that outer water from the rocks between 6 and the shore, without disturbing the confluence water where the tributary joins in. If it is possible to fish from point B in the

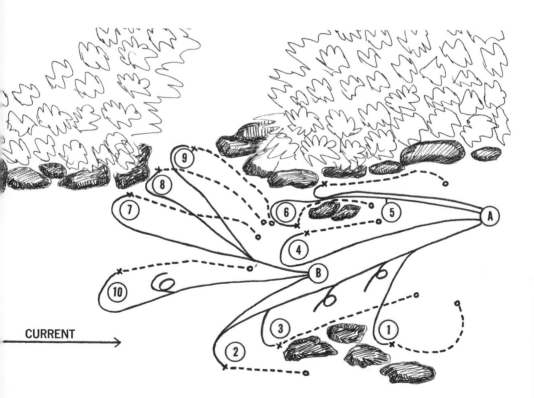

CURRENT

Figure 77. Fishing Tributary Entrance Upstream.

early spring, do so. A hatch of Hendricksons will drift straight down to you and offer dry-fly fishing *par excellence*. Drift your wet flies and skitter during the first stages of the hatch.

Wonderful bit of water, isn't it?

And, we haven't yet begun to really understand it at all. We've merely road-mapped fishing potentials and recommended techniques to follow. Late spring and early summer we can work the section in a combination of all the methods and ideas written above. This is also a great place for night fishing.

As April passes and May introduces many of the principal hatches, the character of the two streams becomes more apparent. By this time, unless someone is building a road up the tributary, this water is clearer than the main stream. It is also colder, bringing with it hatches ordinarily not found on the big water. Midges hatch in the pools of this tributary, and countless thousands of mosquitoes and tiny species of May flies. Since this sort of tributary flows through the woods and broken fields, land-bred insects are constantly falling into the water. All of this loot is flowing right into the main current at one potent spot.

During the hotter months ahead, the big fish that generally inhabit the deeper parts of the pool and the broken water below in the distinct flow of the tributary water will come up to the tributary junction and immediately above it, to sit there and take their hand-outs as they come along. When a hatch of flies comes down the main stream, the fish that are comfortably settled in the cooler water from the tributary will then move up and out and, particularly just ahead of the "Y" and take the floating insects. Meet them there!

While we do not show the other side, or side across from the bottom of the picture, I have been able in May and June to wade into that center water and, with a long, stiff dry-fly rod, place dries to the rocks just under those two dead trees. The flow of the flies is short, since the currents drag them quickly. The only hope in this situation is for the trout to grab the fly before the current does. The center rocks are easier to fish from that distance. Between these two spots I've taken some nice trout. One big rainbow grabbed a fly just as the current dragged it toward the rocks, right along the edge of the joining currents. I had to rollcast the line over and below the center rocks to avoid a snag. From that point on the rainbow headed downstream and I had to wade ashore, away back to my side, hold the rod high while he jumped unmercifully all his way downstream. I finally netted him a hundred yards below. I've often thought of him as a miniature salmon, for that's the kind of trip those brutes usually take you on.

When the water is extremely low, I approach the hole a bit closer. In the early morning I place a nice juicy-looking bucktail up above the white froth, let it sink during the slight drift and, as the current catches it, zigzag the fly back over the water, letting it drop down to the head of the rocks. Makes me drool to think of it and remember the times I've connected in this manner.

I prefer this water during the Leadwing Coachman hatch. The two rocks near the shore down from the join are usually littered with the nymphs that crawl out on the surface to shed their shucks. The midstream rocks usually gain a contingent of the same flies. When that action is going on, the trout from the hole, from the main stream, both up and down seem to get the message. Never have I seen so many trout—big ones—feeding with such utter abandon.

Low water of late June and into July finds stone flies hatching sporadically and the late species of May-fly spinners usually flit above the water enticing the trout up from their daytime hiding places. Now, wading to the area is easy, so I begin downstream on the near side, out of the picture, and work the flies over to the froth, and, with rod held high, dapple wet flies, spiders, heavily dressed dries, usually in that order.

Now the cooler water of the tributary brings all the trout to it and such concentration is bound to produce a rise. This advantage can be completely destroyed by undue wading disturbance and, particularly, by sloppy line handling. Make only a few casts. Then rest the area by changing your direction.

Don't underestimate the tributary itself. Most anglers bypass this most potent spot—the overhangs immediately up the stream. These can best be worked by the downstream cast, even though dry flies will be used.

A brace of small wet flies in very thin leaders worked in under that overhang especially during the bright time of the day will connect you with at least one of the big trout that has forsaken the main stream for the cover and coolness of the gin-clear, in under the brambles. As a matter of fact, it will not be out of place to fish that tributary well up from the main stream, for the holes there will be loaded with escapees from the warmer waters below.

The stretch downstream of the tributary should actually be considered as part of this entire picture. The reason why we have separated them into two sections is because of several definite conditions that should be seen and consequently met in order to fish the lower water properly in ways that the actual fork would not generally be fished.

CHAPTER 25

Below Tributary

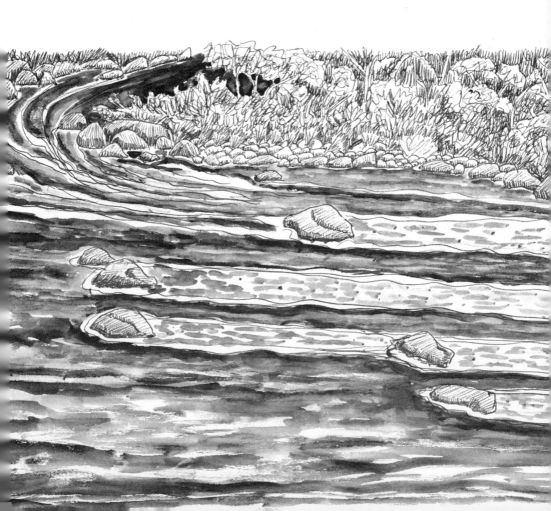

AS you can immediately see, this stretch is not the same as that of the preceding chapter, although the principle is the same. I've merely picked a more complicated one about five miles downstream on the same river. Much of what we did in the last chapter can be duplicated here, but we will see in dramatic examples the big difference between the water of the tributary as it enters and stays by itself for quite a distance before blending with the main stream, and the basic river itself, an entirely separate entity in most respects. The narrow, deep, and fast strip of water starting out between 7 and 1 has us virtually fishing two rivers at the same time.

In the early spring, the first of the little flies to hatch to any degree is the little black stone fly. This insect drifts down during the day from the tributary where it has been growing as an underwater insect for a whole year. The fly will be carried down in the current directly and will not be exposed to any degree to the fish lying in front of and behind the midstream rocks of the main river.

By the same token, a Quill Gordon hatch that originates in the main stream in the pool immediately above will float down in good clusters in the main water and there will hardly be a Gordon seen drifting in the tributary water adjacent to it.

In June no Green Drakes will ever be seen coming down the little brook. They'll float their way from above on the big water.

This separation calls for astute observation and fishing techniques as previously outlined in the many chapters before this. The main point here is to watch what is actually happening in the two pieces of water. Quite naturally, with this two-party system of events, the trout will be acting likewise. Where, in one case, all the trout will be rising in one section of the stream in a given circumstance, a change of activity will find them all moving into the other lane for their feeding spree.

From the first week in April when the main stream and the tributary are high until the drought-ridden days of late August and into September, there is more diversification on this bit of water than on most stretches. A whole day can be spent here, provided you do your wading with a bit of care and caution, and your casting is held to a minimum and is well directed.

Follow along with me on an early-morning vigil in late June. The water level is normal, the color clear, and the air invigorating, with a good rising barometer. Since the flats at 2 are now bare, we can look on the rocks for the cast shucks of stone flies. There are many, telling us that there must have been a good hatch here the night before or during the past few nights. From position 1 we can work a small bucktail or, if you

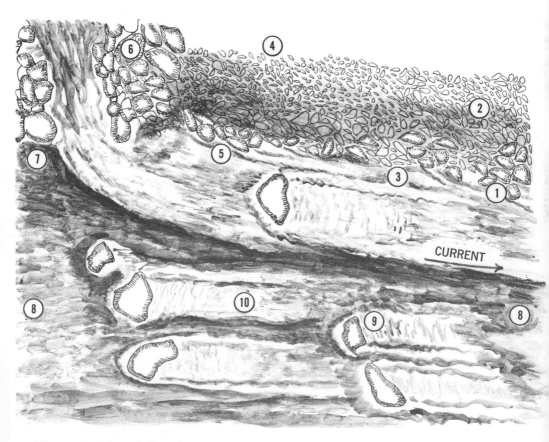

Figure 78. Below Tributary.

prefer, a couple of good-sized dark wets, first in an across-stream cast toward 8 with the drift down out of the picture. This will give us the feel of the current before venturing into the hot spots above. A cast close to 9 reminds us of the problem of the deep center current where the fly can be whisked away by the fast line of water before it does its duty. Remember how to solve that one. Casts go to above those two rocks and we also comb well the washes between and below them. At this season, many trout that otherwise hang out in front or beside the rock will drop back during the night into the shallow wash and stay there until anglers or too much sun drive them into a shady side of a boulder. If we see by skittering our flies that there is the possibility of taking a trout on a floater despite the lack of signs of encouragement, we can move to 8 quietly and take in the two rocks at 9 and the water just below the rock down from 5. We either allow the fly to drift back down almost to the rod tip or rollcast and pick up the fly for a recast. Having snared a small trout from 9, we know that the area has been disturbed, so we can wade up there and be in a position to fish the big rock below 5 and the lower washes in the rocks above 10. Some nice choices here? You can stand for an hour throwing everything in the book before the sun comes up.

From 10 we can reach over into the tributary water with a dry fly, which usually brings a rise even from a small fish if nothing else. I like to follow up such a rise with a bucktail, just in case an "old ragged fin" brown has been awakened.

Since it is possible now to wade across to 5, we can do so after we have turned around and wet-flied the rocks at 9. I did this one morning and hooked a good fish that fought heavily, rolling its course downstream until I ran out of line. When he reached the end, that was it. It was fun while the line supply lasted.

While wading in the dark strip on our way to 5, we can work diagonally downstream and across to 3 with wets and a bucktail, changing to the dry fly for an upstream thrust to the midstream rocks and over into the pause water below 7, similar to the spot described in the preceding chapter.

But the most perplexing time on this stretch is when there are two distinct hatches in progress. The trout are crossing from one to the other and it is a pretty problem to try and pick a pattern that will suit them. Specific hatches bring on selective feeding, but how do you handle two meals at once that are quite different in taste and form?

The unorthodox usually wins. Remember that if things get really tough and your dry-fly collection is drawing you a zero, you can always switch to a spider, particularly in the evening, a Fanwing Royal Coachman, or even a succulent bucktail, my old standby.

Fishing this stretch down with a brace of wets in the evening can be pleasant, although you will have to be prepared for the strike of a good fish that will have all the advantages of the current with him. Better be armed with a reel that has plenty of backing, or he'll make you either run down the stream or you'll have to swim to keep up with him.

When the Leadwing Coachman nymphs are clinging to the rocks above 10 and I'm located between 3 and 5, we have a perplexing situation. That's tough water to handle. You can stand there, watching the big trout flipping up and down along the rocks, and once in a while one will slither over the top of one knocking the nymphs back into the froth. Spinners, drifting down from above, will be in the deep center strip and the water will be alive with busting trout. The problem? To get that fly to float for a long enough distance to bring a hit. Remembering that a spinner does not spend too much time on the water, we really need not be concerned about this. Just a few seconds, that's all it takes.

See, there's a smashing rise. Look at 'im travel downstream. I'll sit on a rock until you return with your trout.

Take your time with him. After dark, we'll refresh at the bar and then return for some sporty night fishing with the big wet-dry flies that were tied first by Ed Sens, a fishing expert who handed me this pattern (see Appendix, page 326). The pattern is the Giant Stone Fly.

It's pitch-black when we return. The stream is no stranger to us since we've worked over it and have begun to know most of the wading pitfalls and difficult casting angles.

Our fishing now, however, will be simple. No fancy casts or tricky drifts. For one thing, we couldn't see enough to perform anyway. In the black of night it's calm, quiet, ghostlike. A slight mist is on the water, for it has been a hot day when the sun was beating down. The moon is in the black, so we have no light except that from the stars. As we have in previous situations, we douse the cigarettes, and, of course, the flash-light is put away. We carry one in case of trouble, of course, but do not use it generally.

The main reason why so many anglers do not fare well in their night fishing is because they insist on bringing light to the stream. There is nothing other than a thrown rock into the pool that will put trout down quicker than a strange light.

Coming out of the brush at 4, we stand by the gravel beach for a moment until our eyes become accustomed to the dark. Soon we begin to see and hear and feel. Our night radar is beginning to function. Our rods are rigged and there is nothing to do now but to cast. We are armed with Sens's Giant Stone Fly. We sense and "hear" a bat flying. It zooms out over the water. We can "see" some stone flies in the air. The sound of the water seems far different than it did during the day. As we walk down to

2 for a different perspective, we notice the change in the sound of the waves and bubbles as they curl around the rock below 5. Now that our eyes have opened a bit further, we can see the white wakes behind the 10 rocks and the wash from 9. We know all about that fast, deep run of main current down the middle of the picture. We also remember how difficult it is to float a fly there for any length of time because of the confusing currents.

We cast a glance behind us to survey for backcast room. There's just enough for about a fifty-foot cast if we are careful to keep it high and up off the grass and blueberries.

But there are no rises. Should we wait before casting our first try? Yes. We'll wait a moment, but let's take up a position near 5 so we can work that water from 7 across to the center rocks. We'll plan to throw an almost straight cast to 7 and, hopefully, keep the fly afloat for at least fifteen feet of drift. Our next cast can enter the picture at our side of 10 without our having to move.

Still no rise, no sound of feeding trout. We wonder if we should walk downstream to the big pool to see if any action is going on there. We begin to question the merit of this midnight business. It is cool, though, and a pleasant walk with its contemplation of taking a really big fish.

Let's make a cast anyway and see what happens.

Nice drift. Nothing.

We try below. Nothing.

We have learned the feel of that big fly in the air on cast and also know how it drifts down in the current. Let's quietly walk to 6 and cast the Stone to 7. We'll feel the current pull the fly under when it is carried into the white water of the tributary. Right at that point we should get a strike.

Bingo. There's the current pull and a yank that only a big fish could make. There's a splash, the slap of a big tail. The spare line in our hand vanishes. We find ourselves playing the fish directly from the reel now. That doesn't happen with the majority of trout.

Our line is as tight as we can safely snub, but where is the fish? All we can do is to feel generally that something, somewhere out there is pulling at us and thumping around in its big bathtub. What a ruckus!

Now the line is holding steady in the main current, slowly moving upstream. He continues right up into the rocks below 1 and we half feel the need to rollcast our line over the first rock on our side, to keep the trout from winding us up on the rock's jagged edges.

He discovers that he's been found out and that the ruse did not work and so he slashes high and heads for the center rock and its wash. Holding the rod high we throw a bend downstream as a suggestion for him to

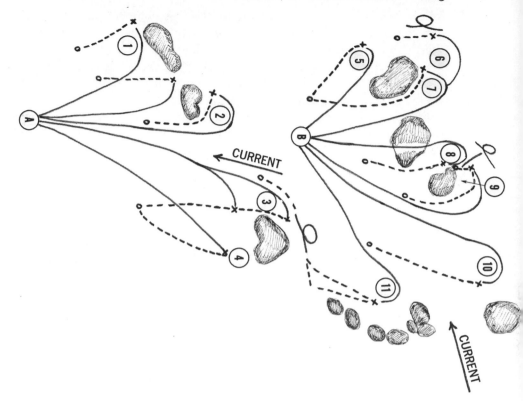

Figure 79. Study of Typical Casts and Retrieves.

Here are eleven casts to look at and try to perform on the water, fishing wets or dries. They are similar to everything that we have covered so far in this book, yet they have their individual problems. With the general current and rock picture and the two streams, the washes in your mind, place yourself first at A and work casts 1 and 2. Fairly easy drifts plus the one in the center. Two casts can be made to cover 3 and 4 is a distinct right-hand bend. Note all retrieves are made well down from the area in question.

Now at B are some tricky ones. Cast 5 is a typical right-hand bend, drift, and pickup. Casts 6 and 7 are also right-hand bends, although 6 must be picked up unless you can easily flip the line over the rock for a longer downstream drift. It's worth a try. Cast 8 is intentionally laid over the rock and then flipped up in a roll so that the fly fishes the water first on its downstream drift. Cast 10 is a normal one with the drag showing at the point of pickup. 11 lets you have a good drift down and a retrieve across the head of that rock. (Review Appendix for these casts.)

If you can perform these when there is fly action on the water and the trout are feeding, you should come home with a basketful.

With some twenty-four situations behind us, the downstream bucktail casts should be almost too obvious to diagram.

follow. This is always a good trick by the way, whether you are fishing day or night. Quite often you can turn a fish by directing him with a spare curve of line in one direction or another.

Down he goes to 10, and he's tiring. How we are going to get him into a position for netting is quite beyond reason at this point. We hate to wade into that water and disturb it, besides it is tricky going at night.

In a series of body-rolls and surface slashes, he drops down to 9 and we are able to pressure him over just above 1. From here the netting will be an easy project. This fish looks almost large enough to beach if necessary.

Another taste of night fishing. One fish like that is quite enough, unless you are a real hog.

CHAPTER 26

Waste Water

WE are about to show you the miracle of the trout stream. You are going to take trout from what anglers term as being "waste water." Our crowded Eastern streams contain many miles of long stretches of such water. Drive along a stream like the famed Beaverkill in New York's Sullivan County in any season of the year and you find most if not all the anglers wading where they should be fishing—right in the pools, or all ganged up at the pool heads and deep holes, sharp-angle bends, and riffles. The vast part of "our" water will be walked by, given an occasional flip of a wet fly while they are scurrying from pool to pool.

That's just fine, for it leaves all that good area to us.

In contrast to the better-looking stretches, these wide-open spaces look barren, especially after the floods of early spring have subsided. There seem but a few ridges and strings of deeper water where trout might hide. Logic argues against this water, since the trout, if he has any sense of reason, would surely work his way out of such openness and take up residence where trout fishermen would prefer him to be.

Those few hardies who have suspected that fish might stay in this type of water usually slap their lines at it in a haphazard way, and, getting no rises, conclude that their observations were right. Off they go to cluster with the others and complain that the Conservation Department isn't stocking the water thoroughly enough.

Good.

Leave them be.

Yes, and even those who have "accidentally" taken fish from such water consider it luck, and away they go too.

Which leaves us quite alone in our desert of "fishless" water.

So, let's look at a couple of views (see figures 79 and 80) of so-called waste water. One is aside "good water" and the other embraces the entire stream as it flattens out into one big shallow, cut only by shallow current ridges and narrow grooves that anyone can see should never contain other than trout fry or minnows. Wouldn't we be better off, especially in the bright light of a May morning, to seek deeper holes for our trout?

Well, as the upstate native says, "Mebbe."

It's your choice. Either stay with me or skip this chapter and move on to the next. I'm going fishing right here.

Let me ask you a question that might convince you of the possibilities here. This is a big river and it bares lots of this type of water. But, let's just suppose you were to cut the picture into quarters. You'd find that this is about what you would find on a small brook of mountain heritage as it wends its way down the valley, pausing now and then to breathe a bit of thinner air, only to collect again into holes and pools. You would fish all that water religiously and you'd catch fish in it, wouldn't you? Let me answer: "Of course you would, and you have, many times."

So, for the sake of our sanity and logic, let's pretend we are not now

Figure 80. Waste Water.

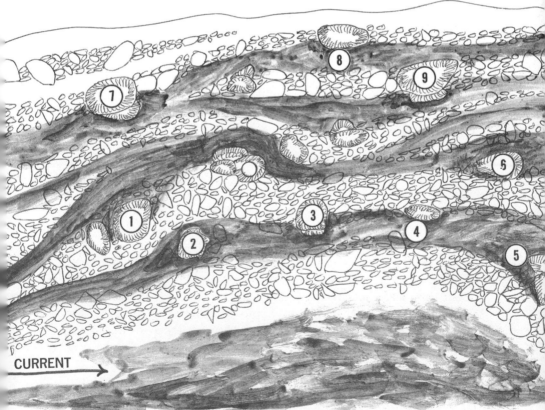

CURRENT

on a big stream, but are following the course of our little stream or big brook, if you will, and so go forth to war on its veterans.

For several reasons, however, we will need the basic stream illustrated.

Let's assume again that there have been many fishermen working the tail of the pool above and the faster, deeper water astride our wasteland. They've been working it wrongly, or if they have pricked fish, those fish and the ones they have scared have all gone into the waste water and are hiding there for the rest of the day, or at least until the shadows begin to lengthen and the traffic subsides so that they can return to the heavier water. There are fish also in the waste-water section that prefer the open terrain, for they find that hiding under a rock even in foot-deep water is better than the false security of the greener pastures in midstream. So, all in all, we have a chance to connect. Also, much of the food that drifts down to waste sections astride big water, or in the case of figure 81 of the entire stretch made of such terrain, the food tends to gather by force of the current to be carried down in a long steady line right by their noses. They don't have far to rise to grab at it and like the trout of the brook, they have adequate hiding facilities and little or no disturbance from booted feet, and slapping lines. They tend to strike fast and hard—to our advantage.

Prospects look a bit brighter? Wait until that sun goes under that puffy white cloud. We'll have about fifteen minutes to work out some small wet flies over some of this water. We'll work the water of figure 80 first.

We have diagrammed and numbered only the interesting spots—not the locations for the fisherman to cast from, seeing that this is hardly necessary in this instance.

Casting two wet flies, size 14, say a March Brown and a Leadwing Coachman, let's stand in the inches-deep water above 1 and 2 and merely flip the flies in and around those rocks, letting the flies light for only a few seconds. There is little need for a drift here. Either the fish will see the fly as it approaches him directly and instantaneously, like a blow-in or a drift-down, or he'll not bother with it. I have shaded the picture dark for the deeper water, almost-white or white for the very shallow. I saw no need to grade this, since it would detail it too much for easy reading. Naturally, when more water is flowing down, the whole area is flooded; even the rocks that are marked with lines as being exposed and above the water level at the moment would be covered. When it is drier, of course, the white areas are out of water and the dark areas would be more shallow.

This is not drift-fishing, as we stated above, but merely spot-casting, not allowing the flies to dawdle except in rare instances where an overlapping rock might hide a good trout. Give that kind of area a couple of tastes of your imitations. Work slowly, dropping down slowly and covering the entire length carefully. No need to reach out to the farthest waters, since you can work your way back up after you have finished to 6. Use either the wets or a dry fly. I have found, under daytime conditions, that it doesn't matter which, and wets are easier to flip around than dries.

Working up from 6, you can cover all the lanes if you like, but it is a problem reaching out too far since your line will be landing and catching in the rocks. Your leader will be the first to foul and, more often than not, an inaccurate cast can bust off a barb. As is our usual advice, take it easy. You are not going anyplace, and *here* is as good as *there* anyway.

Now, with some nice fish in our credit list, let's take on the big desert. Notice that it is devoid of fishermen, and while we have been fishing the water above not an angler has even walked by it.

This water is about fifty yards wide and about two hundred yards long, so we'll divide it up into four streams and fish it that way; down with the wets, up with the dries. At sundown, if there are no hatching

Figure 81. Waste-Water Run.

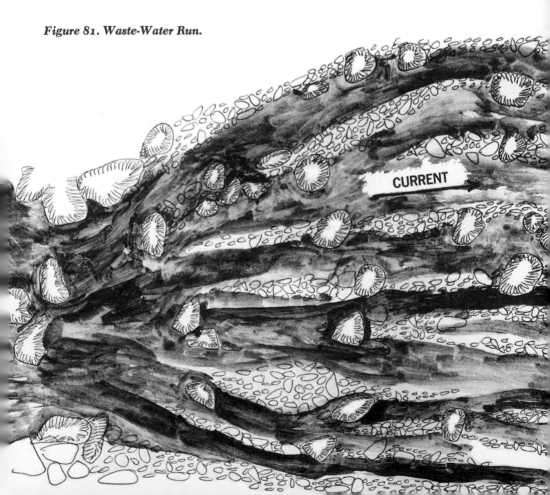

insects or evidence of feeding fish, we'll throw a few very small bucktails just to prove that this water can be fished by all normal techniques, and that trout can be gotten from such water.

This is the same type of water as before except that the entire stream is made up of it. The "run" begins at the left of the picture, breaking out into the barrens from the cluster of three rocks that start its dispersement. From here more rocks split up the wakes and shallows begin to develop from the constant runs of water, heavy and thin that gradually carve their roadway downstream, trying to make a river out of the flat, but at the same time building up ridges that conflict the current into many streams. Think of this again as several small brooks and fish it that way, using a short line, fine leader, and the two wet flies or some of your own choice. Since this is the main stream, and not a side kick of flat, it remains even better throughout the season than the side water of figure 80, since the main stream takes care of the traveling fish going up and down. Fish it carefully, paying particular attention to the bigger rocks and the hold-out spots ahead and behind them. Twitch the flies a bit when they land, but remember that it is a game of spot-casting, not drift-fishing that is called for here. Your rod will be almost always in the motion of forward or backcasting in a nice easy motion as you gently move downstream pausing only to unhook an occasional fish.

So, now that you have fished four streams in one and have taken more than any mortal's share of the profits, it's time to head for supper. A good day of fishing, wasn't it? Pick the waste water, particularly in the spring when the heavy current washes the wounded or soft hatchery trout to the holes. If the state stocks brook trout, you'll find most of them in such water, for they prefer rocks and slashy currents to deep holes and much disturbance. If the stream is crowded, fish this water and be a loner. Try and not show by your actions that you are hooking fish. Keep that rod down flat, and for heaven's sake, don't tell anyone where you got the string of fish, even though yours may not be as big as the ones the wormers jerked out of the bridge pool.

Figure 82. Rock Eddies.

CHAPTER 27

Rock Eddies

THIS is the section of my stream that separates the men from the boys. This is tough fishing at best and if you are not the careful, quiet type, willing to sacrifice grandstand casting and exercise of your talents, forget it. Just pass on to the next chapter. There are big fish here of course, but they are big simply because not one angler in twenty has the least idea of how to fish this water even when the fish are rising in so-called abandon. I've been skunked here when the pool has been alive with fish that were actually seen rising to hatching or hatched and floating duns, returning spinners. I've also missed any connection when I've seen the big fish chasing minnows, cruising the surface like small tarpon, looking for drifting shrimp or young shad minnows.

This is deep, quiet, slow water. When it is muddy or murky, the trout are somewhat easier to approach and sunken wet flies and nymphs will sometimes rouse them, but not often. There is so much food available to them right at their fin tips that they seldom need to move an inch. It's like living upstairs over a supermarket. It's all there for them. Also, even in the murky conditions of early spring when the water is high and there is more of a current to move your flies, they are still not prone to dash out at your every beck and call.

During the lower-water times of late May, June, and, particularly, July, the midday finds the trout sleeping under or beside those rocks, moving with the shadow as the sun changes the angle of beam. Approaching them from the sun side requires tricky rod handling, and line control. Approaching them from the shaded side would divulge your presence and your line would be a much too obvious give-away and element of disturbance to their scene.

During the hatch, they work from a well-studied position, having figured out just how far and how fast they must move in order to pick off a good-looking hatching or hatched insect. They have lots of time to inspect, and I've seen the times when they have nosed up to a perfect specimen of a May fly and deliberately let it float by. Their feeding action is slow, deliberate—a sort of up-glide, slight pause just under the surface, a short lunge to the surface, usually without even scaring it into waves, and then the quiet retreat usually backwards into their former waiting position.

Their minnow-chasing activity is another thing altogether. Then they seem to change character a bit, becoming more active, yet retaining that same sort of respective quiet. They know too well that any minnow can outdodge them in the clear and that it is largely a waste of time to go cavorting all over the pool chasing one minnow. They prefer to wait until a group of the little fish are feeding unconcernedly. They watch their prey like a cat watching a mouse. I've seen, right in this pool, right from this angle, four fish suddenly dart out from their various rocks to converge upon a half-dozen minnows all bunched together in one area. The resultant splashes and surface ruckus is something to behold. Once they scatter those minnows, they drive them right into the air. By then the whole pool is alerted and fish, big ones, are seen cruising everywhere for a few moments until the whole place takes time to gradually settle down again to the watching and waiting bit.

To hold back from casting, and to merely watch this going on takes a certain amount of patience, but to learn how to fish this water, casting for the fun of it here and there with hope only is not the way.

I've pictured this stretch as if these rocks, those exposed and those bulging up from the bottom but still well covered, were just sitting in the mud and ooze. I've done so because this sort of rock-eddy fishing usually is made up of both elements; big rocks and sand and ooze plus snags and refuse, perfect bottom for many of the stream insects not found in the faster, rock-bottomed stretches of any big trout stream. A similar drawing of the same general scene but with gravel and rocks in between the boulders could have been done. If you come upon either sort of bottom, you will find a mixture of all sorts of insects, but the problems of interesting the trout without scaring them will remain the same. Their attitude toward their meals and to your slapping line will be likewise. They are not in a hurry to feed, generally, but are in a hurry if you scare them. With the surface of the water barely scarred and rippled by the slightest currents breaking by the rocks, their position from down deep, as deep as maybe six feet, their angle of vision is much greater than in the usual stream water, hence your need for caution.

One would deduce that the problems of fishing such water would make it more worthwhile to skip over it. As I have said, most anglers do just that. Oh, sure, they'll place some nice casts here and there and even

shoot out some nice upstream bend casts so that their line will not precede the fly over the hot spots. But they won't usually waste time here,
preferring the pooled-up waters, the deeper runs, and the sections of
the stream that seem to be easier to fish.

One of the smartest tricks for summertime on this water is the use of
a big dry fly, of size 10 or even 8. On a bright day, I like the Fanwing
Royal Coachman, and in the early morning and early evening, a Wulff-
type dry fly, again with white wings so that I can see it even if the trout
can't.

Now, you don't just merely cast indiscriminately all over the stretch.
If you haven't looked a bit before entering the water to see if you can
locate any specific fish, you can try and figure the best spots around the
rocks within easy casting distance. I use a very long leader in this type
of work, and since the fluffy and large dry fly is a slow actor in the air,
I select a big rod with a medium-soft tip. This rod will give me just the
right action in the air, throw me a wide and slow bow, and put the fly
where I want it. Its length will enable me to keep most, if not all, of the
line off the water. I do, of course, rollcast forward and then pickup, rather
than use the conventional drag pickup. (You must be getting sick of my
referring to this, but I've just returned from a day on my pet stream and
NOT ONCE did I see an angler using this pickup. They were scooping their
long lines and sawing up those pools unmercifully. They were not catching any trout, either. "Weather too warm, light too bright, water too low
and clear. No fish.")

So, we enter the stretch, preferably from below, wading VERY slowly,
for every time we breathe a ripple goes out from our waders. If there
are periodic breezes that ruffle the surface, we move during those times
to partially cover our intrusion. We don't wave our rods around in the
sun, allowing light to bounce all over the water from our well polished
rod surfaces and silver ferrules. Paint your ferrules black, by the way.
I meant to tell you about this in Chapter 1, but, after all, it all can't be
included in the first chapter, can it?

Looking up ahead there are so many good-looking rocks and consequently such fine places for trout to hide that we are a bit at a loss as to
just where to cast. So, we wait for a moment to see if any trout are nosing
around in the surface film. If we spot one, we wait until it settles down
and then cast a bit above it. If we see no trout, we just pick a rock and
place our curve neatly about five feet above it, being careful not to reach
out to long positions, but to work the rocks nearest to us first.

Now it is time to hold our rod high, so we raise it slowly to the vertical
and actually reach up as high as possible. The drift of the fly is slight and
slow, so slack is no great problem. On our long leader and extremely
light tippet, the fly needs a little slack in case a trout does hit. We note

how well the fly dances as it comes in contact with the slight wavelets as it glides into the rock, guided by the current. Now, behind the rock we can't see it for a few seconds.

But we see a splash and the leader tightens immediately. We've hooked something and from that first lunge we know it isn't any chub. Before the fish surfaces, we note that several wakes from sudden underwater spurts of scampering fish crisscross the pool. There must be twenty fish in here— all picture fish. "Our" trout means business; heads for a rock and winds us up pronto. The only move now is to let out slack and try to rollcast the line away from his rock. The ruse works and he's away again. With rod now held lateral to the water and at right angles to his direction, we try and hold him from other rocks and force him into a surface or body-rolling fight in the open. It's quite a battle of wits, and he's got the props on his side.

I like to fish this water from above, when the water is higher, the current a little faster and the water cooler.

Approaching the trout from above is particularly tricky since they are heading upstream and any motion and sound will alert them. Big fish, I've found, alert much faster than the brash little ones. This type of water seldom holds little trout, so the stakes are high.

In all but flood conditions and murky water, I prefer my very small minnow imitations (see Appendix, page 326), and, if the mood strikes, I have two flies tied on a leader tip which I tie onto the 3X tapered standard leader of ten feet in length. The butt of this leader is heavy to conform to the rather heavy end of the line. The major portion of the taper is in the leader for this fishing, not in the line, since little distance casting will be done, nor is it at all necessary.

Again, look for the signs of movement underwater. Pick a stretch of water when the morning sun is at your back and shining right down the middle. This will tend to put the fish behind the rocks, or at least well under them and away from the glare coming from upstream. In this way, they are also a bit more blind to your movements. Position is everything in life in trouting in relation to the source of light.

Now, drop the flies about five feet above the rock. If the current is slow, make it a little closer, since the flies will sink readily and far enough. Then, as they reach their goal, a few inches aside or in front of the rock in question, gently snub the line, lower the rod tip to the horizontal, and, with the rod at right angles to the line, you are ready. The fly slithers up toward the surface, hangs there tantalizingly for a few seconds and, just to frustrate the natives, you twitch it a couple of times when it breaks the surface.

That does it, and you are fast again to a trout that will winch your line around the rock before you can gather in the slack.

Nice work if you can land him.

No, rock eddies are not for everyone. That's why big trout are there and grow old because nobody disturbs them with barbs, although slapping line, wading brogues, and other disturbances will move them about.

I spent a lunch hour overlooking this stretch of water not too many seasons ago. While waiting for my companion to arrive and share lunch at this appointed meeting place, I watched at least ten anglers fish the pool. Not one of them caught a trout, although some of them did display various aspects of good tackle handling and a smattering of stream know-how.

My friend, who was the one who first showed me how to fish this water, appeared, as he usually does, about an hour after the appointed time. He approached from below. It was a hot day and I was glad to watch the show from under the shade. Four times he removed his hat, mopped the sweat from his brow, doused his hat in the water for a cool-off, and then resumed fishing.

Now, remember, several fishermen had been through the stretch just before him. The water was not exactly undisturbed.

Yet, before he came into the beach and wound in his line, he had hooked and released four good trout, none under the fifteen-inch mark.

"Hope you kept one for lunch," he said, calling out, knowing that I was back in the brush with my head propped against an old stump.

"Nope, figured you'd keep that last one. Boy, that was a whopper."

"Well, damn you," he said. "I'll just have to catch another one."

So, he waded out, unceremoniously, making the ripples you are not supposed to make. On his first cast a fish thumped down on the fly before I was able to see whether he was using a wet or a dry. It is fortunate for the fishing industry that there are few alive who can stick big trout with the ease this man displays.

Sure, he knows this water like the back of his hand, to use and old expression. But, that's a big part, if not most of angling anyway. A stream like this one and its rock eddies get to you, eventually.

Figure 83. Stream Split.

Stream Split

A generous bend in the stream with big rocks to hold some good fish on one side and a slight cove on the other for more possibilities. Between them, a nice, big, fat, deep, quiet, easy-to-cast-to fishin' hole. What else could anyone want on a June day, when the sun is warm and the air light and clean; on an April morning, when it's cold and forbidding; on a hot August "dog" day that makes you want to give up fishing, especially wading—like now?

Humidity is also tiring. It's time for lunch, and I've brought you here on the off chance that what I found at the head of this split some years ago you may find to your satisfaction.

First, to get settled for lunch. Now, that cold tea you brought in the thermos. Right there ahead of you under those birches is a fragrant mint patch, just as it grew ten years ago. Mint for your tea!

From right here, we can survey this pool for present moment, fishing, and also look at it from the seasonal standpoint later. I have included a page diagram with eleven casts you can make with a bit of subtlety and luck. You SHOULD take a trout even though the weather and the heat are against you.

Hardly any breeze. This eliminates any blow-ins to feed the trout. No hatches other than the odd species of stone or May fly that didn't make it earlier. August is a good month for the late hatchers. Sometimes as many as ten species can be found on the water at once—only two or three of each, but a representation.

Is that water clear! The sun is high overhead, but, theoretically at our back. A slight ripple is flipping the tree and sky reflections over the "hole," but if we are patient and eat quietly with our eyes peeled on that water, we may see some action from the trout, even at midday. Other than eat and take a nice nap, we might just as well look busy.

While we are surveying the possibilities of the present, the scene at other times also presents its portents. We can make a mental note for instance to work that deep overhang at the right hand side of figure 83 with wet flies at almost any season, including now. The white water that is coming down in bunches is made that way because of underwater rocks. Note that it is different from the flow on the other side. There should be a trout among them that might take a big wet fly, a very small dace, or praise be, I almost forgot, a dry fly. If I approached up the other lane, on the left through faster white water, I'd obviously try dry flies first unless it was too early even for the Quill Gordon or the Little Black Stone Fly. But the "hole" is still ahead and I become anxious to take a whack at it.

But, how about the approach? Coming too near from either fork would spook the fish. Better go ashore and rollcast upstream into the hole and to the rocks on either side.

In May, this is the spot for the drifting Hendrickson hatch. The nymphs come down like sailboats in a race when the duns are hatching or have hatched in the pool just around that upstream bend. Just about here, they pause, circle around in the "hole," and offer an aerial fashion show for the trout. What dry-fly fishing, no matter from what angle you present your wares!

Or take a June night when the Leadwing Coachman spinners are descending to lay their eggs. They too, have come from above and many will be drifting dead on the water when they reach here. The trout just suck them in.

The Green Drake hatch? A few, but not many on this stretch of the river, since it is mostly fast and rocky bottom. But the Cahills, the Little Marryats, the stone flies? Boy, what a fly fisherman's dilemma. I've seen 'em all at once and the fish bustin' at 'em all at once until I lost what little logic I have been able to retain under such circumstances and—you guessed it: I fell back on the Royal Coachman Fanwing, bless it.

I took trout, and it was shameful.

I like to time my arrival to this portion of the stream for just after daybreak. There is a time of about fifteen minutes before the sun comes up over the hill that usually offers some of the best wet-fly fishing you can imagine—especially after a generous caddis hatch and their return to the water the previous evening in the egg-laying ritual. They hug the grass, flowers, bushes, trees, and rocks by the hundreds. That first bit of morning breeze comes down the valley and whoosh . . . handfuls of the insects are blown in. They come drifting down the very center of the run above the hole and then, meeting the confusion of the center pool, either sail around in it for a while or are branched off, like traffic at a crossroads, to descend the river either to the left or right. If you watch closely, you may see insects coming around in opposite circles, meeting at the apex at the bottom of the hole and then, like partners in a folk dance, alternating to the left and right. Some are momentarily caught in the deep tublike run just in under and above the mint.

Speaking of that, drop your sandwich for a moment. Don't knock over your tea. Without telegraphing your attack, carefully elbow your way over there and peek into the water. There just might be . . .

Three? The stream is doing better for me than I thought. Getting a fly to them is going to be fun.

Carefully ease your rod over to you and slowly string out about four feet of leader from the tip. Whatever fly that's there will do. You'll connect at once or you won't. Now, slowly inch that rod out vertically, keeping it close to the trees as possible and gradually lower it until that fly just barely touches the surface. Don't let the fly sink or rest on the water. Just touch it.

I'll relax now and eat the last sandwich. You get your kicks while I draw the last card without opposition. That tea and that mint . . . It's wonderful to be alive.

I suddenly thought of my Audubon friend who is constantly bugging me about my keen appreciation and interest in nature and the silliness of the trout fishing having to be the device to study it. He believes all trout fishermen are either delayed, strayed, or something. I can hear him now. "Why look! You're enjoying yourself in the woods beside the stream. Why couldn't you go on a picnic, and a bird and animal walk instead of parboiling yourself in those waders? You don't keep your trout anyway, which makes you look even more ridiculous."

But, why did I bring that up? That's thinking and such activity has no place out here . . . only observation.

Ever notice that, given the proper light conditions in each case, that it is easier to spot trout action underwater from downstream rather than up? Well, it is. So, before we leave here, let's just go into a sort of Buddhistic trance and fix our eyes on that hole and see what we can come up with. There are bound to be some fish down there. If they are resting quietly, I know what to do. NO! Not sleep. You wait. If they are at all active, we see what they're up to.

Over in the bushes there's a plop of something.

Probably a frog? Your eyes didn't make the switch soon enough. If that was a frog, then what was it doing with white brook trout bars on its tail?

Right from here, without even getting up, make yourself a nice cast laterally on the water and plop a fly right below those rocks upstream of the dark spot in under there. Worth a chance. I believe that more fishing should be done from a streamside armchair. That one fish you just caught is almost enough for one person. One more fish and we can set up housekeeping right here and to heck with the diagram that follows. After eating those trout, who wants to sit around and analyze diagrams?

So, make the cast. That's it—fine.

Wait, don't disturb the fly, even though the fly COULD have been put in under a bit more. That's the trouble with most casters. They are so intent on casting perfection that they would, in a case like this, retrieve the fly and take perhaps three more shots in order to get the fly in under. When they did, the trout would have taken off for the reservoir ten miles downstream!

No take. Try again. No fair getting up. Only one arm and elbow for your pivot.

Good cast. That should be right.

It is. How do you like your trout, medium rare? Broiled or broiled—I didn't bring a frying pan.

That's a pretty native brook trout. The Conservation Department has never stocked them in here. They say that brookies would not prove out in this stream! Ha!

Cup of MINTED ice tea? You deserve it. Two tries, or at least one foul tip, and two trout.

Now, let's remove this terrible humidity and this mad, midday sun. Let's put it over there, at about six o'clock. It is still burning down on you, but the air has changed and the angle of the sun has helped to bring more shadows to the river. Some insects are hatching.

Oh, yes, we'll also adjust the season, too. Let's make it late April.

We're late for the Quill Gordon hatch, and the fish will have likely had a ball and will be well-fed. We can't kick, though. We took several in the pools below on Cahill nymphs and later on dries. Perhaps some spinners will be about later.

But, for now, let's try some casting from the positions laid out in the diagram. These are not the only casts that could be made, of course. If I tried to put them all on here, you would have the devil's own time in following the routines. It's crowded anyway.

Let's take it from position 1 or 1A. We are approaching the center hole with the care of a golfer making his chip shot to the green. Cast A is almost too obvious to mention. We throw an upstream bend (we are dry-flying, by the way, despite no insects on the water). Dries are chosen so we can see what this difficult bit of current does to the fly. When we want to actually fish for meat, we'll go under with something more succulent. The line drags and we skitter the fly back to us. A small chub bumps it. Our second A cast goes out and presents a nice drift until the spare line is absorbed. We COULD mend upstream for more drift but the real business is up ahead. Now, to C, first the nearby cast and then the one farther up. Another chub—oh no, it's a small brookie.

Now for the try off those rocks to your left. Another curve cast lights the fly just where the diagram wants it and the drift is clean.

Funny, there should have been a trout there. Give it another foot of drift. Rollcast pickup. OOPS. Another small fish that tore from the hook due to the power of the upgoing fly. He'd have nailed it down if he'd been a bit bigger—say about a pound.

Step ashore onto that rock and with the elevation you can throw a good cast right on target on the black dot. Good. Let it drift. It is going straight down. Remember last summer and those trout under the mint. You can see the hole now: the mint's not up yet. There! Trout enough for anyone. It's not fair though, you KNEW that trout would be there.

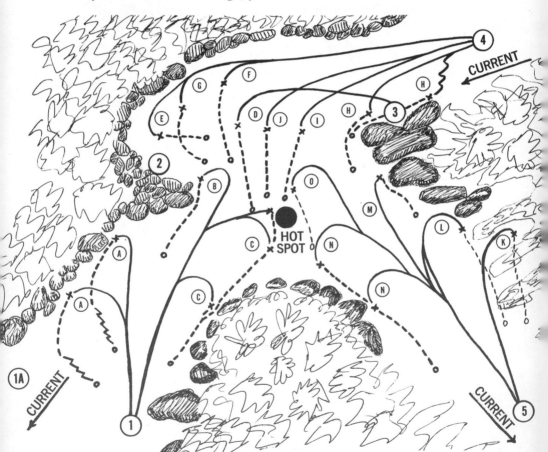

Figure 84. Typical Casts and Retrieves.

So, now for the business of practice and learning this water. Let's cross over the island and enter below 5 and fish up again. Maybe there are bigger trout, or even bigger chubs on this side. It's shaded, which can be some help. Even though the brambles are still to be leafed out, they are there. Stone flies, Gordons, small caddis, and even a spider or two might be feeding what ever is under there. Maybe we'll find another one of those brook trout that are not supposed to be living here.

Two casts and two trout? Isn't that enough?

Okay, work yourself to death and follow from K, L, M, the two N's, and the O. With your luck, that last one should bring your jackpot in and we can go home. It's getting too cold out here for me.

On another day, study that approach from 4. It can be very subtle, and the way you handle your drifts, be they dry flies, wets, or streams, will determine the weight of your creel. Just made for a bucktail!

It's getting too cold even for a should-be Auduboner, so let's call it good for today.

You never waded where you should fish. You never fished where you waded. You made no unnecessary movement in or by the water, except to reach for a sandwich which I ate when you were catching that trout.

Now, you are getting somewhere. Someday you may write a book about it!

Figure 85. Stream Rejoin.

CHAPTER 29

Stream Rejoin

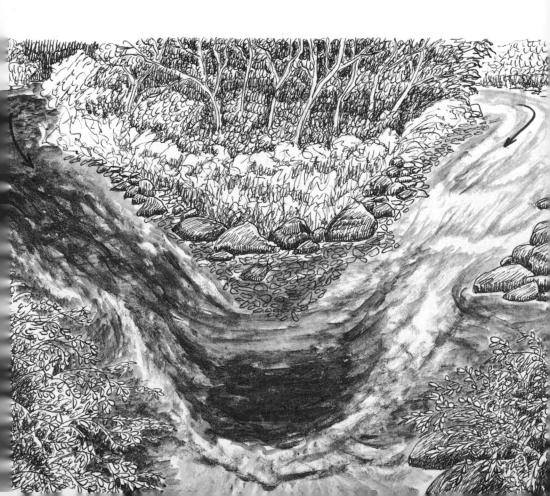

ALWAYS a good spot, mainly because of the joining of two currents into one whole, where, inevitably there is a deep pocket where all the food collects that has been drifting down from above. This situation we have copied from an actual stream. The branch on the left is deeper than the one on the right. It is slower and perfect upstream dry-fly water and good small bucktail water if you are fishing down to the pocket. The right lane is more broken, good for skittered wet-fly and surface bucktail action. On the bottom of the pool on both sides is a generous amount of overhang that drapes shade and potential insects over sandy bottom. When the light is right and this area is in the dark, the fish move in. When the anglers who wade the stream improperly come along, this overhang is where the trout head after being ungraciously dislodged from the hole. In the evening, when the trout in the center are urged to take in a minnow chase, the sand and gravel bar at the toe of the island is the place. This is also where the stone flies hatch and some of the floating May flies from hatches above congregate momentarily before drifting down into the hole, around the backwaters and finally down the spout.

Fish this water at all hours, allowing the direction of the sun to guide your presentation and wading angles.

Suppose you are fishing downstream and pick the left branch to fish down with your wets. The sun is coming from the right, which means the right bank is in shadow and the right-hand side of the hole will have some shade. That last big rock at the bottom of the picture should produce at least a keeper fish.

To cast to that shore from your position requires that you abstain from lashing across the pool or wading any farther down into the overhang off 6. So, you go ashore to the rocks *on the island*, shoot short casts across

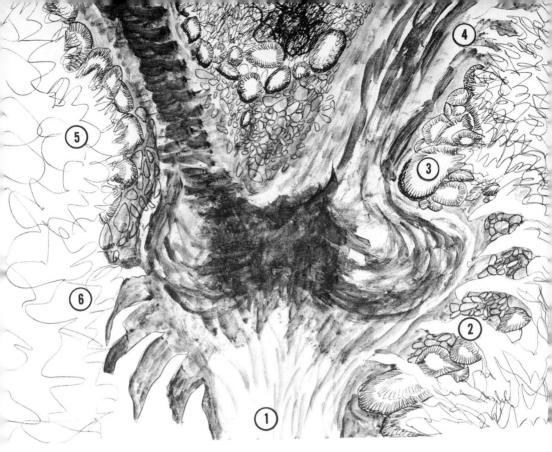

Figure 86. Stream Rejoin.

the right stream in and around the rock at 3, and allow your flies to drift into the back current and into the lane just by the overhang. Taking up the position above 3 and below 4, you throw a couple upstream and then turn toward the shaded area between you and 2. There should be a nice trout there. The final drift of the fly should include the top of the big rock just below.

From here you can drop the flies practically at your feet and let them sink into the hole and drift down into the spout. You have worked the best part of the pool from one stance without disturbing the water.

When the sun is directly overhead, fish both overhangs, being careful to keep the center of the pool unscathed. Later, sunken flies allowed to feed into the very bottom of the rocks and gravel of the hole will take trout, especially if seen flashing in typical bottom-feeding activity.

I try to arrive at this pool in the late twilight. The hole is shaded by big trees not shown in the picture. Quite often, if no other anglers have been near, the trout in the center will be seen hanging in the middle. They might be there just waiting for something to drift down, or they might be turned on to a hatch of tiny May flies or even midges. It's quite a sight to see them, nice big fish, just hanging there. From below, the problem of casting to them is not too easy. If you throw a left-hand curve cast, the current will take it, as you can see, and drag the flies away after only a very short drift. If you were to go ashore and downstream stop cast to them, chances are they'd see you. Problem?

There they sit. Waiting.

Wade over toward 2 and rollcast into the very top of the right-hand center of the run, make a quick mend to the left. The fly will then precede the line flight into the center of the pool. You have a good chance to connect, this way.

In the early morning, I like to hit this spot from dead center down the island. I usually stand by the rocks in front of the beach and look at the water for a few minutes to try and figure what, if anything, is happening. It is a beautiful sight, with the dew still sparkling. The glinting rays of the sun dance on the water. If a splash or two breaks the silence and the surface of the hole, so much the better. From here I can employ almost every technique and fly type in the book. I can also work both sides of the two runs, the two generously overhung beaches, and the lip of the spout. Quite often I will pick up a nice trout, usually a rainbow, just below this lip, so I never leave without giving it a whirl.

Just before dawn, I use a bucktail here. A stop-cast dry fly is also one to provoke a rise, even this early, if the month is May or June.

In late season, the pool becomes more defined and the trout are more confined. If I notice that there have been other anglers through this water, I invariably skip the pool and work the flies right in under the brambles, simply because the trout will have been driven in there by anglers wading directly into the center of the pool.

The best time to fish this in the spring is when anglers are clustered at the head of the island. The pool is bigger there and they'll remain there longer. As they wade, they disturb insects from the bottom. These drift down both lanes and by the time they reach the hole, they are well off the bottom. This stirs feeding action. I merely sink wet flies in the same general pattern. I've taken more trout when anglers have been active upstream of me than I have when the stream has been quite alone. This is a good thing to remember. Always fish below a cluster of anglers if it is possible, particularly in the early spring when no hatches are about. This artificial movement of larvae and nymphs from the bottom stirs the trout and makes them far easier prey.

Some awfully good hatches come off in this pool. The insects that have drifted down from above in the act of hatching suddenly burst forth right in dead center—the March Browns; Cahills in particular.

The bottom of the pool is loaded with caddis. I remember one afternoon in May when an early green caddis hatch came off. All of a sudden the air was full of the insects. I had just arrived and had not seen any action underwater.

The pool came alive with trout and insects. The flies were so thick that I could hardly cast through them. When this was over, a wave of caddis from the pools above came down on the drift and the action was again one of frenzy.

The next morning, wet-fly fishing was excellent as many of the caddis began their trek from the leaves and branches of the overhang to their egg-laying activity.

This is a good pool after a sudden rain or thunderstorm. The water from upstream suddenly bears down to converge here and with its cooling influence in the summer, the trout become active. I've seen such times when they would take anything you threw at them.

It is not easy to get to know a stretch like this. Unlike the more obvious, though just-as-potent, "open" stretches, this kind of water demands several visits over the seasons at various times of the day. Actually one can spend a full day here, starting out at dawn, fishing for a while, perhaps quitting to rest or read a good book. It is a favorite meeting place for me and a fishing pal. I've spent many hours here, just watching the water. It is somewhat like having your own aquarium and arboretum. It is a quiet place, too, plus the musical additions of the verios and warblers that nest nearby.

CHAPTER 30

Road Pool

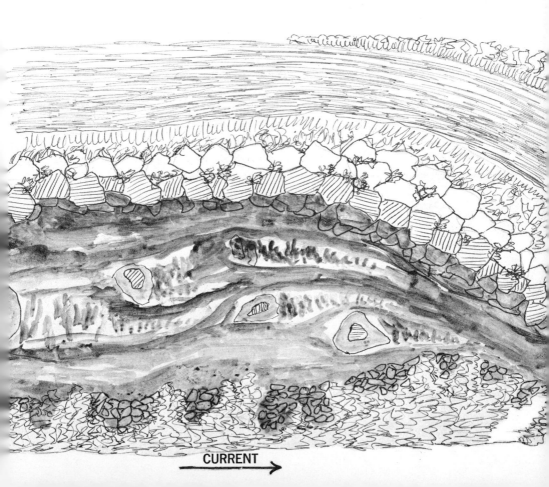

CURRENT

THIS is one of those stretches of trout water that has been blessed by the addition of a proper road bank along its side. Actually, in this case, the stream has not been altered. The rocks in the center have not been disturbed. And, of course, the far bank is untouched. What has been added is a rim of big, rough, and sharp boulders put there to bed the curve of the road against flooding out. This addition is a grace, because before this was added the pool was nothing much in the way of a trouting center. Now those rocks offer countless hiding places for trout. The bottom, being of silt and sand, has been washed out from under them, making additional shaded place when the sun beams down mercilessly in the summer. Even at low water, trout can be seen resting in under those rocks, while only a few had the privilege of taking up positions around the four exposed rocks and the one duo of under-water rocks in the center of the picture. The level of water is represented by the lined rocks with their tops exposed. This is the high-water level that is normal in spring. The lower contour of the rock is what is exposed later when the water level has dropped. At that time the washes of the rocks become more defined and the deeper runs in the center become shallower. The big boulders, however, always offer hiding places for the trout, no matter what the level.

Another good point about the road is that the high bank, reaching some fifteen feet above the water, offers a vantage point seldom enjoyed by the trout fisherman. From up here, one can observe the entire stretch without disturbing it. But how few are those who will take the few moments to stand up there and look down. Some will clamber down the bank in mid-pool and enter the water, driving every fish to cover. Others will enter either above or below with no thought of care in wading or

244

line presentation. I like the way they fish, because I know just where to cast when they have left.

The angle of the sun is great for morning fishing. The road bank is in full shadow then and the rocks throw shadows into the current beside them.

The approach, then, is a simple and direct one.

I park the car near the bank and walk below the pool, cross in the fast water there, making a couple of casts as I go. Then I take off into the bushes and hit a game trail leading upstream about ten feet from the brush at the edge of the bottom of the picture. I poke my head through the alders and willows at a point just below the lowest rock and stand there and look for a few minutes.

Are there any rises to surface-floating insects? Naturally there will not be a hatch at this hour, but night-hatched stones or caddis might be drifting. If there is a slight breeze, maybe some land-breds will fall in, offering a varied fare.

With no signs of either, I look for any minnow-chasing activity. If no anglers have preceded me, there is a chance that the big fish might be about foraging for big stone flies or minnows.

Without this sign, I look then for flashing of feeding fish as they might be nosing the bottom for caddis. The bottom here is varied from mud and ooze to gravel and sand, so it has everything in the book.

Still, nothing. I have about a half hour to fish before the bright light bangs down on the surface.

No, I don't cast into the bank of boulders quite yet. There is a chance that there are still some trout near those rocks that have not retired to the bank. I'll work them with rollcasts from the brush and then, when I've worked the nearby rocks and their washes, I'll step out just into the cover of the alders that can still hide my form and work as far upstream as possible. Then I make many casts with a small dry fly, and I'll have stirred some action.

Then, I'll work my way upstream, staying out of the water, in the protection of the alders. I'll move slowly and cast with the rod in the horizontal position. I'll watch the water for any trout that might dart from rock to rock or into the shade of the boulders.

When I've worked my way to the top, I'll still resist the boulder side, for I still have fifteen minutes left. I'll nymph it in the spring or skitter wet-fly those rocks from my upstream position, using all the tricks we've been through together in other chapters.

Only then will I venture out to exposure and enter the water for a good casting position for the first coverage of the boulder water. This calls for the dry fly fished down and across, though I'll stop cast it and at the same time throw a generous loop on the upstream side so that the fly will drift in the rocks, not away from them. I'll hold the rod high and when the slack is absorbed, not try to extend the cast, but roll pickup and gradually move down the stream.

I've got five minutes left before the bright sun hits the pool.

From a mid-pool position, I still continue with the dry fly. Fishing down first and then throwing some nice targeted ones into specific rocks and their deep shadows.

As the final shot, I trek upstream carefully, tie on a small bucktail and work those ledges to a froth, throwing short lines and almost dappling the fly wet-fly style (see Appendix, page 308).

Other than this, the road pool here is no different than most of the waters we have been fishing throughout the book. The addition of the high bank is what makes this water. We can be thankful for good construction and attention to some basic conservation principles.

Remembering that this pool is pounded to death by every angler who visits the stream, we are thankful for the times when it has been our luck to find it unmolested. Realize that with the techniques recounted here, we have fished the pool carefully and thoroughly without disturbing the water. I can remember one day having fished it just in the manner described. I climbed back up the bank from a position below and sat in the car, eating a sandwich and sipping coffee. Another angler and then another came to the pool, one from below and one from above. They both took fish from water I had just left, which shows that it is possible to fish properly without destroying the water for the next fellow.

This is good brown trout water. I can recall a late May day when I came here to try my luck. I knew I'd have little chance of even seeing a trout, let alone even fishing for it.

I stood on the bank by the edge of the road for some minutes. The whole place looked barren of fish. Then between rock 2 and 3 in the center just beside those two sunken rocks, there was a dimpling rise.

I could not tell what kind of a fish was making it, whether it was a chub, a new hatchery arrival or a big old brownie. I didn't wait long to find out, for I saw the shadow of a fish. That shadow was about two feet long, give or take four or five inches. The light shone down so that the trout itself became invisible, but its shadow was not.

This was all I needed. I watched him for a few minutes, as he hung in the current, dropping down to cover once in a while and then rising, ever so gently, again.

I felt a dry fly would take him, if I could place it just right in that run. I slithered down the bank of boulders with its poison ivy and willows and made one rollcast upstream of his position.

That fly did just what it was supposed to do.

Back at the diner, I was asked by an angler where I'd taken the fish and when I said "the road pool" he just laughed and practically accused me of being a liar. "I've fished that pool for many years, and the best I could ever do was bare keepers."

I saw the reason for his lack of success one day when I stopped the car after having spotted him from above. He was wading right up the middle!

Leadwing Coachmen like to hatch in this pool. They usually congregate on the top rock and the bottom one, leaving the other two alone for some reason. Late-evening hatches of Little Cream-Colored Light Cahills come off for about two weeks, but I've never seemed to connect with trout during this hatch in this pool. I've had my best luck in the early spring during the Quill Gordon hatch. Also, when the water is much higher then, I like to fish those boulders with a black and white bucktail. If the water is murky, I used the one with a tinsel shank.

How to dapple wet flies over these boulders and their lairs?

Sneak down the bank of rocks, hang on tight, and dangle the flies in the current below you, on a very short line. That's the way the kids fish it with worms.

Figure 88. Big Boulders, Fast Runs.

CHAPTER 31

Big Boulders, Fast Runs

HERE, again, is water that literally separates the beginner from the expert. It calls for experienced wading, care, and judgment in moving about the fast-moving, deep, and "holey" water. It also demands the best use of tackle and the employment of all the tricks we have so far developed over the waters of past chapters. There are big fish to be hooked, played, and netted here, and with their natural environment all in their favor, most of it against you, they have the advantage. Watch your wading with care and use a wading staff.

Although we were not able to show it, the bottom of this stretch of river is as uneven as a cross-cut saw. It is consistently dangerous in that any gravel stretches among the rocks are always unsteady due to the pressures of the water. This is especially true in the spring freshet season when the bottom is continually being shifted. Only the biggest rocks and boulders maintain their hold. These rocks can be round and smooth or sharp and coarse. Some of them can be dislodged if you walk on their tops or, in wading, knock them off balance. Add to this the pressure of the water forcing anything into its path into submission and you have the makings of a broken or sprained ankle; a good wetting at the least.

So, before thinking of fishing this stretch, we first have to take into consideration just what we are getting in for when we venture forth. And venture we must, for in order to fish it properly, we must place ourselves in a position for certain drifts and angles for proper presentation of our lures.

Looking at the stretch from our vantage point on the bridge, it becomes apparent that we should plan, at least some of our trip, in advance, to avoid the deep holes and runs and to chart a course in the washes. With the light in the right position, see what lies ahead.

To wade this properly, we must have the right footgear. While some of this can be waded with hip boots, the water really demands waders of chest-high dimensions.

The selection of proper wading gear is fully as important as the choice of rod and line. A few years ago comfortable and adequate wading equipment at a reasonable price was practically unheard of, but now the manufacturers have developed waders that are not only durable and waterproof but actually featherweight. Some companies manufacture waders in three weights: heavy, medium, and light. The heavyweight type offer years and years of wear, but are bulky, heavy and hot. The mediumweight waders are what the name implies, and with care, will last several seasons. The lightweight variety are very flexible and relatively cool, although care must be taken not to pull or snag them.

The basic material has always been rubber, either all rubber or rubberized fabric. The most modern development is the use of new plastic materials that have had relatively good success, once the sealing process has been perfected to some degree, to withstand the stretch and strain called upon. The lightweight varieties are very handy in that they can be rolled into a small package (the stocking-foot type) and carried in your jacket pocket. Carrying the old-fashioned boot-foot rubber waders over the shoulder on a long hike uphill to a favored wilderness pond can be quite fatiguing.

Waders come in hip-boot length, waist-high, and armpit or chest lengths in rubber, rubberized fabric, or in plastic. For water such as you see here, you are better off with the chest-highs, unless this extra margin tempts you to wade too deep and to go into dangerous water beyond your capabilities. The temptation that comes with the high waders is sometimes hard to resist.

All waders sweat from condensation due to the temperature difference between the inside and out. Actually, you are encased in a thermos bottle. The fabric waders become damp to a much less degree than the plastic or all rubber, but their cost is much higher, their life less long, and their tendency of wear and splits is much greater.

Correct fit is the major point to remember in the selection of your wading gear. If your build is such that the regulation waders will not fit properly, don't buy any waders unless you are willing to pay the price for a special factory-fitting job. Waders that are too short or tight in the crotch will split open almost immediately. Waders that are too deep or loose in the crotch are even worse, because they tend to constrict leg movement. When you buy waders or boots, try them on in the store. Ask the sales clerk for a pair of heavy socks so that you will be sure you are getting the correct foot size, then test the crotch length—the most important point in your selection. If it is necessary that you buy a size larger in the foot to accommodate the body fit, by all means do so, and figure on filling up the feet with another pair of socks. Put them on, complete with the suspenders, bend your knees and kneel down with one knee on the floor. When you can do this with ease and without undue strain on the material, then stretch one leg up and see if you can touch the countertop with your toe, easily. The wader that will allow you to do this should enable you to fish with a minimum of restriction.

Boot foot or stocking foot? Each has its devotees. I prefer the boot foot, that is with boot foot attached, simply because I'm lazy. There are a number of accessory slip-on sandals of chain, felt, and deeply grooved rubber. Felt is for slime, chain for gravel, and grooved rubber for rocks and gravel and, to some extent, slime. You can't win this one, with all the variations found on any stream, but you can try. I know a stretch of the Ausable in New York State where you will slide on your tail no matter what's underfoot unless you have the balance of a ballet dancer. Usually, the ordinary boot foot with its grooved soles is sufficient. For the water down there in front of you, especially with a strong head of spring-cold water coming down on you, I suggest the use of accessory chains.

Wading equipment is expensive, but it can be made to last for many seasons with a few precautions and simple care. Remember that, other than the plastic variety, boots and rubberized fabric waders contain rubber, and rubber rots sooner or later. If you happen to be fishing a long time out of the water with the upper material exposed to the hot sun, sit down in the water occasionally to wet the fabric. If perchance your waders become wet inside from a spill or you want to dry them from internal sweat, do so in the shade. Turn them inside out for air circulation and if excessive perspiration or condensation is evident, wash them in a mild solution of castile soap and thoroughly rinse. Do this often, as the salt in perspiration rots rubber quite soon. When storing, hang by the feet in a brace that will hold the boot foot open. Place them in a relatively cool spot in the house or barn where they will not mildew or freeze; never where it is excessively dry or hot.

When a scratch, tear, or worn spot develops, be sure the area is completely dry before attempting a patch. Periodic inspection is in order and special attention must be paid to the seams. Rinse waders and boots. Keep them clean of grit. Take as good càre of them as you do your tackle and you can fish the water in front of you with me and be reasonably certain that both of us will keep dry, fractureless, and at ease on the stream.

Forgive the lecture, but it is better to get it off your chest now and know what's what before learning it all the hard way on this water. It is tough enough even under the most correct conditions of personal equipment and abilities.

As to actually wading it, we have discussed this in general before. This time we'll be more specific, paying as much attention to wading this water as fishing it.

So, now from our vantage point, let's look at the water and then let's in the next hour go catch a limit of trout, or at least one good fish.

The places they will be found, unless a hatch comes off, are in the pockets behind the rocks and the dead-water holding spots immediately in front of the rocks. With so many of these areas, plus the runs beside the rocks, the holes and underwater rock obstructions, this means that trout can be literally covering this stream.

This is true, but it is also a fact that you can fish this water until you wear out your casting arm without getting a strike—unless you are lucky, very lucky. I have picked this particular stretch simply because I have been left fishless after three hours of working over it much more often than I have taken fish from it, yet it contains more big fish than the average pool.

Why?

I can only suppose that the angle and art of presentation must be improved, or at least made to be more constant, eliminating the luck entries.

So, I guarantee you nothing.

We can fish it up or down, or we can enter at the middle and fish both ways for a while, just to get the hang of it. Let's try the latter.

Since the light is coming from the right, let's fish the right side that's in the shade and wade in at a point out of the picture just below the cluster of big rocks.

We'll arm up with bucktails first, since there is no sign of hatching activity and no wind seems to be about to blow in insects. Everything seems quiet. The season is about a month after Opening Day, and this would put it about at the end of the Hendrickson hatch. There might be a few spinners about or a new May-fly hatch might begin sometime during the day. Perhaps we might even get a caddis attack. The water is not clear, but it is not foggy either. Just enough clarity to watch your fly and for the trout to see it easily too.

Now, you don't go prancing out on this stage before testing the water every inch as you go along with a toe point. It may look shallow and that not too strong a current is passing, but test it anyway. If you don't, your first "step" may be right into a hole or on a rock that slides and you've a bad ankle before you have wet a line.

First one foot tests until it hits the solid needed, then the other. You are facing upstream and still have one hand grasping a spruce bow. I forgot to mention that a wading staff would be a good assist in this type of water. You haven't one, nor have I today, but I'll guarantee that your first purchase after a couple of beers when we return will be a wading staff, unless you are handy, have a broomstick, a small drill for a hole, and a piece of leather or rope for a handle not unlike that used on ski poles. An old ski pole with the hoop removed is excellent for this purpose, by the way. So is an old discarded golf stick, though this might be too short for most uses.

So far you haven't even made a cast.

With the fishing objective lying out there right across from your position, it is best to try and wade out from under the trees for a decent casting position and angle. You are now in the wash of that big rock and the water pressure is normal. Already, you are up above your knees. You can't see very much through that foam and the reflections. (Do you wear Polaroids?)

Now, about five feet from the bank of rocks and trees, you can safely turn around and face downstream for a drift cast into the wakes of the rocks. Gradually work your way to a fishing up-and-across cast, which will now have to be rolled, and fish the water as you have countless other times in similar stretches of water in this book, paying particular attention to allowing the flies to drift down and sink into the pocket.

Now what if a good fish hits? Have you figured just where you would go to land it? Of course, you'd want to bring it right in to you, but figure a path of downstream movement so that you can get below the fish for the landing. In this fast water, trying to scoop up a fish that is below you while you try to hoist it upstream, even with a heavy leader, is bound to be precarious.

It would seem logical to stay in this position and wade little, at least until you have exhausted the possibilities with wets, nymphs, and even dry flies. A dry flecked into that wash behind the boulder cluster should take something even if it is only a small hatchery fish. Worth a try anyway after the underwater flies have been found wanting.

As usual, we recommend that you don't try to cover the entire one hundred feet of width here from one position. Be content to fish the first forty feet up and down, gradually working upstream, rather than down. The reason it is better to wade upstream, especially if you are trying gradually to work your way out into the center, is that if you are breasting the current you can better judge its force. If you turn your back on it, it helps you along nicely and fools you. If you have to return by a cross-stream or upstream return, you might not make it, since wading against it would be too fatiguing.

Stick to the washes. They look bubbly and fast, but remember that the rock above has broken the current and thereby offers you a place to move about.

Look at the diagram.

Notice that there is a fast and deep main stream just outside the rock

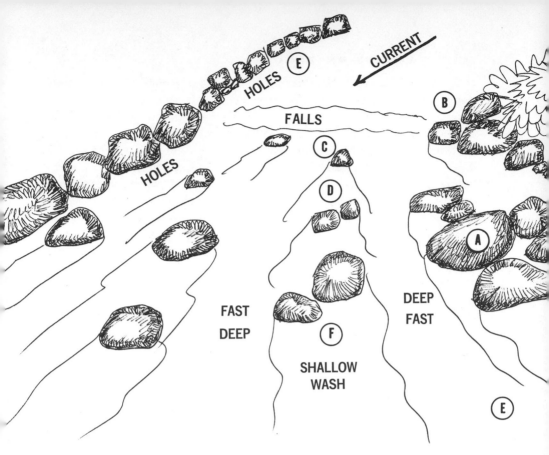

Figure 89. Below the Falls.

cluster A, which you must pass through if you are going to get out there in the middle. Survey this. Poke your rod tip into it for depth and current pull. It is deep and fast. Being fast, there are few big rocks to wedge your feet into, in order to move ever so slowly out into it. It is very likely, without such props, that you'd go head over heels or slip in the current without sufficient holes to step in. Try it for size, if you like, and see if you can make it. If I am right, you won't. You'll have to turn back. Before you make your decision, look downstream. It might be better to cast upstream toward B and work the rocks there, or even slide along the big rocks and around them, moving upstream by inches in order to cast out by the rocks C and D from the safe edges. Later, you can wade in below at E and, quite possibly, work your way up into the center to F by means of dodging between the fast runs and the wakes of the rocks. (You can, because I've done it many times before.) You can actually find a path through that maze, as indicated (- - - - - -), which will allow you to wade and fish all the way to the other shore. Fished up or down it is all excellent water. The bucktail and streamer are best while fishing down.

255

While we've been fishing, an angler has been working his way down the other shore. He's obviously a pro the way he is casting and wading quietly and carefully. Let's watch him. He's just about to the lip of the slight falls at F. With one hand on the rocks, he works his way around each one testing with his lead foot before he places his weight forward. The rod, in his other hand, is constantly working, casting wet flies below him and down and across. He stops once in a while when he can stand upright, makes a number of casts up, across, or angled down.

Actually, the fishing of this water is only half of the exercise and most of it, by now, is obvious. The only part that is important is the transportation angle. You must take care and plan your movements. Even if your plan is good, make sure that it conforms with the hang-ups and tricks that this type of bottom presents to you.

There is no time when this water cannot offer up good fish: from early spring on the first day when the rainbows are running and the browns are hungry to the very last day of the season when the water is low, the rocks slimy, and the air thick with humidity. In August you'll be able to work your way from rock to rock. Slime will now be more of a problem than current pressure. You will also be able to rest awhile on the rocks actually cast from a sitting position. I've eaten my lunch on such rocks and have enjoyed watching the trout come out from the rocks to watch me.

There are hatches like mad here, all season long, and drifts from the hatches above. Bucktails are good at any time of the season, all day and under all conditions. Dry flies will take trout, even small ones when the August sun is blaring down, and big dries will take 'em at dusk. Fish it up or down, one side or the other.

But, wade carefully and easily.

This water is for the pros.

And the patient.

The fish here are big and they don't fool around.

Figure 90. A Typical Hole in a Little Stream.

CHAPTER 32

Little Streams (Four Types of Water)

Type I

IN this day and age, not too many anglers work the little streams, for small waters require much difficult wading. There is little chance for the angler to display fine casting ability and long-line handling. The open-water conditions of the bigger waters are not present and working the holes and hot spots must be a more clearly defined and planned operation. Yet this is the stream that the kids love to fish with worms. It is a kind of water that bids for the quiet angler, the one with patience, the one who is not in a hurry to snag that lunker. Fishing it is an intimate experience. You are close to the rocks, for they give you stance, protection, and they offer good holes for the trout you seek, washes for the fish to lie behind. The small stream has instant changes of pace, not long stretches of the same character as the big stream. A sudden bend, like the one we have waded up to in figure 89, comes from a pasture, where the stream has meandered quietly for miles, and lurked its way through the sieve of a marsh and swamp. Below it is a series of cascades, and it pools up in a dead water. But, this spot here, unlike the water fifty feet above it or ten feet below, offers a specific sample of nature's design—a contest for you and a special kind of promise if you fish it wisely.

You won't need waders today. In fact, if you could become really simple like the local farmboy and fish it barefoot or even work the spot from the rocks above and merely dangle your flies into those pockets of dark water—dawdle them into the crevasses between the rocks—you'd tangle with a trout. You'd probably have to get down to the water if you did hook a good one, especially if your leader is small.

This particular cascade is from my memory book. It is located on a stream in New Brunswick, Canada, where I spent many summers after square-tail trout and, in the stream into which this brook flows, Atlantic salmon. I used to love this "hole," if you can call it that, for it would invariably offer me a good trout, maybe one of ten inches, which would be head and shoulders larger than the other ones on my forked stick. I first learned of trout flies and patterns on this water. My first trout here was taken on a Royal Coachman, wet. Twenty years later, I fished this hole and took a nice trout of eleven inches on a Dark Cahill dry fly. I used my pet dry fly rod of six and one half feet in length and its gossamer leader. What a battle! By then, the old snag spruce had long since rotted away and I was free to make a long cast up into the lip of that falls. Holding the rod tip high, I could get a drift for about three feet, which was just enough.

How can I tell you how to fish this kind of water? It is virtually impossible. You must learn this small-stream fishing the delightful way of trial and error, but I'll guarantee that it will be an unforgettable experience and, perhaps more important, one that will stand you in good stead when it comes time to fish the big streams. For, as we have intimated several times in the past, the big stream is virtually a collection of little ones, though running side by side. In the preceding chapter, you could easily divide that big brash water into four or even five stretches and fish each one as a little stream. By the same token, you can take this little incident on this stream and work it as a pro would work the big water.

The holes for the trout are obvious and readily accessible only if you sharpen your eyes, scale down your casting to almost dappling. (I learned to fish this water with an alder pole and a length of black string. I took as many trout on that gear as I have on a one hundred and fifty dollar rod and reel.

It's fun to fish such water. One can not know what's ahead until upon it. Each bend, each stretch has its own surprise, mood, problem, and solution. If you are graced by enough action from the fish, even though they be little ones, remember that this is the life. A special taste is to be found here, but you must try and approach it in quiet and in peace. Don't attack it, or it will fight back. Black flies will slay you. Spiders and their webs will crease your eyes. Rocks will turn under your feet; every rock, fern, snag, or tree leaf will have its rewarding answer to your invasion, and your temper rise will soil the experience.

Type II

This is only a fifty-foot stretch of a stream that tumbles like this for about five miles down a valley. It bubbles, crashes, and pauses between big rocks, forms into gravelly circular pools, bangs up against boulders, and foams into falls in a pace that is quick and ever-changing all the way down to the mill and the flat water of the duck marsh. What water to fish! There is a trout behind every rock and several in those dark patches where the water deepens suddenly only to spill out again. It can be fished upstream with dries and wets, using dry-fly delivery and drift, or down, with miniature bucktails and wets in active manipulation. It is a brook trout farm, but browns and rainbows also frequent the pools, although they don't stay there long, except to migrate to and from their spawning.

I remember one hunting season when I walked along the stream looking for deer sign and I spotted a whole school of trout slithering along the rocks and up the falls and bubbly runs. They were on their fall mating and spawning mission and were bright and spotted in their mating colors, brighter than I'd seen them during the open fishing season. There were some big trout among them; surprisingly big. One I touched with a stick was about twenty inches and there were many in there just under that mark. For some reason some of these fish stay up in these pockets all season long while their brothers go below.

The rainbows also migrate in the fall, somewhat against tradition. They also come up in the legitimate spring run for the same reason. That's why this particular stretch is a potent one all season long.

Spot casting is in order. Wading is not necessary unless to cross. It is better to dapple, or roll a cast from the shore. No sense wading right up the middle. It's tough going at its best.

I like to worm this water, or at least I did many years ago before my trout fishing became complicated. It might be a good idea for some of us old-timers—steeped in the literature of the experts, laden down with technique and organization—to get into an old pair of pants, wear a discarded pair of sneakers, and go forth with the traditional bent pin. This is the water for it.

Oh, sure, you can fish this with dainty dry flies. Believe me it takes caution, care, and casting ability to keep from becoming snagged in the overhangs. (None are shown in this particular stretch because our attention was really to the water type.) To spot cast and plan a good drift is a constant game of billiard shooting. Quite often, good trout will rise to dry flies but will refuse to take them. Just how they can make that dash to the fly and actually touch it but at the same time change their minds has always been a puzzler. All you can do is to try. I've found that either a low-floating dry fly, or a wet fly, even if it is tied with bulk, is a better cure for short hits. Work it slowly, work it bit by bit. Move along by inches. Each little change of angle in your walk either up or down presents problems that vary like the whims of a spring breeze.

Fish it in the early spring when the leaves are not yet out and its mood is one of almost forbidding silence and sharp, glassy tones as the water lashes at the rocks. Try it in May, during an early morning when

Figure 91. Rapids and Holes.

the birds are trying to outdo each other and the May flies are hatching and the trout are seen jumping once in a while. Leaves are out now, ready for your flies.

Come here in late August at midday under the steam of a humid period. The water will be low and much quieter, but the fish will still be there. In fact, due to the lower temperature, trout will have moved up from the wider stream below. Chances of good fish taking a fly are even better now than they were in the early season.

Small bucktails, dropped from a position above the holes and allowed to merely drift into the deep, will usually provoke a rise. Remember, these trout are constantly on the alert and will not be too choosy. That's why streams like this one are usually fished out early in the season, by the wormers. It is surprising how, in the face of this fact, that the careful and unhurried angler can take good fish from the fished-out pools, when he gets to know them.

Type III

Here our stream breathes a sigh of relief from its hard work of pounding the mountains into valleys. It can run along laughingly, easily, and serenely at times, even bend a bit as it carves a shallow roadway through the gravel and soil of the valley. Here the sun beats down, but all along the length are bushes and grasses offering food for trout (and snags for anglers).

Fishing it is easy. You can walk it along the bank, for sometimes there is a game trail or open stretches where the going is easy. From this vantage you can cast either with a roll or, if angle permits, a fore-and-aft cast to put the fly well ahead or below to a good pocket.

The bends are, of course, always good for a trout or two, even though

261

Figure 92. Meadow Creek.

they be small. This is not a migration route. Any trout found here will be natives, for the stream is not stocked, simply because anglers demand that bigger waters be attended to. Few anglers will be seen here. Oh, perhaps a farmboy or two will fish it in the early season with worms, and they'll deplete the trout population quite a bit. But, again, it is surprising how many trout these experts miss.

It's better to fish this in the early morning or late afternoon, when shadows make the trout less scary. A dry fly is really the most fun and I prefer to fish it upstream, using very light leaders and tiny flies. I'm not after monsters. There is something about those little aquarium-sized trout that offer some sort of feeling far different than the big fish of the big river. For one thing, they have a beauty all their own. Those that mature at about ten inches are beauty in the hand. I seldom if ever keep one, since they are so precious. Besides, trout that small are hardly worth the effort of cleaning.

How to fish this?

Take a moment off. Take a big breath. Sign off all the tensions of life and business. String up a small, light rod with its light line and leader.

Don't become scientific about choice of fly or even the size. Don't worry about technique. Just let your feelings fish this river, not your brain or your logic. Neither brain nor logic belong in nature—only in man's complication. This stream will unravel you.

Type IV

There's a subtle difference in the "tumbler" that we have just fished and the step pools in the next chapter. This little brook has now grown a bit, or perhaps it could be the representation of a smaller brook in a high-water, almost-flood stage, typical of early spring. The "pools" are beginning to be more defined, yet you can hardly call them pools in the classical sense. The stretch at the top of the drawing fits the pool description better and so does the water at the very bottom of the illustration.

There's trout all along here. They are not big, or at least were not when last I fished this brook. In fact, I have never taken a big trout from

Figure 93. Holes and Steps.

it, even in relative terms. For some reason all the fish in here are small, they mature at around a foot in length—browns and brooks. There are no rainbows and nobody has ever thought of stocking the reds.

Because there are other stretches where it is wadable, you wear boots here, although you need not go in very often. It is a sort of miniature of the water described in Chapter 31, "Big Boulders, Fast Runs." You fish it as an individual, dealing with each situation as it comes. Wade or walk the bank foot by foot and the problems and advantages of the water change with you, much like the moon that moves as you walk under it by night.

There are hatches of very tiny flies on this brook, though, to be successful here, one does not need to wait for the evening rise, or be at all conscious of hatches and feeding periods. I have seldom seen trout in any amount actually on a mass feed. There is simply no need for them to do so, since the food they get here is on the bottom, jammed in between those rocks that form the bottom and those that break the fall of the water. It also comes down from above in a constant stream—land-bred insects, particularly in the summer and long into the fall.

The main staple is minnows, if post-mortem inspection of random samples is any indication. Believe it or not, I've taken trout on small bucktails in those two middle flats—spots where one would hardly expect to see them at all.

I have come to be an avid user of the very small bucktail or streamer and the "buck-streamer" fly that is a composite of both. It seems to catch trout in all types of water. Whether it looks more lifelike as a minnow than the usual large patterns, or actually imitates an insect like the stone fly or any one of many swimming nymphs, I do not know.

It works on this water, and pattern seems to make little difference, though, again, this may be because I've tied only a few combinations in this size (see Appendix, page 326).

They are also easy to cast.

Fishing upstream as you see the brook now, I wade the center of the pool below and spot cast to the ledge rocks on both sides, gradually working my way up to the falls. I never plan any kind of a drift or action. The technique I find best for such water, and that includes all four of these situations in this chapter, is the spot cast and the almost immediate withdrawal of the fly. It is as if I were tempting the trout rather than trying to let them see the fly. Fish with a regulation-size rod so that you can dapple the rig and not have to bother reaching to the sky all the time to keep the line from bulging on the waves. At the most, right after the spot cast, I twitch the fly, if the current isn't doing it for me, and then retrieve for another shot a foot away in either direction, or usually above, if still fishing from below.

The tendency in fishing this kind of rapid-moving foam-and-deep is to skip all but the "pools." This is where most anglers make their mistake and so leave most of the fish in the stream for me. If you watch them, they make their casts only to the bottoms of the falls and then move on.

I can say with certainty that most of the fish I've taken from the very stretch you're looking at were taken from the rocks IN BETWEEN the pools. That's the real tip-off for fishing the brooks. Work the pools, sure, but don't neglect the actual white water and the rocks around it. Even the shallow edges of the "pools" is good, too.

When fishing this brook downstream, I like the dry fly because it is easier to control and slack cannot develop. Again, use the spot cast and the mere drop. Never mind about drift and don't worry if the fly is pulled under—as it surely will be after even the best of delivery. Any natural fly would be pulled under too, so don't fret about this.

Obviously, when casting the floater it is not necessary to wade. Wading downstream in this situation would be a difficult and precarious operation, and a highly unnecessary one. Spot cast the pools, dead center. Then, work the edges, flipping the fly to let it light; take it away with a slight bit of drag; send it right back to the same spot again, or at least nearby, and then take it off the water for another cast. Cover the water like a blanket this way. You'll take trout.

Generally speaking, the best time to fish it is in the morning or evening, but if your plans bring you here at high noon, the trout will still be there and almost as willing to feed then as in the more pleasant hours.

Your trout will not be large, but they'll be full of fight, deep-stomached, and intensely colored. Since they are hardly meat-market size, and you want to see action here often, use barbless hooks. The whole point here is to see and feel the little guys hit—and they hit hard.

Step Pools

IN Pennsylvania and New York State, there are areas in the hills and sometimes in the mountains where the terrain seems to descend in steps or sometimes in actual ledges similar to the ledge pool a few chapters back in our fishing. The pool shown here is not made from actual flat-stone ledges, but is, nonetheless, a series of gentle cascades broken by generous and sometimes very deep pools. For some two hundred yards this stream gives us a series of these pools that have always harbored many good trout of reasonable proportions, especially brook trout. They are not easy pools to fish. Or, to put it this way: they are easy to fish, and to cast over. You can make quite a demonstration here for the photographers, wading, as you might, right up dead center and shooting long lines in an up- or down-stream direction, carefully missing the branches of the nearby trees.

But you wouldn't catch anything but leaves.

Most anglers wade right up dead center, scaring the trout in under the falls and into the rocks at the sides. Or some of the trout run down around to hide behind them and wait for peace to return.

Let's fish it the right way, or at least the way that has been most successful for me.

We'll work upstream first. The season is May, or even the first week in June. Flies are hatching sporadically, since big hatches seldom come off in bulk on these pools, with the exception of the caddis.

For practice, let's use a dry fly, so we can see the action of the current and also better spot the strikes or passes that trout may make.

Remember that this water is not quite as small as the tumbling pools and falls, yet not as large as a legitimate big-stream pool where long-line fishing is called for. Here, you split the difference between spot casting

268

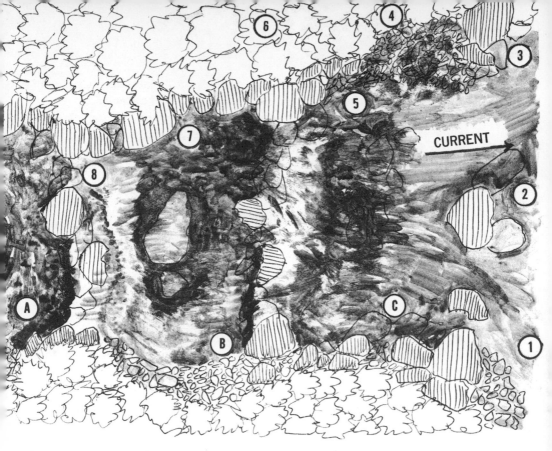

Figure 94. Step Pools.

and the quick retrieve and the longer planned drift. You can mix both techniques and most of the time alternate when the water allows. Drift and drag offer a problem that does not have to be solved in the conventional way, for drag and drift can be considered added attractions to the fly in most situations.

So, we start from the corner approach below 3, since the other bank is the shady side to work. After obvious casts to 2 and to the current that splits by that rock cluster, we shoot a cast to 5 and let it drift down to us. (We have sent out a left-hand upstream curve so that the fly descends that shallow first.) After pickup we shoot one to the dark and deep outside of 5 and, as the fly descends, we mend an upstream bow to the right to allow the fly to descend straight to the rock for pickup. A cast goes to C and lands just under the deep and we mend an upstream bend so that the fly approaches the rock below C. Just as we are about to pick up the fly, a small trout interrupts the procedure.

A nice cast now to the lip of the center falls. The fly dallies for a few seconds. A small trout pops out at it. We quickly roll the pickup and recast to the same spot. Again the small trout. Again the pickup and recast, this time a bit farther out into the center of the stream.

Wham! There we go. That trout must have been watching the little one and then decided to take when we presented it to him just right. Down he comes for his body-roll fight in the center of the pool. Trout are seen spurring in all directions. Some go into the falls and hide under the lip. We'll remember this and work a bucktail over them on the down-stream fishing.

And you haven't moved from 3 as yet.

From here, you could move to position 2 or up to 5. Remembering that it is better to work the other side of the stream because of the shade and save the center from being waded, we can move up to 5 and use a buck-tail or brace of wet flies, or even stick to the dry fly we have on the leader and stop cast downstream directly below. We can, of course, work the rock from this angle. We can also fish the falls, by casting to the near water first and then extend our cast to the other side and let the flies dapple and zigzag down to and below C and around to the front of that big rock.

Looking upstream, we see a deep hole just above the lip of the center falls. Wading any closer from our position at 5 would scare any trout that would be there.

A careful look and we see a nice brown trout rising, or at least he's there off the bottom too. So, we go ashore and poke our nose out of the bushes at 6. From here we can half dapple, half rollcast our dry to a spot near 7 and let it drift down. That does it. Another fish—the brown that we had seen. That's calling the shots.

As we had to come to the rocks to land and release the trout, we can now dry-fly the lip of the falls above and let the fly dance over that big submerged rock in the center of the pool. That's a good spot later for the downstream bucktail or wets. Moving to 7 VERY QUIETLY, we can now place a cast to a spot above B and let the fly dance to B for a pickup. We roll pickup the fly. Wading to 4, we are now in a position for stop cast, downstream dry-fly dappling, letting the fly bounce a bit. Frequent casts, short drifts are the measure here and we work the pool as if it were a smaller one in the smaller stream.

If the light were reversed, and the right side of the stream, or upper in the picture, were in shade, the hot spots would be the corners just below the falls and, of course, the deeps in the center of both pools.

Before we begin our descent with the wets, we can throw some nice ones in what appears to be a much deeper pool above. That's all good water and it is my bet that we may pick up a trout right above A if we land the fly right and let it drift down to the very lip. That's where the trout will hit.

He does. Right as directed. Nice one, too!

Now, to work the stretch downstream. We could use the dry fly all the way, but, for fun, let's dance a small bucktail and a tippet wet fly just to see if the trout are at all selective if given a choice.

We take a helicopter to the brush above A and work the flies in the dark where we just took a trout. Before concentrating downstream, we throw them to the opposite bank where that big rock overhangs. A small trout comes out but does not take. Notice that he struck almost the instant the flies hit that water? That's the trick here. Quick casts but don't let them look at the flies too long.

Now, an easy one, but a tough spot to be in if a fish hits, for it would be impossible to land it unless we go below the falls.

Work the lip by allowing the flies to slide over the falls, but pick up just before they enter the dark and deep. Don't give them time.

Whoops, there's a hit. Another just as you pickup.

See what I mean?

Spot cast. Never mind the drifts and long lines. Keep the casts short, the rod tip up, and since you are using a light leader, manage the spare line with care, as this is the cushion against the hit and fight of a big fish.

Cast out and across as you proceed to B, working the favored run from 7 down to the hole above the falls. Another cast to the hole and allow the fly to dance over the falls, picking it up just as it goes into the slack water below. There's another small hit. Another—and this time the trout took and he's a good one. Remember, you were standing there quietly a moment ago and that trout was not scared down by your wading.

And, so on, down the line.

At twilight, if you fish carefully, it is possible to wade right up the center of this water, going very slowly. There will be hatches of very small flies and you can get a good work-out with size 16's and even 18's. I tie a Light Cahill on an 18 that does the trick on this water at this time of the year. Earlier I like the gray phase of color. Later, I prefer the bivisible black and white. This is small-rod fishing, short casts and gossamer-thin leaders. The trout may not be big by the usual standards, but on such light gear that can be a lot of fun. Again, I use barbless hooks, for during the evening hatch I can usually bank on hooking and letting go at least forty fish in these and the several pools above and below this water. Most of the fish will be hitting almost under the rod tip. Many are the times I've had trout rise right under my rod hand, and one night one hit a fly right in front of me and then landed right in my net! He was a good little brookie, spotted pink and blue—a real native.

This is dainty fishing, the kind that really send the pulse high. It has a charm that big-rod, big-water fishing simply does not possess. There is the intimacy of smaller water, more obvious problems and more interest as we move along a foot at a time. The stream changes dramatically with every footstep.

There's no danger of losing a too-big fish here, for there aren't any that can't be handled on 5X unless you horse them unduly.

Sure, you can work the light and small gear on the big water, but it doesn't have the same feeling. Usually when I use the small gear on big open water I tend to feel helpless and restricted and then wish I had more formidable gear.

Fish this stretch of pools in the early spring. The water will be cloudy and higher. Bigger flies are in order, particularly a trio of wets, or even two nice fat bucktails. Nymphs can produce if you weight them and fish them as you would a worm. Dunk them deep and let them drag the bottom.

Late in the season, go even smaller into the midge class. Here's the place for midging even during the day. If they don't produce, don't forget the old standby for such water—the spider fly.

If all else fails, go back to the Royal Coachman Fanwing, especially if there is a breeze to flutter it a bit during its short but potent run on the wavelets.

Fish this stream carefully, quietly. Don't be in a hurry. There are many subtleties to be learned here that will stand you in good stead when you are on big water, but are faced with exactly the same situations in the runs on your side of the river.

If you happen to reach this area at lunchtime, plunk yourself down on a rock where you can look into the water. Sit there for a few minutes and watch the show in your private aquarium. You'll learn more about your trout this way than by casting all over the pond with no idea of why you're doing it.

CHAPTER 34

Watching the Trout

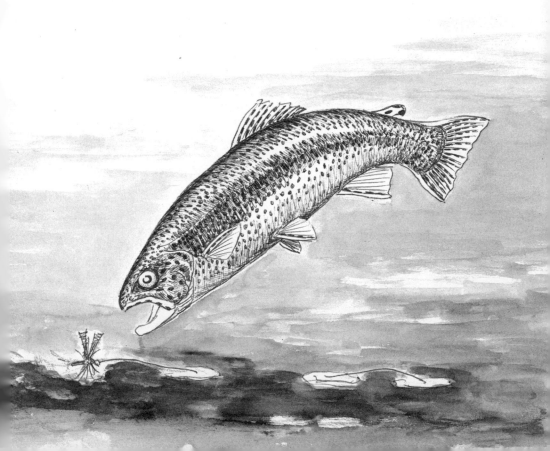

IN this chapter, we drop our rods and tackle in a safe place and for a good while fish with our eyes—pick up a pair of binoculars, peer through the single-lens reflex with a high-powered telescopic lens, climb a tree, or don skin-diving togs—any and all for a closer and more exacting look under the surface of the water. What we can learn from this will tell us much about the mysteries of the current, the habits of the insects and their relationship to the trout, and, finally, our relationship to them.

For learn we must, if we are to become more than mere "chuck and chance it" anglers.

On the following pages are many examples of the ways trout act under various stream conditions, stimulants, food availability, and seasonal aspects of water temperature, speed, and light.

Usually, the trout fisherman can only see a very few of these activities; mainly the ones that are visible on the surface from where he is fishing. If the light is right and all conditions concur, including very clear and glassy conditions, the angler can see some of what's going on. But, even the plain-sight surface splashes can be misinterpreted. Splashing water CAN look as if the trout is taking an insect from the surface, when, in reality, his tail might be causing it—his head being pointed down, straight down. Naturally, in this pose and action, the trout would not likely show any interest in a floating fly. The angler, then, rightly concludes that he would be better off with wet flies, nymphs, or even a bucktail—anything but a dry fly, unless he wants to disregard this tip-off and play the way-out odds.

For many years the author has watched the stream and the trout by the hour. The study is reflected in the pools and ripples of the various situations you have fished with me throughout the book.

One is constantly impressed with the magnificence of the "big picture"; the completeness, the oneness of it all under some seemingly great directive force. It's awesome to behold! To become aware of this, is, in a way, prying into nature's secrets. If so, let's pry!

Here we have all three trout species, the brook, brown, and rainbow, feeding together on a rocky bottom section of a medium-fast stretch of water, perhaps near the end of a pool before the water shallows and splits into individual watercourses. This can also happen along the quieter edges of main currents, quieter water sections near the heads of big pools and away from the actual drop-offs from shelving riffles. Here are found the various species of caddis larvae and a grand assortment of the several species of May-fly and stone-fly nymphs that abound in this type of water, and on this kind of bottom.

Usually, the springtime finds the trout feeding almost exclusively on the bottom and in this fashion, since not too many hatches of insects have attracted their attention to the top of the water. Here, you see the trout dislodging the nymphs and caddis-fly larvae that are still living in

Figure 95. Bottom-Feeding on Nymphs.

their cases; some swinging in the current—all easily spotted by the trout. Since these "bugs" abound in great clusters, the trout congregate in these areas, picking off the insects at will, slithering along the rocks to uproot them, or, in the case of the distant rainbow, nosing along in a permanent "mudding" nose-down position.

This action can be seen plainly when the light is right. It is not limited to the early season. Quite often in midsummer, in the period of hatches, they will feed in this manner, even when a hatch is in progress, and will only give it up when enough of the passing nymphs and hatching insects distract their attention from the bottom. The obvious lure is the wet fly or nymph fished deep—actually bumped right along the bottom.

This is a variation of the bottom feeding shown in figure 95 except that it occurs in shallow water either aside from the main current near the top of a pool or in the "deep" feed lanes that string out near the waste-water sections near the tails of pools. Numbers of fish will be seen tailing in this manner and the usual deduction would be that a rise was taking place to surface insects. Only a close look will divulge the tails of the trout, not the snouts. A dry fly used here would be, of course, a far-fetched bit of nonsense, for the attention of the fish is obviously down, not up.

Tailing is done at all times of the day and all season long when the light is not too bright over the water, for, remember, these shallow areas are generally well exposed. Similar to the deep-water bottom mudding, it is done when there are no hatches in evidence. They will return to it long after a hatch has passed on. Still hungry, they returned to their "gardening."

Rainbows and brook trout tend to feed in this manner much more so than brown trout, since they are not prone to lie in the open current or stay in relatively exposed areas during the bright time of the day.

Freshly planted hatchery fish quickly take to this manner of feeding. I've seen "day-old" trout in the stream already bottom feeding and it is usually quite a hatch that will cause them to rise to the surface. Maybe the hatchery men should train the trout by giving them "floating" pellets rather than the "sinking" kind!

When you catch a trout, no matter on what type of fly, inspect it for gravel and bits of leaves in the gullet. If it is full of such material you have the evidence of this type of feeding.

The alert angler can see the nymphs drifting perhaps a few inches below the surface of the water preparatory to hatching. When they are seen doing this near the surface, you can be certain of a good hatch coming on within a few minutes. Flashing will be seen in the fast water as the trout pick the nymphs off before they reach the surface film where they begin to disrobe from their nymphal shuck. As the nymphs begin

Figure 96. Shallow-Water Tailing.

to actually cast their shuck in the surface film, the trout will be "nymphing" for them and will break the water surface with their tails or by a follow-through from taking the nymphs as they lunge upward from below. Many trout will be seen in this follow-through, actually jumping into the air. A close look at them will show, as have fast-action photos, that they had their mouths closed and that there was no insect "ahead" of them on the surface to jump down on.

This all-important surface-film activity is where the wet fly, skittered or manipulated in an escaping-form-of-life technique of short jerks, is the method to employ. Look closely during the next few minutes and you'll see the actual substage, or dun stage, of the May fly actually taking to the air, freed from its shuck. In the case of May flies such as the Quill Gordon or March Brown, this change takes a longer time and the insect struggles both with the film and the shedding process. A wet fly fished very light on the top film or a sunken type of soft-hackled dry fly is recommended. Finally, when enough of the duns are floating on the surface, it is time to shift to the dry fly.

To really get the "feel" of this situation, allow one of the drifting

277

Figure 97. Subsurface Feeding on Drifting Nymphs.

nymphs to lodge in your hand in a bit of water. Chances are it will perform the change right before your eyes and fly away to shore. Now, you
are really bearing witness. Again, inspect the innards of the trout and
you find they were recently feeding on nymphs, some with their cases
already well cracked open.

So, you SEE. It's all there in front of you.

This is a composite illustration of three types of rises. They are all
typical in their approach. It is an impressive sight, especially when the
action is unexpected. A single dun can be hatching above your position.
Or the rise can be to any one of a dozen flies about to hatch in the feed
lane, working, as they will, right in and around your artificial. Note that
they are freely turned by the current, your imitation is not, so here again
is the recommendation to use the finest leader practicable to give the fly
freedom of movement. Keep a sharp eye out when the trout glide near.
Hold back on your trigger finger when you see a trout break the water
nearby. Nine times out of ten, if your line is tight, your strike will be too
early and you will claim that the trout are only making light hits. Actually, you pulled the fly away from the fish.

When you see the naturals close together, place your artificial in among them—one of slightly smaller size and same general color and shape. Control of drag here is important, so keep it to the absolute minimum.

The brown trout is pictured here in a characteristic airborne leap, as this species is prone to aerial acrobatics. Note that even in this "rise" he is headed *down*. Of course, brookies and 'bows will do this, but not so generally. Browns usually rush the fly as shown and brooks merely roll up under it like a shark taking a surface bait.

During the middle and late times of the season, usually at twilight, during the dun hatch, the evening rise is the most dramatic in this respect. A pool which half an hour before looked entirely devoid of life suddenly becomes crowded with action. Big trout seem to come from nowhere and one wonders how it is possible for the pool to hold so many that have gone so completely unnoticed during the foregoing hours.

This is the most conventional of all the rise types, and the easiest to identify. Other kinds of splashes may be confused with it, but sharp eyes can detect that actual taking of the dun from the surface when conditions are right. Usually, it is more obvious below the actual location of the hatch, since the transition from the taking of the emergING duns and

Figure 98. Rise to the Emerging Dun.

the emerged duns can be quite confusing. Below the area of hatch when there are quite a number of the duns "sailboating" the pool, the rise to individual floating insects can be easily spotted.

The typical rainbow rise can and is performed by all three species, but the rainbow is the better-looking performer. The type of rise is naturally dictated by the other conditions around it. If the water is fast, the chances are that the trout will rush into the foam to the fly. When the surface is calmer, he can and does come up and over.

Now is the time for the dun patterns. The dry-fly technique with all its subtleties of cast directions, including the right- and left-hand bends, the upstream bends and mends and the rollcast pickups is in order. When the trout are feeding on emerged duns, it is best to keep drag to a minimum, since the fly is not actually performing any movement other than walking slightly on the surface, not fluttering or struggling as in the hatching sequence.

As to pattern selection, I have found that a pattern slightly smaller and, on a clear day, lighter—dark day, darker—is a GENERAL idea to follow. During the dusk-time hatches, a darker fly is usually recommended, although this is hard to follow in the bad light. A white-winged pattern or a bivisible is used.

Figure 99. Dun Rise.

The biggest trick to hooking fish that are rising to the emerged dun is in making sure you do not strike too fast. Often the quick response pulls the fly away, particularly during the aerial rise.

This is the rise that can literally drive the dry-fly addict crazy. It is the rise to the adult or spinner stage of the May fly. Actually, three things are going on here. The adult flies, having cast their dun skins in the nearby bushes or trees or on the rocks, are now returning to the stream to find a mate. In the early season, this flight comes off before sunset, when what little warmth has cooled down. In the later season the flight occurs at twilight, and in midsummer it usually starts just at dusk. Some of the insects are blown to the surface, some light for an instant only to take off again. The brook trout in the illustration is heading for a mating pair of spinners.

The adult fly has little or no food value, since its energy is now all centered in the eggs. The trout know this and are really after the eggs of the female. She dips down to the water in a tantalizing dance that is the continuation of the mating up-and-down zigzag, not unlike the ballet dancer performing her light, bouncing motions. When the insect touches the water ever so gently, the eggs drop off into the water, quickly descend, and attach themselves to the bottom stream rocks. The trout like those eggs.

There is hardly an angler alive who has not wondered at the reason why trout will sometimes bump the knots of even the thinnest leader. Those knots look to the trout just like the egg clusters the May flies are depositing. If you don't believe this, take a 7X tippet and tie on three short tippets. On the ends tie a size 20 or 22 hook with a small bit of light yellow or gray yarn. You'll take trout!

With insect species overlapping in the middle of the season, some will be hatching at the very time the spinners are performing their return flight. It is interesting to watch the trout turn from one to the other. If you are fishing a spinner and see the trout taking the duns, try that pattern. If the trout become selective to the spinners, switch to a spider or a very lightly dressed spinner pattern. Tricky business, and one which requires that you see before you can do.

Despite the extreme activity of the life of a trout, he seems to find time to rest. Contrary to some authorities, he is not always on the feed. During the summer months when the water is low, clear, warm, and the sun bright and dazzling, he prefers to sit out the midday shine in the comforting shade of a ledge rock and await the coolness of the evening before venturing out. Many times I have waded by "sleeping" trout and, despite the fact of trodding almost upon them, have actually prodded them with the rod tip to dislodge them from their hold.

Figure 100. Evening Rise—Spinners.

You'll find them almost asleep, since there are no insects hatching, no minnows moving nearby. Even a sparrow flying overhead will not cause them to move a fin.

Look at our nice fat brookie, snuggling close in under the rock . . . his dorsal fin swaying gently in the current. He's not alone. If you were to carefully inspect all the bigger stones and rocks of the average run, particularly in medium-shallow stretches down from the heads of pools, along the edges of main currents and in the holes at the pool tails, you'd find many such fish in hiding. Only a general over-all glance at the pool would bring on the impression that there was not a fish in it. Those are the ones that make the place look like a crowded dance hall on Saturday night once the air and water has cooled and the lights are low.

How to catch this fellow? Personally, I wouldn't bother him. Let him rest until sundown. There are fast runs and eddies where the trout are bound to be more active. Oh, sure, just for target practice and for kicks, you can float a few flies over him and possibly anger him into striking. This can be done if you have the patience to throw a fly, maybe twenty

282

times and drift it right over him, drag free with an expert delivery each time. He won't bolt if you goof, but, since he's not hungry, he'll just let you practice while he snoozes.

This is a touchy type of rise. The fish are just hanging there in the current with their snouts hardly breaking into the surface film. They are merely waiting for the insects to drift by and tickle their noses! It is seen over a deep hole where the water surface is ruffled and so offers some protection from the penetrating sunlight. It also happens at twilight or where the forest shades that particular part of the stream. Note that the snouts are almost breaking the surface film. The trout are not rising to any specific insect and may hang there indefinitely, changing positions occasionally as the current itself moves them about. They'll gently wave their tails, but you'll see that they keep returning to the actual feed lane where the food will be drifting by. They won't waste time out of the path of circulation.

Trout that normally will not put up with fish their size in the lairs on the bottom will feed in the open like this almost side by side, rarely chasing each other away. This is a very difficult pose to cast a fly to, since the least line or leader disturbance will send the whole lot of the fish scampering back to their homes behind rocks or into the deepest

Figure 101. Asleep in the Shade.

parts of the pool. When the fish do open their mouths it is ever so slightly, and appears as a mere ripple, hardly discernible if the water surface is at all churned or flexed by the current or breeze. Seen from a distance against reflection and glare, one would swear that it was only a tiny chub or minnow performing, but it could be a trout of magnificent proportions if one were in the right position to see the "fact."

This attitude of the trout is also part of the picture when they are actually feeding on drifting black-fly and "midge" larvae. These insects drift in the surface film by the thousands and it is the trout's habit to merely nose into them and, usually by touch rather than sight, feel the insects with their lips and open their jaws for the flies to be sucked in. Quite often a big old brown will be seen cruising along with his snout making a very slight wake on the surface. A close look shows him with his mouth cracked open just a bit all the time.

To present a tiny size 20 to him under these conditions is quite an art and it works when you can pull it off.

*Figure 102. **Dimpling Rise to Drifting Flies.***

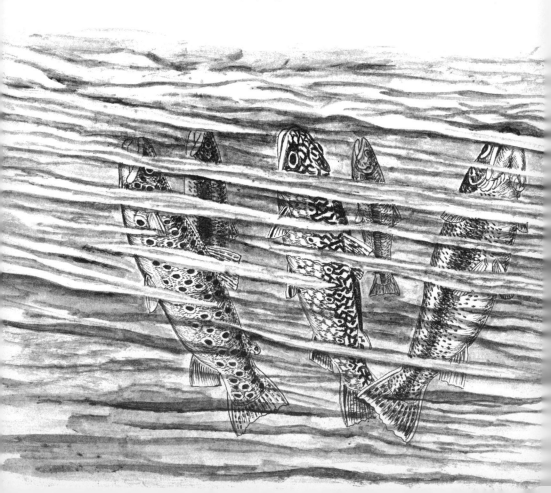

Figure 103. On the Alert.

This is the pose that most anglers hardly ever see. This trout is well hidden, perhaps between rocks and submerged branches. At least he is in a position where any insects floating down in or on the current will flow by him and become tangled in the branches of the snag or be swayed out to him by the current slipping by that rock behind him.

He's there because this is his domain. No other trout will be nearby. He may have had to fight for the position, or has taken it up after some lucky angler caught his predecessor. Every fin is poised for quick reaction if a succulent insect comes near, or a minnow ventures in too close.

He's a sucker for your flies, no matter what pattern or style, just as long as your delivery doesn't scare him down deep and out of circulation. If you do frighten him, you'll not be the wiser. You'll merely conclude that there was no trout there or, if there was, he simply wasn't interested. Walk along the bank of any trout stream where there are overhangs or underwater rocks that jut out offering such positions of "watch." You'll see trout there that you never realized lived in the stream. Again, this is taking time out from casting, but the evidence in this case will pay off once you are on the water. You'll automatically assume that there are fish waiting to be caught in these places. If you have any doubts and want to see first and fish later, you can go ashore, peer down, and your evidence will be yours alone.

This fish in this position is rarely selective. I've taken them on whatever lure I've been fishing at the time. It is merely a matter of good, careful presentation technique, such as we have been detailing in the countless situations similar to this throughout the book.

APPENDIXES & INDEX

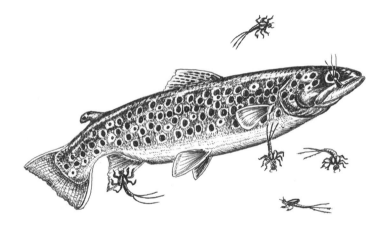

AS I went along in this book "fishing" with you, I realized that there would be the need for an appendix—a sort of "off-stream classroom" where the mechanics of casting could be detailed along with necessary techniques and discussions of tackle as referred to in the text. Also, there would be need for the subtle line-handling techniques, various types of methods of fishing the flies, and the combinations of fly manipulation and retrieve. Also, again, I would have to detail in some place other than the main part of the book the various flies, rigs, or other pertinent information needed—whether the reader be an expert or novice.

Bit by bit the Appendix grew and finally I found that I would have to give it a table of contents!

I must assume that the reader may or may not be expert or at least adequate in handling tackle, tying flies; knows the various knots and the hundreds of aids that are known—and in many cases forgotten—by most of the time-tested anglers. I don't want to insult the expert, nor do I want to leave the beginner hanging. To bridge the gap and attempt to keep everybody happy is the purpose here in separating "action" from "mechanics." I hope this division of the book meets with your approval.

APPENDIX I *Equipment*

Fly Rods

A fly rod, like a wife, is an individual creation. The personality of the angler, the way he fishes, and the way he acts on the stream must be taken into consideration before the marriage—in this case with the fly rod. Actually, a strong-arm man, used to the athletic approach and liking the display of force in casting, will be able to push most rods well beyond their normal possibilities. Others, of the more gentle type, may need rods with more built-in strength.

There is much nonsense floating around fishing circles about rods and types such as the "ideal wet-fly rod," the best "fast-action dry-fly rod," and the rod for "heavy big-fly fishing."

Buying them all is fine if you have a rod caddy following you along the stream. You'll find that quite often in these pages we suggest that you shift from heavy bucktails one moment to tiny dry flies the next. Without a floating tackle snap tied to your waders, you are going to have to get used to one, two, or perhaps three rods for basic fly-fishing needs. If you can trim this to two rods, so much the better. A third rod can be a very specialized one, like the very light and fine dry-fly rod when you know you won't be throwing heavy flies, at least long distances that day. By the same token, when the water dictates heavy fishing, a big "almost salmon" rod could be used.

I'd rather have two well-made rods with good actions, tight-fitting ferrules, proper mounted guides, and a variable action than five rods of lesser quality. Besides, I have found that all the rules can and should be broken once in a while. We are supposed to be having fun.

For instance, I recall the day I first fished with a very stiff "dry-fly-action" rod. I caught nothing with it, at least while using the dries. Then, rather than return to the car, I decided to tie on a heavy leader and cast a bucktail with it. Did that work fine! I have come to love a dry-fly rod for bucktailing! On the other hand, I have had a long romance with a soft English-style wet-fly rod. The tip is as soft as limp spaghetti. Yet, when I'm not trying to break distance records or snap flies off leaders, this rod is just perfect for a relaxed evening of dry-fly casting. The action is slow, easy, gentle, subtle. And, yes, it also casts wet flies well, even a brace of them if they are not too large. It will not perform well in a gale, nor can I cast a single wet fly seventy feet with it, but for normal fishing it is a perfect "all-purpose" rod.

So, generally, it is a matter of mood and needs, not what some experts dictate, that counts.

When I bought my first fine rod of beautiful bamboo from William Mills in New York many years ago, I'd saved up for that day for more than a year. That rod was to be with me for many years and I fished it under all types of conditions. Its big lesson showed me that by becoming familiar with every inch of its action, I could bring various "parts" of the rod into force when needed. I could soon throw a tight bow for quick false-casting of the dry flies one minute and, then, by a switch of pace, throw a wide bow for the three wet flies without having them hang up on each other on the back or forward cast. I was able also effectively to rollcast, and when the right line and properly tapered leader was used, easily cast two bucktails well with the same rod. True, I could not throw them across the county line, but, as you will discover in these pages, most of the fishing and more exacting and productive casting is done at much shorter ranges than most anglers realize.

True, there is no substitute for a rod for every purpose and whim, but the same thing can be said about fly patterns. Of the thousands invented over the years, only a basic few are *really* necessary, unless, of course, you are a special and constant experimenter, tying your own patterns for an extension of that particular phase of the sport.

The choice of line to the rod, for these various types of uses from fast, slick dry-fly casting to heavy bucktails is, of course, actually more important than the choice of the rod, despite the fact that the line is really an extension of the rod, and so is the leader.

You have heard and read a great deal about "balanced tackle." In nine situations out of ten, the angler is the one who must become balanced.

True, it is no good to go to the stream with tackle that does not fit your personality or your needs on the water. There is a compromise point, however, or better stated, a point of "meeting" where the angler marries the stick.

As to glass or bamboo, I have always preferred bamboo over glass and am still considered a hold-out. True, I've fished with many glass rods that I've designed myself for the manufacturers, so one would think that I'd arrived at the perfect rod at least for myself. This is not the case. When I think of glass, I unconsciously begin to push hard and slash at the water, fighting the elements. Bamboo, on the other hand, sets me calm and quiet, and I find that if I "feel" the rod and almost go along with what it wants to do with the particular rig I have attached to the line at the moment, my efforts are more than rewarded.

I find that becoming sensitive to the tip action is half the battle. It is possible to work the tip, the middle, and even the butt section by subtle wrist movement and arm action together with timing.

For instance, suppose I'm using a typical 8½-foot medium-soft-action fly rod suitable, most people would say, for wet-fly fishing. I "change it" into a dry-fly rod for that narrow and tight bow, that fast drying snap of the leader and fly, simply by timing my push and impulse so that only the very middle section of the rod is flexed. This leaves the tip section more or less stable and so the line snaps back and forth well. If, on the other hand, I wish to throw a wide and high bow and make a slow cast so as not to tangle the flies in the air, I try and reach my power to the very tip of the rod, bending this section in the timing action. Obviously, when using three flies of medium or heavy size, or a big bucktail, I have a heavy butt leader and usually do not taper the leader too thin, except when fishing in or around snags. This cast uses the entire rod from butt to tip and is a much slower action and smoother swing throughout, making the fly do what I want it to do.

Rollcasting with this same rod can be accomplished by the same sensitiveness. I try to "think" my pressure into the middle of the rod and my timing comes out pretty well nigh perfect.

The stiff rod of the legitimate "dry-fly action" type is not quite so adaptable to this sort of handling, so I generally use this rod least of all. The big 9- or 9½-footer used for the big water, fast runs, big rainbows, and heavy leaders and flies only comes out when that specific type of fishing is going to be done. Even with this rod I can always change to the dry fly if I use properly tapered leaders.

The selection of the line, too, can make all the difference in the world, and it is easier to carry reels in the fishing jacket than rods.

So, we have, basically three types of rods with which we fish this book. We use the medium-action rod most of the time. We try not to false cast too long a line, nor pick up long lines unnecessarily. We make all casts below the fifty-foot mark, most of them nearer forty feet.

I feel that I am not dodging a responsibility by omitting specific rod weights, but merely referring to soft, medium, and fast action. You must learn this for yourself. If you are an old-timer, you well know why I say this. The beginner must experiment, and as he becomes sensitive to rods and to fishing needs, he will arrive at a true marriage. Bamboo or glass? That's up to you!

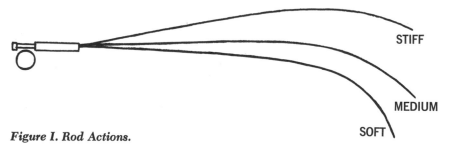

Figure I. Rod Actions.

Fly Reels

As to reels, remember that the reel on the fly rod, for all but the very biggest trout in the very fastest waters, is merely a line carrier. Most trout under the two-pound mark are seldom played from the reel, or should I say, it is not necessary or advisable to play them from the reel, since the line hand can govern the tightening or feeding of line under most circumstances in relation to the pressures exerted by the rod on the fish. (See the section on "Striking, Playing, Landing.")

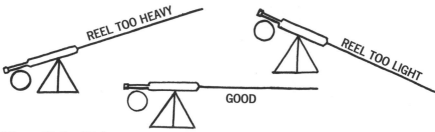

Figure II. Reel Balance.

So, pick a reel that does not weight down the wrist heavily. Try and find one which, first, will hold a standard double-tapered or weight-forward tapered line. If the rig is going to be used for small streams and small fish, allowance for twenty-five or fifty yards of backing is not necessary. For big streams, big fish, and fast water, better have a bit of backing under the line, at least fifty yards of it. This can be ten-pound-test braided nylon and tied to the basic line smoothly or, better still, wound and varnished. If you don't already know how, have it done by an expert. Don't just tie it together in a knot that will jam in the rod guides!

Single action is desired in a fly reel, not multiple action. Strength and quality is a matter of the pocketbook. Most of the English reels are tops and the best American-made reel I have used for years in several sizes is the Pflueger Medalist. I have used their big salmon-size reel for both bass bug and Atlantic salmon fishing and have never found it wanting.

Lines

I like silk lines best for fly fishing, especially for dry-fly fishing with a bamboo rod. However, they require more care than most people would care to be burdened with. If you are a beginner, use nylon lines and only try the silk after you have become selective. You may never find the need of the feel of a silk line and so avoid unnecessary care. As to the correct taper, follow the manufacturer's recommendations (rod specs.) for this. You will also want to vary from the usual for certain circumstances. For instance, for fishing braces of wet flies, especially large ones or weighted flies, or even streamers and bucktails, I like to use a heavier line than recommended for "standard" use. I also tie on a three-foot butt section of bigger diameter ahead of the tapered leader so that the cast will flow better in the air, straighten out, and in general be easier to control.

Sinking lines have become common in trout fishing in the last few years. I've tried them, and I don't care for them, even though I might sacrifice getting the fly down deeper by the use of the floating line. If I wish to compromise this, I simply use a line at that moment which has not been dressed. It will sink, generally, just enough for my needs. But again, this choice is yours to make for yourself.

The weight-forward or bullet-tapered lines are for long-distance work and are an abomination for close-in, shorter-line fishing. They don't really begin to function until you are reaching out to longer distances than fifty feet. Under that distance, a double-tapered line, for me at least, is sufficient. Also, the weight-forward line requires a stiff "dry-fly-action" rod and I use one of these so seldom that for general work, including all of the situations in this book, I would not even carry the rig in the car. I also find that managing the double-hand cast with the double-tapered line will suffice even up to sixty feet with an 8½-foot rod with all but a very soft tip.

Sure, you can get all gooked up with a lot of gear. That's fine. I went through this years ago, but I find my needs now are really very simple. Perhaps you've found it this way, too.

As to terminal tackle, in this case leaders, I *am* touchy about this since it is the fuse that lights the bomb. The improper leader will kill the best rod in existence. Quite often, if you were to inspect my leaders, you'd find butt

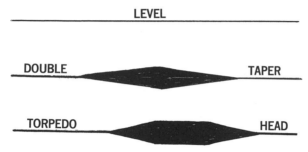

Figure III. Tapered Lines.

ROD	ROD ACTION	NYLON TAPERED LINE	SILK TAPERED LINE
7½ ft.	Medium to Stiff	HDH	HEH
8 ft.	Medium	HDH	HEH
8 ft.	Stiff	HDH (Cut taper to suit)	HEH (Cut taper to suit)
8½ ft.	Medium	HDH (Cut to suit)	HEH (Cut to suit)
8½ ft.	Stiff	HCH	HDH
8½ ft.	Very Stiff	HCH (Cut to suit)	HDH (Cut to suit)
9 ft.	Medium	HDH	HEH
9 ft.	Stiff	HCH (Cut to suit)	HDH (Cut to suit)
9 ft.	Very Stiff	GBG (Cut to suit)	HCH (Cut to suit)
9½ ft.	Medium	HCH	HDH
9½ ft.	Stiff	GBG	HCH
9½ ft.	Very Stiff	GBG (Cut to suit)	HCH (Cut to suit)

extensions beyond the standard tapers. You'd also find that I have cut off a large portion of the double-tapered line and substituted a long, heavy butt leader section ahead of the recommended tapered leader. This balance is needed in dry-fly fishing specially. But it is also necessary to have a strong and stiffer butt section to the leader ahead of three wet flies and particularly bucktails. If you fish three bucktails or even two, the standard leader will be too light. You'll need three feet of heavier butt ahead of it, sized to your needs. There is no formula I can give you for this.

Fly rods I recommended for a rounded selection include three from the William Mills catalogue. A 7½-foot medium-stiff-action small-stream bamboo rod for dry-fly fishing, light nymph and very light wet-fly work. Second, their 8-foot medium-fast-action all-purpose-type rod for everything but small-stream and heavy-bucktail work. Third choice is their 9-foot soft-tipped rod with a good strong middle section for use in casting bucktails and big Wulff dry flies long distances. A general line-up of rod recommendations follows.

I use Pflueger Medalist reels exclusively in all their sizes.

Leader sizes and pound tests vary even in the manufacturer's stock. The listing that follows is a bare guide. The best way is to use a fine measuring device and accurate pull scale; it is better, of course, to experiment by casting the leader on the line and rod it will be used with. This is the real test and the only one that amounts to anything.

GAUGE DESIGNATION OF SIZE	AVERAGE (NOMINAL) DIAMETER IN INCHES	MINIMUM PERMISSIBLE BREAKING TEST IN POUNDS
7X	.004½	¼
6X	.005	⅜
5X	.005½	½
4X	.006	⅝
3X	.007	¾
2X	.008	1
1X	.009	1½
0X	.010	2
10/5	.011	2½
9/5	.012	3
8/5	.013	3½
7/5	.014	4
6/5	.015	4¾
5/5	.016	5½
4/5	.017	6¼
3/5	.018	7½
2/5	.019	8¾
1/5	.020	10

NOTE: From 7X to 4X the permissible variance in each gauge designation or size is ¼ thousandths plus or minus. From 4X to 1/5 the permissible variance in each gauge designation or size is ½ thousandths plus or minus.

Casts

Basic Casts

Many angling books deal with the basic casts; what we present here is therefore really nothing new, but must be dealt with for the benefit of the beginner.
However, I find that the actual instruction experience I've had with many
anglers from six years old to old-timers requires a very simple approach to
what some make into a veritable intellectual drag. Fly casting is easy, despite
all the dogma handed down by purists from the old country.

Actually, casting a line with a fly rod, if it is the right line, is as simple as
throwing a stone. Some can hit the barn the first time, others will take a little
longer. It is all a matter of "feel." I once taught a blind man to cast and he
was good!

So, very simply, here is all there is to it. The subtleties will come as you go
along in actual fishing. We'll try to make it look and read simply for you.

Fore-and-Aft Cast

You are now hip-deep in water, facing downstream. Your rod is already
strung up with about twenty feet of line out from the tip. Your rod is a very
sensitive thing—so is your hand, your wrist, your arm, and your body. From
now on they all have to work together. On the end of the line is a seven-foot
leader, but no fly. There is no need for the fly—it goes along for the ride. When
you can cast the line and leader so that it goes out straight and lands lightly,

Figure IV. Getting the "Feel" of the Line in the Rod Guides.

you are ready to fish this cast, and so tie on a fly. Hold the rod parallel to the water. Feel the slight drag on the line as the current pulls on it? Flip the top of the rod up and down a few times to feel its action and to get used to the line drag on the water. This slight pressure against the rod is most useful.

Now grasp the line coming from the reel between the reel and the first guide and pull it in from the rod and release it. Now pull some line from the reel and release it. Do both of these a couple of times to get used to this action and movement. You'll need it in all your fishing as well as your casting.

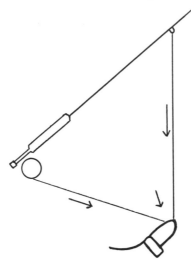

Figure V. Drawing in the Line at the Beginning of the Cast.

Step one of the cast is the raising of the rod tip to bring the line back and up off the water in preparation for the back part of the cast, or the backcast as it is called. This is the first of three parts of the cast. The second part is not a separate action but a strengthening or powering of the same motion in order to raise the line farther off the water and make it begin its ride up and over your head and behind for the stretch-out before the forward cast begins. This is what happens in stage one.

Figure VI. The Line Pickup for the Cast.

To perform it, begin again. Let the line drift downstream until it straightens out. Grasp the line from the reel at midpoint to the first guide. As you begin to raise the rod tip up, pull gently on the line coming from the guide. This will add additional pressure on the rod during the pickup and supply the energy needed to send the line back over your head. Now, the line is over your head beginning to make a "bow." When your rod reaches about the two-o'clock position on your watch, add a bit more pressure to the backward swing and pull down on the line just a bit. (Actually, this line handling in addition to rod work is a modification of the double-haul cast, which is only a pressured version of what we are showing you.) Now, the line is in this position:

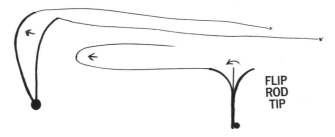

FLIP
ROD
TIP

Figure VII. Showing the Rod-Tip Flip.

You relax your line hand by letting the line pressure from the backcast pull on the line, and so your hand goes back out toward the first guide. The line then begins to go straight out behind you like so:

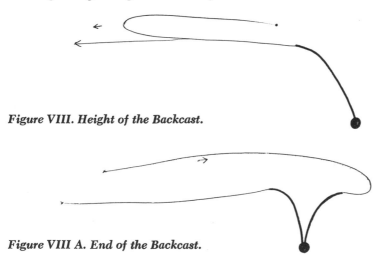

Figure VIII. Height of the Backcast.

Figure VIII A. End of the Backcast.

AT THIS MOMENT

you begin the reverse of what you have just done. You now push the rod forward with a bit of wrist kick and go downward with the forearm, developing a little more power than you needed on the backcast. Now, with the line in the air and high, you have to keep it that way and make it travel forward over your head. At the instant you begin the forward drive, you again tighten on the line with the line hand to add pressure. This sends the line in a nice unfolding "bow" forward and the bow develops up and ahead of you. When your rod tip reaches the level of the water, the line will have straightened out and the whole cast drops down to the surface. Like so:

Figure IX. The Forward Cast Drop to the Water.

The False Cast

In order to get used to all the swinging and arm and wrist movement, to say nothing of the actions of the line hand in concert with it, learn the false cast, for it is a necessity in all of your fishing. A primary use in dry-fly fishing is that of drying the fly. The other is to get the line going back and forth properly before releasing it on the actual cast. Gradually you will being to feel when it is going smoothly and at right tempo and height. On the next forward throw, you let the cast go down to the water as directed. A bit more pressure is needed in the false cast to keep it flying neatly and evenly in the air. Remember, that it will be only as good in front as it is in back. Since you cannot see how it is straightening out in back, you must begin to feel when it is going down too low. Try and time the forward throw so that the line will not have

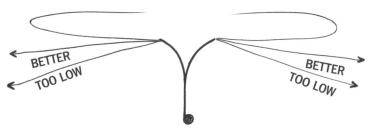

Figure X. Keep That Cast High.

to be lifted up and shot high in front of you on an angle. It is best to have the whole cast going flat above the water. To regulate the action use a combination of line pressure from the line hand as you pull or release the line coming from the guide. Added or taken pressure on the rod will develop into a skill of timing and perfection.

Now it is a matter of getting used to all this in concert and in fluid motion. When you arrive at a smooth delivery, to extend to greater distance you merely strip more line from the reel AT THE TIME YOU PULL ON THE LINE FROM THE FIRST GUIDE. If a lot of line is going to be used coil it in your hand. The added line will require more casting pressures and a longer pause on the backcast to allow the line to straighten out. To shoot the line (in the case of using a torpedo or weight-forward line), you false cast only the heavy front section, coiling the flat running line in your hand and allowing the rod action to pull it from your fingers.

See the difference in the "bows" in the line on the cast? There is a good reason for both kinds, and to perform them the steps are really quite simple. The wide bow is for use in wet-fly fishing, particularly when two or more flies are on the leader. A flat bow would obviously tend to tangle when the line loops forward or back on the cast. A dry fly of a wind-resistant type, such as the Royal Coachman Fanwing, cast on an exceptionally light leader would also tend to tangle with the line, especially if the breeze whips it about in the air.

The flat bow is cast in the wind for accurate delivery and also for drying the fly in an almost snapping motion of the leader. The flat bow is preferred for most dry-fly work when accuracy is demanded for the letdown on the water.

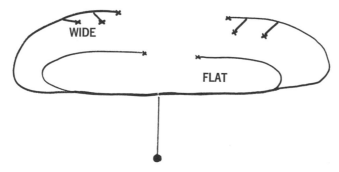

Figure XI. Wide Bow for Wet Flies—Tight Bow for Dry Flies.

Most so-called dry-fly-action rods are stiffer on tip than the softer so-called wet-fly rods, so they perform the flat bow exceedingly well without much need for that extra pressure and split timing. The stiff rod must be given a waving motion in order to perform the wide bow well. The soft rod, on the other hand, performs the wide bow easily because of the slower pace, and takes twice the pressure to perform the flat bow. In both instances and with both rods, the wide bow is aided in the start by lifting *up* on the first stage of the backcast and followed by a very slight pause before continuing the pressure to send the line again straight out behind—well up off the water. The same goes for the forward cast. The line is allowed to dip slightly below the horizontal before beginning the forward throw and at the peak of the pressure is off before the big push forward. A subtlety, of course, but you'll learn it by practice.

The flat bow is the result of guiding the line horizontal or flat in the air with no pauses and, in fact, with almost an anticipation of power before the line straightens out (behind or in front). In the case of the wide bow, you were aware of the entire rod working slowly and with pauses. Here the TIP of the rod is pressured. The rod with a stiffer tip will deliver a flatter bow. Obviously, you'll have to work much harder to flatten the line with a rod that has a soft tip. Actually, dry-fly fishing with a single fly, when you want to dry the fly quickly, is about the most important use of the flat bow.

From here on it is practice and learning the timing of the three motions, the pickup drag in relation to the length of line out, the bit of pressure sending the line back, and finally the push forward.

Right-Hand Curve Cast (Right-Hand Bend)

Much of the time you will need to know how to cast the fly, either up or down stream, but swing the fly and most of the leader in what is termed throughout this book as a bend or curve cast. To perform this you simply follow the directions for this cast with the only change being that you flip your wrist over (or turn it over sharply) to the RIGHT as you drive forward on the forward part of the cast. For more of a curve add some forearm motion to it. Note that the ends of your rod-hand fingers will be seen when the wrist is fully over. This motion sends the line in a curve as it goes forward over your head and it continues to curl to the right just before it drops to the water. To ensure a good bend, come up on the rod rather sharply to the LEFT just before the line hits the water in a sort of whipping motion.

The left-hand curve cast or bend is done by turning the wrist to the LEFT showing the back of your hand. Remember to bring the rod tip up sharply to the RIGHT before the line touches the water.

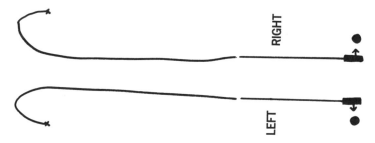

Figure XII. Right-Hand Bend Cast.

Change-of-Direction Cast

This one happens almost without your knowing it. Actually, it happens if you are not careful when trying to direct a straight cast to a specific target!

It is actually hard NOT to perform the change-of-direction cast!

So here is how you perform a sloppy direct fore-and-aft cast, known as the change-of-direction thing.

You have just picked up and wish to send the next cast to the right. You simply false cast and in one or two slight turns to the right, you direct the cast by degrees to the target area desired. Simple?

Same thing for the left, except direct to the left.

If, however, you wish to change direction without false casting, you can do so with an obvious swing of the rod on the pickup, and an equal swing in the opposite direction on the forward throw. We'll show you. Look at the diagram. You are seeing it from above.

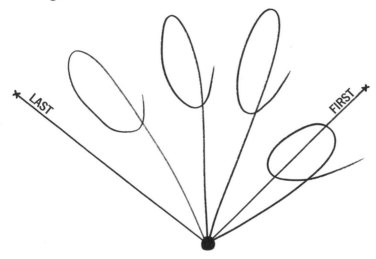

Figure XIII. Upstream Mend Cast.

Suppose you wish to cast to the left. Pickup and swing back, curving your arm and the rod to the LEFT. On the forward throw, curve the rod to the RIGHT, which will send the line to the left.

Reverse all this for the cast to the right.

Now, there's no big deal about that one, is there?

As you have experienced, the conventional pickup is the beginning of the cast. Later you'll learn the rollcast pickup.

But if you have a long line out that cannot be picked up easily by merely grasping the line in the line hand and pressuring the rod in its initial backcast phase, strip in line with the line hand, reaching as close to the first guide as possible and pulling down sharply. If two grasps of line are necessary, release the first line at the bottom of the arm swing and quickly reach up for the next grasp. You'll be doing a lot of this in playing your fish and also in manipulating the fly in a combination of fishing action and retrieve in all directions and in all current situations. Therefore, get used to doing it now. If necessary, HOLD ON TO THE LINE at the bottom of the first pull and bring it back up to the next grab. Now you have a loop. On exceptionally long casts and retrieves, you'll gather several loops of line. One of the most effective fishing retrieves is the stripping type described here, so practice it. You can also drop the coils on the water as long as you can keep them from tangling. You'll learn to let them float in a bow in front or alongside, depending on the direction of the current.

The Rollcast

The rollcast is a bit more difficult for the beginner to master than the fore-and-aft cast, but fortunately, through learning that first cast, you have become acquainted with your tackle—the rod, line, and leader—and how all must work together with your fingers, hands, wrists, forearms, and your entire body.

Actually, I know many anglers who use the rollcast almost exclusively unless they are fishing dry fly over very placid water or they wish to reach out farther than a normal rollcast permits.

The main purpose of the rollcast is to make it possible to get that line out under conditions where there is no backrest room. It is also a very good cast to use in a headwind. The fore-and-aft is a back-breaker in a wind, but the roll-cast seems to perform against the wind with much more ease and with just as much accuracy.

The cast does have one limitation, however. It is hard to make the cast properly unless the line and leader are balanced to the rod for this purpose. Too light a line will make a fairly good fore-and-aft cast, but it will be most difficult to make an equally good rollcast. Also, a small wet or dry fly on an exceptionally long and light leader made from very soft nylon will be most difficult to handle.

So, to learn the cast, we'll go properly equipped. Our line balances well with the rod and we have a good tapered leader that is not too thin at the butt. We'll cast the rig with no fly attached, for, here again, the fly goes along only for the ride. A heavy fly on a light leader would be out of place, at least at this first session.

As before, we are standing in a mild current, facing downstream. Twenty feet of line is out below us, and our rod tip is down, preparatory to the cast.

Figure XIV. The Rollcast Steps.

In this one, the entire action takes place before your eyes. The line never comes back toward you closer than the rod tip. This makes the learning all that much easier.

The first step is to get that line in motion to create pressure against the rod, so you pull back to about the two-o'clock position and the line begins to come up and off the water, dragging a foot or so on the surface.

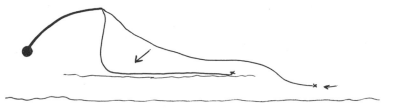

Figure XV. The Rollcast Steps.

Then some line falls almost at your feet.

   At that instant you bring the rod up to the vertical sharply, and as quickly as you do this you snap it down quite hard back to the horizontal position, like so:

Figure XVI. The Rollcast Steps.

Here's what happens to the line during these motions. Step one, raise the rod up. See the line? Now the second flip to the vertical causes this:

Figure XVII. The Rollcast Steps.

and after the downward thrust, this happens:

Figure XVIII. The Rollcast Steps.

How about that? That's the rollcast. Pretty sight. Using a longer lighter leader will require more pressure. A thicker line and thicker leader would require less pressure all around.

Now to give more force to the cast, you apply the double-haul technique in both motions, rather than merely hold the line in the line hand. You haul in line from the first guide in a downward motion of the wrist and arm, and at the peak movement, just as you begin the downward pressure action, you haul again and quickly release after the line has come out, gone skyward, and shot its way to the target. Note that invariably the end of the leader will hit the exact spot from where you withdrew it.

To extend the length of the cast, strip a loop of line from the reel and hold it in the line hand. On the forward throw open your fingers and the rod pressure, if sufficient, will take all the line and even ask for more. Accent the forward thrust and make sure that you do not pause at the peak just before it.

Rollcast Pickup

This modification of the rollcast can and should be used as often as possible with the fore-and-aft cast, or any cast where it is desired to retrieve the line with a minimum of water disturbance. Make the ordinary drag pickup as described in the previous cast and then execute the roll pickup often referred to in the book, and you'll see that there is about seventy-five per cent less water disturbance since the line is being lifted UP rather than through the water.

You do it thusly. Your line is out. Start the usual rollcast but with a much shorter first raise of the rod. Now snap forward sharply and the line will rise up and off the water similar to figure XV.

At the same instant, haul down on the line and give a hefty start to the conventional backcast. Now you are in business for the fore-and-aft cast.

But let's use this with the conventional rollcast, where you cannot have any line going behind you. Start the rollcast pickup as just described, start the backcast in phase two, but instead of continuing to pull back as in the backcast, you roll forward *again*. This gets you into the conventional rollcast and your fly goes out perfectly. Try this a few times. It's tricky at first.

Roll-and-Mend Cast

We use this a great deal in the book; also the one that follows, the roll, mend, and bend cast. Let's mend our first one to the left.

First things first, however. This is a pretty cast to watch and fun to execute. You start out with the conventional rollcast steps, but as you do this, you swing the rod back, pointing it slightly to the left, bringing it back in a slight curve to the right as in figure XIX, as seen from above.

As you snap it down, you swing the rod to the left in a curve path. This lands the line to the left, and as in the fore-and-aft cast, you stop the cast short a bit just before it lands. In order to execute the roll, mend and bend to the left you aid the action by twisting the wrist to the right (showing your rod-hand fingers) and apply a bit more stop action as the line almost hits the water. This brings the line around, mended to the left and curled to the left in the bend technique.

It is obvious now how to perform the same cast but mend and bend to the right.

This is what has happened on the water.

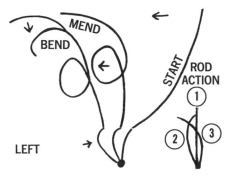

Figure XIX. Upstream (Left) Mend Cast.

If you wish to drift a cast a long distance downstream and cast it again in an almost ninety-degree switch, this cast will do it.

It all sounds easy, and it really is—like dating a girl, you may be awkward the first time, but you'll soon get the hang of it!

Special Casts

Forward Rollcast (Also Roll-and-Pickup)

The conventional rollcast is simple to make. A great deal of fishing must be done with it, since backcast room is not always available.

To start the cast, have the line out a little distance in front of you. Lower the rod tip to let the line go out on the water (for practice, preferably downstream to add pressure on the line). As the line straightens out, raise the rod tip to the twelve-o'clock position with some force and quite fast, and when it is at its peak and you feel the pressure of the tip, snap it down quickly and forcefully. The line will pull the fly back toward you and up into the air in front of your face. The fly will then flip out again in the direction from which it came to settle in the exact spot. To lengthen the cast, simply take slack line from the reel and release it as the line goes out for the final drop of the fly on the water.

Quite often we mention using the roll-and-pickup cast. This is done so that the line will not have to be dragged through the water in the manner of the conventional fore-and-aft cast pickup. To pick up via the roll method, start as described by flipping the rod tip down sharply. As the fly and end of the leader raises out of the water, pull back VERY SHARPLY on the rod to start the beginning of the backcast, done in the usual manner. The fly will rise straight up into the air and then be whisked back into the conventional backcast pattern and you proceed as usual.

Right-Hand Mend

You have made the cast across-stream. The current is flowing downstream from the left. You wish to mend or send the fly to the right for a better drift. (Usually this is done when additional distance is also required.)

Raise the rod tip to gather in the slack. Most of the line is now off the water and the fly and leader is still drifting. Now, snap the rod down and to the right, about twenty degrees. The fly will rise to the surface, go up in the air, and sail to the right, leaving the leader behind it in a semicircle. If additional distance is required, simply shoot line coiled in the hand. When the line goes out in the direction as given, the added line will be pulled from your fingers if enough pressure is applied to the rod on the downward thrust.

Left-Hand Mend

You have made your cast across-stream. The current is coming from the left and your desire is to place the fly UPSTREAM to the left from its present position. This is the left-hand mend and is accomplished by raising the rod tip until most of the line is out of the water. The fly and leader are still drifting at this point. As you feel tension on the line, snap the rod tip down quickly and strongly about twenty degrees to the left. The fly will rise to the surface, go up into the air, and sail to the left, UPSTREAM, being led by an upstream bend in the leader and end section of the line. If additional line is required to reach out, this can be accomplished from coiled line in the line hand. The rod action will pull as much as you need for the distance wanted.

Left-Hand Forward Cast

The conventional forward cast, made of the fore-and-aft false cast in the usual manner, goes straight out in whatever direction you choose. Now, you want the fly to go to the left of your usual center line, leaving an upstream bend or bow. Start your false cast as usual, and keep it swinging in the air as we direct you now. When you are set to deliver the left-hand curve cast, you simply turn your wrist sharply to the LEFT, showing you the back of your hand. This will sail the line in a curve over your head. To shorten the curve at the other end, that is where the line and leader falls on the water in its curve, simply come up sharply with the rod BEFORE the line hits the water. This will tighten the left-handed circle of leader. Usually you need a circle of bend about five feet across with plenty of the bended line or leader UPSTREAM from the fly. This will do it. It is a matter of practicing the wrist flip and the shortening of the drop as the line is about to settle on the water.

Remember, to make the left-hand forward cast, get your false cast going smoothly, and then on the forward release throw, turn your wrist sharply so that you see the back of your hand.

Right-Hand Forward Cast

The conventional forward cast, made of the fore-and-aft false cast in the usual manner, goes straight out in whatever direction you choose. Now you want the fly to go to the right of your usual center line, leaving an upstream bend or bow. Start your false cast as usual and keep it swinging in the air as we direct you. When you are set to deliver the right-hand curve cast, you simply turn your wrist sharply to the RIGHT, but this time you see your fingers to the second knuckle. This action on the rod will send the line in a curve over your head.

To shorten the curve at the other end, that is where the line and leader falls on the water in its curve, simply come up sharply with the rod before the line hits the water. This will tighten the right-handed circle, bend, or bow of the leader. Usually you need a circle about five feet across with plenty of the bended line or leader UPSTREAM from the fly. This will do it. It is a matter of practicing the wrist flip and the shortening of the drop of the line as it is about to settle on the water.

Remember, to make the right-hand forward cast, get your false cast going smoothly and then, on the forward release throw, turn your wrist sharply to the right so that you see your fingers to the second knuckles.

APPENDIX III *Working the Flies*

It may be a big assumption, but let's consider that most trout anglers have spent some time, perhaps years, to select the proper fly rod and balanced reel, lines, and leaders. They have learned at least the two basic casts, the fore-and-aft and the rollcast with their variations and intermixing as we have shown previously in the appendix. Fishing with dry, wet, or nymph flies and buck-tails, they have enjoyed moderate success, but realize the need for subtleties of line, leader, and fly action through studied manipulation, which must be mastered and correctly chosen for the situation of the moment. Many of us have learned that no amount of casting perfection, alone, will put fish in the creel consistently. Putting long distances between themselves and the fish by the mastering of a long cast is only half the answer to a prayer. If sufficiently lucky, they have noticed that shorter and more accurate casts often pay off better. Both types of casts have their rightful place, but they are the means to an end only—the proper presentation of the fly being the most important.

The main part of this book is about this presentation business, and the way we have shown it is to actually take you fishing in exacting and often perplex-ing situations and show our way of solving them.

Come this far, it is time, in case you are not yet acquainted with the tech-niques mentioned in these situations, to open the classroom on the water and take these various presentations and retrieves, one by one, and show how they are done.

Then, we can return to the river with a bit more purpose and confidence.

Basically, the manipulation of the line is performed by two defined move-ments and combinations of movements in order to bring life, or dead drift, to the lure—life, in the form of action that imitates a hatching or fluttering insect; or death, to imitate a dead insect being drifted in the current.

It is a matter of pulling and releasing the line. This is done by twitching the rod tip, pulling on the line as it comes from the first guide, or a combination of both. In order to see how much or how little of these two methods to use for a desired effect, we have to know what pressures to apply under the con-ditions of the moment. If there is only a short amount of line out and the water is fairly quiet, little tension is needed for immediate movement of the fly. If a long line is out and the water is fast and currented in swirls, more pressure, or at least more defined pressure, is needed. If the line is slack on the water in a drift and action of the fly is still wanted, still more pressure has to be applied while allowing the whole cast to drift in the current.

It pays to experiment with this problem and the result will be to know whether your applied action of rod tip and line is actually REACHING THE FLY. I have seen many anglers patiently manipulating their line. Watching from above, from a bridge or a high rock ledge, I've seen just how little they were aware of exactly what (if anything) was happening on the other end of their line.

To experiment, tie on a bright fly, preferably white, and manipulate it in several ways and watch its action in relation to the tackle you are using. If your rod has a soft tip, naturally more pressure or sharper pressure is needed to register. If your rod has a stiff tip, less pressures are needed. Then, try the same actions upstream and downstream and across the current, and note the subtleties here. LEARN TO BALANCE LINE JERK WITH ROD-TIP ACTION and the difference of the two pulls on the line in relation to current direction and force.

For example now, let's take the simplest "fishing retrieve" and see how it is done.

Downstream Techniques

Face downstream above the run in figure XX. The object here is to drift a brace of wet flies down into that run. They must drift and at the same time be manipulated to imitate darting flies or hatching flies. Then, when the drift is completed, they must be retrieved upstream over the same water in a life-like active manner.

Cast the flies to a spot above the run A. Use a longer line than that needed to reach the first landing-target spot. Stop the cast by pulling back on the rod tip just before the line lights on the water. This will supply needed slack line for the drift. As the line and flies hit, raise the rod tip and begin to wave the rod tip from left to right, allowing the line to form a snaky series of three loops. This action alone will cause the flies to swim back and forth across the run, and is quite sufficient. But let's add a jaunty kind of jerk to the flies. This is done at the top of each bend of the rod, by a slight twitch and a short snappy pull of the line by the line hand. This is the effect as shown in B.

As the line absorbs, and the run is still to be fished, strip out more line from the reel and feed it out in jerks by slipping out from the rod tip, again with a healthy jerk of the tip, either sideways or up and down, and at the same time pulling back and RELEASING the line. This will add motion to the line release and at the same time control the amount of slack. Notice that you are in touch with the flies all of the time and that when a trout hits you'll feel it instantly.

The upcurrent retrieve back up through the water just fished is accomplished by snaking the line again by waving and holding the tip to the left or right. The swim of the flies upstream is accomplished by the combination of rod-tip flips, line retrieve (by bunching the line in the palm of the hand, or merely pulling it in slowly and dropping it). Only when a couple of yards of line is in, do you need pause to reel in or coil the line in the line hand for use on the next cast. The path of the fly in the upstream retrieve looks like C.

This retrieve is deadly on smallish streams where the trout congregate in runs, or in big streams where you fish the water run by run as if you were working a brook. Bucktails and streamer flies are fished in the same manner; the wets, and nymphs, likewise.

If still more length is desired in the fishing of this cast, roll line forward for an added loop of about two feet, rather than merely feeding it from the reel.

Now, suppose you wish to work across and down, as in D. The water is fairly fast and about three feet deep. You wish to sink the flies. Make the cast across the stream, above the run, throw a loop of slack bent upstream as the flies alight, and turn your rod in a position in right angles to the line bend as shown. This will allow the flies to drift naturally and yet slack will be controlled and action felt immediately since your line bend acts as the bobber to feel as well as watch. With the flies now entering the hot spot of the run, throw another bend of line, raise the rod tip, and follow the bend at right angles as shown E to give action to the flies and still allow them to move downstream naturally, start the rollcast pickup to lift them and then drop them, repeating this process as they drift to a distance where control is no longer possible. Retrieve by allowing the whole leader to swing gently across the bottom of the run. Now, to work back, rollcast to an almost pickup and mend to the left, placing the flies on the far side of the run, and begin the retrieve up and across the run as shown F. Roll and mend again and you can now repeat the whole performance. In this action, you have given the flies both dead drift and motion, fished the entire run properly with no unnatural actions to the

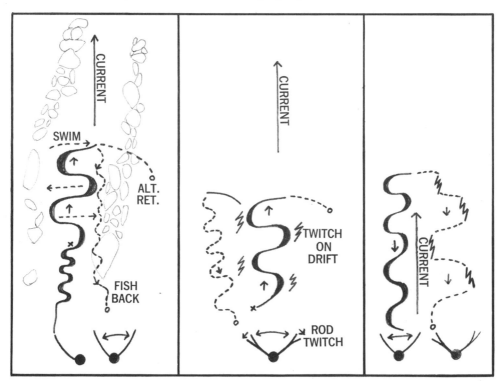

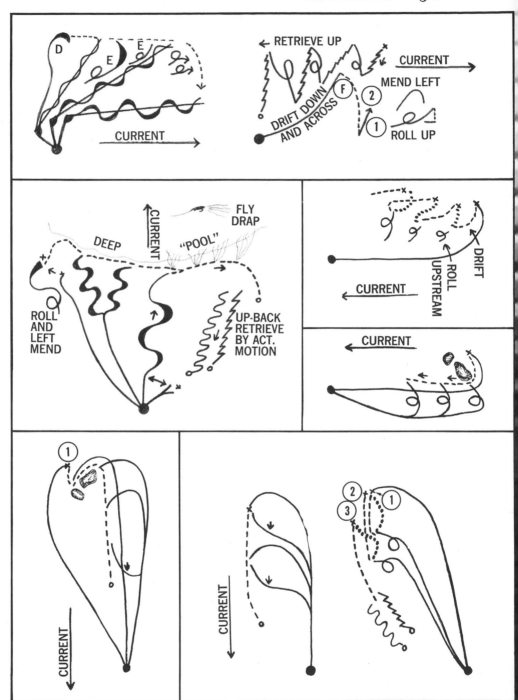

Figure XX. Retrieves.

flies. To dead-drift throughout the entire cast and retrieve, you merely eliminate the rod tip and hand jerking. This is the way you would handle the dry
fly if you were fishing the run from your upstream position. With a wind coming from upstream and armed with spider flies, this method would be quite
effective during the middle of the day. How a Royal Coachman would react to
that treatment!

Now, for the "pie plate" fishing retrieve. The head of a deep stretch is below
you and you wish to fish the lip of it on the upstream side. The main current
G is dead center down from you and fans out against your natural line drift.
Your first cast goes too far to the left and a quick roll of slack bent to the
RIGHT is performed. This will drift the fly as shown. Now, it is a matter of
line snaking and the unfolding of the large loops as they drift downstream to
work the line across the current to the right. Pickup by rolling to activate the
flies on the surface, and even drop them a bit upstream for a short sink, while
creating the snake for the next portion of drift to the right. Work the whole
"pie" this way. This is quite pretty to watch, and fun to perform. You fish the
lip well, too, without disturbing the lower part of the deep water.

This is particularly effective when fishing the bucktail. If you wish to go
deeper into the "pool," mend and roll a bigger loop and when the slack is absorbed, retrieve, bringing the bucktail to the surface to dawdle a bit and then
let it sink as shown to be retrieved again, working always to the right. The same
procedures can be worked from right to left.

Upstream Technique

The most common cast and retrieve in dry-fly fishing, and also in wet-fly upstream work is the straight-up cast and down drift. The only difference between the dry and wet versions is that with the dry it can be seen.

Standing in a run, and fishing up to a rock or break in the current where
insects are seen to be hatching or fluttering on the surface, the dry fly is cast
after being false cast and dropped precisely in a run where the fly cocks itself
and drifts at the mercy of the current. Down below, the angler has to begin
immediately to gather in the slack line. Now, this line is going to float right
over the immediate path that the fly will follow in, and if the trout are scary
and the water clear, they will likely be affected by the line. Longer leaders are
therefore recommended, but even these will at times scare the fish. Often trout
will be seen coming to the fly only to dart away, obviously scared by *something*.
If the fly is dragged by the leader, this is one cause of their panic. Therefore,
we have to try and eliminate both of these problems.

First, the drifting line that precedes the fly. In order to have that fly drift
clear, we throw a right- (or left-) hand bend and the fly circles out from the
immediate path of the cast line H. As the fly drifts downcurrent, we roll mend
a bend of line to keep the line drifting along parallel to the fly but in water
that we are not concerned with. In this fashion, we have also eliminated line
drag that would have ordinarily pulled the fly down under, no matter how well
we retrieved the slack. The same procedure is used in nymph fishing and wet-
fly drifting when it is needed to "float" those imitations right in the surface film.

To activate the flies, such as popping the dry or skittering the wet, the rod
tip is raised up and you reach as high as you can, fishing a normally short line,

and by the suggestion of a rollcast forward, and the fly is twitched up and bounces on the surface. After a very short drift, the roll pickup is again applied and the fly returned to the exact spot at which it landed on the beginning of the cast. In this fashion of repeats, the fly can be danced for as long as needed right over the same spot, with its run downstream shortened or lengthened as you wish, I.

Rock Flip

Now, let's fish that rock at the head of our dry-fly run. We can circle the fly around it in either left or right direction by the bend cast, but suppose we want to fish out the cast by flipping the line over the rock so that the fly will not be interrupted in its fishing course.

See how it's done? Easy! (See figure XX J.)

Now, suppose we want to cast the dry fly up and across stream into a run. We want the fly to drift downcurrent without the line bothering it in drag or in the way of the path. We cast the fly including an upstream bend of line and immediately when the fly cocks and begins to drift, we throw another mend of line upcurrent and another and another as the fly goes below A. If at any point in the drift we want to stop the fly and flip it upstream, we simply follow-through in the roll upstream mend and the fly scoots into the air and travels up above the point where it left the water K.

Down and across with the dry fly or wet is similar in technique to the retrieve already described.

The only additions to the upstream and up-and-across stream technique are the hand-line pulls and rod-tip jerks that are applied when the actual natural drift has run its course. Rather than pickup at the end of the natural, it is advisable, even in most dry-fly fishing, to fish out the cast. The dry fly becomes a wet for those seconds, and the wet fly skitters like a dampened insect. Trout are likely to hit either.

I've found that good big-wet-fly techniques and small-bucktail techniques are almost one and the same. They are easier to perform than with the big bucktail unless the big fly is attached to a stiff leader and is worked with a stiffer-tipped rod.

One of the most effective methods is the across-stream surface retrieve, which is done by casting up-and-across. The fly is allowed to sink a bit and drift down. It is then rolled to the surface and mended right back where it started from, or almost as far up. The next drift down goes farther and the fly is again rolled into the air. This procedure is followed gradually working downcurrent with line shortened or lengthened according to the rocks underwater or the designs of the current and feeding lanes. It looks like KA on the water. When the end of the drift is completed, a number of retrieves are in store and the choice is yours. One of the best is the drift down, sink, roll up, place it back down a bit, and then zigzag upstream again to be rolled down half way to its former sinking-drift position. Zigzag patterns are also recommended as shown. These are accomplished by the rod tip and hand retrieve of the line as it comes from the first guide.

Another favorite is the stop cast and drift down, which has been previously described.

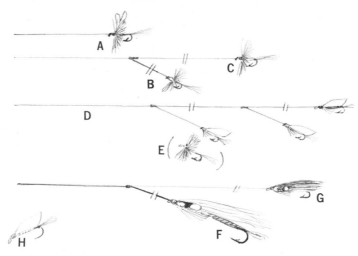

Figure XXI. Various Fly Rigs.

A. *These are various rigs that the author uses at various times. The single dry fly is tied to a tapered leader.*

B. *and* C. *Two flies (either wet or dry or both) on a level leader. I do not use the tapered leader for this purpose because it becomes too fine at the end for a good wide bow cast and has the tendency to tangle on alighting and in fishing if an active retrieve is used.*

D. *The usual three-fly setup with the alternate dry fly as a bobber on the high tippet. If you tie the dry fly as a bobber on the end it does not act properly and becomes drawn under much too easily anyway.*

F. *and* G. *The two-bucktail setup referred to many times in the front of the book. The level line goes to the main fly and a tippet is attached for the smaller fly which acts as a teaser. If the smaller fly is up ahead of the heavier one it will tangle and not swim properly in this position.*

H. *Inspect your fly once in a while especially if you have the habit of dropping your backcast too low on the water or on the rocks behind you. (Of course if you like to fish with barbless hooks . . .)*

APPENDIX IV *Trout Flies*

The matter of proper pattern selection is covered in many places in the book. However, listed and described here are a few of the author's favorites, not because he designed them, or likes their looks, but because they have been proven fish killers over the years. I've cast them from Washington and Oregon, into Mexico, through the Middle West, though this last fishing has been scant. Mostly, they have produced where I've pounded the streams the most—Pennsylvania, New Jersey, New England, eastern Canada and Newfoundland and Labrador. They have worked equally well on Atlantic salmon, steelhead and browns, brooks, and rainbows.

As mentioned elsewhere, I am, however, not a stickler for my patterns, but quite the opposite. I prefer to fish with flies that are known locally as fishing successes. I like to buy flies from local tackle stores and from guides. I enjoy pilfering the boxes of anglers I meet on the stream, though I usually trade quite generously, since I tie my own.

So, I would say, that if I were to fish with you either on the Deschutes in Oregon, or the Beaverkill in Sullivan County, New York, the patterns here would do as well as any I've ever seen.

The brown hackle, the Leadwing Coachman, the March Brown, the Hare's Ear, the Royal Coachman, and the brown, black, and white bucktail, the red, black, and white, the brown and white, the black and white bucktail are standards round the world. You'll find them on the streams of Ceylon yet.

I have included the most valuable Cycle of the Season insects and their imitations which appeared in my book, *How to Take Trout*, first published by Little, Brown and Company. Ed Sens, a fly-tyer extraordinaire, gave me those patterns. In some cases I have adlibbed from them with the labeled "Ovington version." You can take your choice here. I have also included many patterns of the duns and spinners that did not appear in that book, since it dealt almost exclusively with wet flies and nymphs.

There are also rod and line recommendations; some of my own tackle listings for your reference.

I must assume that the reader may or may not be a fly-tyer. If he is not, he can have these patterns tied for him, by a professional or friend who is adept at the art. In most cases, I also include the standard patterns for ready reference and availability.

QUILL GORDON

Order: *Ephemeroptera*
Family: *Heptageniidae*
Genus: Iron
Species: *Pleuralis* or *Fraudator (Epeorus)*
Nymph Type: Clinger
Nymph Size: Body: ¼ inch to ⁵⁄₁₆ inch. Tails: two, ¼ inch
Nymph Shape: Flat and broad
Nymph Color: Body: gray-tan. Legs: tan-gray. Wing pads: brownish-black. Tails: medium brown
Habitat: Fast, clear, rocky stream (lacerated sections)

QUILL GORDON NYMPH IMITATION (Sens)

Hook: Size 14 Mustad Viking 94836
Silk: Pearsalls Gossamer Primrose
Tail: Two strands wood-duck flank feather fibers (long as body)
Body: Gray muskrat dyed light tan (leave untrimmed and pick out with pin)
Hackle: Light gray-tan, two revolutions (clip off top fibers)
Wing Pad: Dark-gray mallard flank feather (clip to shape)
Finish: Whip and varnish
Emergence: Southern New York, northern Pennsylvania, Oregon, and Washington: April 1 to May 9. Noon or warmest time of day

 Figure XXII A. Quill Gordon Nymph Imitation.

QUILL GORDON DUN

Body: ⅜ inch. Wings: ⁷⁄₁₆ inch. Tails: two, ½ inch
Dun Color: Body: medium gray with slight yellow cast. Legs: tan-gray. Wings: slate blue-gray (smoky). Tails: medium gray-brown
Dun Patterns: Quill Gordon, Blue Quill, Blue Dun. Size 12-14 hook light

 Figure XXII B. Quill Gordon, Blue Quill, Blue Dun.

Ovington (dun) Variant: Mallard flank tail, mallard flank body (turned), yellow and black and white hackle mixed. No wings

Figure XXII C. Ovington Variant.

Ovington Spinner: Gray hackle tails, yellow and brown quill body, gray-brown hackle. No wings

Figure XXIII A. Hendrickson Nymph Imitations.

HENDRICKSON

Order: *Ephemeroptera*
Family: *Baetidae*
Genus: *Ephemerella*
Species: *Invaria* and *Rotunda* (similar and appearing together)
Nymph Type: Clambering
Nymph Size: Body: ruddy tan. Legs: tan, dark mottled. Wing pads: gray-tan. Tails: mottled tan
Habitat: Slower sections of fast streams and most semi-quiet waters

HENDRICKSON NYMPH IMITATIONS

Hook: Size 14 Allcock 04991
Silk: Pearsalls Rust
Tail: Three wood-duck flank feather fibers
Body: Gray muskrat fur, dyed light tan (untrimmed)
Hackle: Light gray, dyed light tan, two revolutions (clip off top fibers)
Wing Pads: Black-duck or moor-hen, brown-black covert feather (Ovington variant: brown wood-duck flank feather cut to shape)
Finish: Whip and varnish
Emergence: Southern New York, Michigan: April 20 to May 15. Early afternoon

Figure XXII D. Ovington Spinner.

HENDRICKSON DUN

Size: Body: ⁵⁄₁₆ inch. Wings: ½ inch. Tails: three, ⅜ inch to ⁷⁄₁₆ inch
Dun Color: Body: medium ruddy-brown. Legs: gray-tan. Wings: medium iron gray. Tails: gray-tan

Dun Patterns: Hendrickson (Light), Whirling Dun

Figure XXIII B. Hendrickson (Light), Whirling Dun.

Ovington Variant: Black-brown hackle, tail, brown-tan wool, body ribbed gold, tan-black-yellow variant hackle

Figure XXIII C. Ovington Variant.

Ovington Spinner: Black tails, brown tying-silk body, brown-tan hackle. No wings

Figure XXIII D. Ovington Spinner.

DARK HENDRICKSON

Order: *Ephemeroptera*
Family: *Baetidae*
Genus: *Blasturus*
Species: *Cupidus*
Nymph Type: Clamberer
Nymph Size: Body: 7⁄16 inch. Tails: three, 7⁄16 inch
Nymph Shape: Semi-round
Nymph Color: Body: dark blackish-brown. Legs: black. Wing pads: Mahogany brown. Tails: Black-brown
Habitat: Quiet water, back eddies near fast water

DARK HENDRICKSON IMITATION (Sens)

Hook: Size 12, 3X long Allcock 04991
Silk: Pearsalls Rust
Tail: Three ends moose mane (two black, one brown) used for winding rest of body. Rib with fine gold wire to secure
Body: Build up body in heavy taper and cover with moose mane. Make some weighted
Hackle: Dark rusty brown, two turns (clip off fibers)
Finish: Whip and varnish
Emergence: April 25 to May 9, afternoon: southern New York, Pennsylvania, Michigan, Oregon

Figure XXIV A. Dark Hendrickson Variation.

HENDRICKSON DUN

Size: Body: ½ inch. Wings: ⅜ inch. Tails: two, ½ inch
Color: Body: dark black-brown. Legs: black. Wings: dark iron-gray. Tails: dark brown, banded
Hendrickson Dun Patterns: Dark Hendrickson, March Brown

Figure XXIV B. Dark Hendrickson, March Brown.

Ovington Variant: Black tails, black-brown tying-silk body (heavy), black-brown hackle. No wings

Figure XXIV C. Ovington Variant.

Ovington Spinner: Tan tails, black tying-silk body (thin), black-brown hackle fronted by few whisps of white for bivisible effect

SPINNER
FEMALE

Figure XXIV D. Ovington Spinner.

DARK CADDIS

Order: *Trichoptera*
Family: *Leptoceridae*
Genus: *Psilotreta*
Case Type: (Larval stage) pebbly, sometimes with mixture of sand and refuse. Pupal hatching stage

LARVA
WOOL

Figure XXV A. Case Type (Larval Stage).

Size: Length: ⅜ inch to ½ inch, including sac
Color: Head, wing stubs, and upper body: dark brownish-black. Lower body (pupal sac): dark-brown body color surrounded by gray translucent sac
Habitat: Slower-moving water

DARK HENDRICKSON PUPAL IMITATION (Sens)

Hook: Size 14 Mustad Viking 94840
Silk: Black
Tails: None

Figure XXV B. Dark Hendrickson Pupal Imitation.

Method of Tying: Body and sac: Start with body of stout silk floss. For grayish pupal sac, spin over the underbody a silver-gray muskrat fur that is then picked out to represent translucency. *Head, hackle, and wings:* Two turns condor (black goose) quill tied in by butt ends just ahead of pupal sac, but leave remaining quill free for pointing forward toward the eye of the gook. For wing, select small black-duck wing covert feather. Cut tip in shape of V, with lower stem left on for tying in. Place so that wings fall to sides of body nearly to end of sac. Hackle with one turn or rusty dun. Clip off top fibers. Wind condor quill to eye of hook, making head
Finish: Whip and varnish
Emergence: May 1 to 30; across the country, any time of day—especially twilight
Adult Size: ⅜ inches over-all length

 Figure XXV C. Adult Size: ⅜ Inches Over-all Length.

Color: Brownish-tan wings and dark-brownish body
Standard Patterns: Alder and March Brown downwing patterns. Hare's Ear downwing
Wet-Fly Egg-Laying Pattern: Lady Beaverkill any dark pattern with yellowed floss egg sac

 Figure XXV D. Wet-Fly Egg-Laying Pattern.

GRANNOM CADDIS

Order: *Trichoptera*
Family: *Rhyacophilidae*
Genus: *Rhyacophila*
Species: *Lobifera*
Case Type: (Larval stage) wormlike
Pupal Hatching Stage
Size: Length: ½ inch, including sac
Color: Greenish tinge to body in sac; upper body dark brown Larva imitation green wool on hook shank ribbed with black hackle; sparse black head; heavy hook
Habitat: Slower-moving sandy stretches of streams

GRANNOM CADDIS PUPAL IMITATION (Sens)

Hook: Size 14 Mustad Viking 94840
Silk: Black
Tail: None
Body: Start with body of floss and for the greenish pupal sac spin over the under-body an apple-green wool (very fine), which is picked out to represent translucency
Head, Hackle, Wings: Two turns condor or goose quill ahead of pupal sac, leaving ends free and pointing toward the hook eye. Wing with small black-duck wing covert feather (cut to V as in previous pattern). Wings should fall to side of body. Hackle with one turn of rusty dun tied over free condor quill and clip off top hackle fibers. Wind remaining quill to eye of hook to make head
Finish: Whip and varnish
Emergence: May 1 to 30; across the country, any time of day, late afternoon preferred
Adult Size: ⅜ inch to ½ inch over-all
Adult Color: Brownish-tan wings and greenish-tan body, dark-brown head
Standard Patterns: Brownish-winged wet flies, March Brown, Hare's Ear
Wet-Fly Egg-Laying Pattern: Add yellow floss to base of tail. (Lady Beaverkill good pattern)

MARCH BROWN

Order: *Ephemeroptera*
Family: *Heptageniidae*
Genus: *Stenonema*
Species: *Vicarium*
Nymph Type: Clinger
Nymph Size: Body: ½ inch. Tails: three, ⅜ inch
Nymph Shape: Moderately flat
Nymph Color: Body: cream tan banded with rust brown. Legs: cream tan banded with brown. Wing pads: dark brown. Tails: rust brown
Habitat: Fast water amid rocks

MARCH BROWN IMITATION (Sens)

Hook: Size 12 Mustad Viking 94840
Silk: Pearsalls Light Rust
Tail: Three red-brown fibers (cinnamon turkey tail) or three fibers from cock pheasant tail
Body: Sandy-colored rabbit fur picked out to fluff. Gold-ribbed (thin)
Hackle: Partridge, two turns, clip off top fibers
Wing Pads: Section of medium-brown hen pheasant wing covert with tan stem (cut to shape)
Finish: Whip and varnish
Emergence: Central New York, northern Pennsylvania, Montana, Oregon, May 15 to June 15; midday, sporadic as to weather

Dun Size: Body: alternate bands cream and rust brown. Legs: cream banded with rust. Wings: light gray mottled with black and light tan-olive cast. Tails: rust brown

Standard Patterns: March Brown American, Hare's Ear (evening) add yellow egg sac. Adams Egg Sac (also Adams type tied with brownish-cast hackle), Bradley Special

Ovington Variant: Short partridge feather tail and body. Partridge wings slanted back. Brown hackle. Black head. Dry fly: dark-brown mottled hackle on black-brown body

Ovington Spinner: Black tails, dark-brown tying-thread body, black-brown hackle, yellow egg sac added. White hackle cut to wings only for bivisible

GRAY FOX

Order: *Ephemeroptera*
Family: *Heptageniidae*
Genus: *Stenonema*
Species: *Fuscum*
Nymph Type: Clinger
Nymph Shape: Moderately flat with high shoulder at hatching time
Nymph Color: Body: cream banded with amber. Legs: same. Wing pads: dark brown. Tails: amber brown
Habitat: Fast water amid rocks and gravel

GRAY FOX NYMPH IMITATION (Sens)

Same as March Brown though lighter in phase of colors
Ovington March Brown Nymph: Light-tan pheasant tail fibers. Tan yarn ribbed with gold thorax. Dark-brown wool hump wound on ahead of brown head. Hackle, partridge mottled-brown feather. Wet fly: same body, tail, and hackle, but with brown-black hackle tip feathers slanted over body

Standard Patterns: March Brown, Gray Fox, Hare's Ear, Mallard Quill, Brown Quill

Ovington Dry Fly: Brown hackle tail, light-tan body, brown-tan-red hackle mixed. Gray hackle cut to wings and added in front

Ovington Spinner: Tail: dark-brown hackle fibers. Body: brown-black alternate tying thread, multi-brown-black and white hackle fibers. White added for bivisibility

GREEN DRAKE

Order: *Ephemeroptera*
Family: *Ephemeridae*
Genus: *Ephemera*
Species: *Guttulata*
Nymph Type: Burrower
Nymph Size: Body: ¾ inch. Tails: three, ⅜ inch
Nymph Shape: Semi-oval, fuzzy
Nymph Color: Head and thorax: cream. Abdomen: cream white. Legs: white to cream yellow. Wing pads: chocolate brown. Tails: cream
Habitat: Quiet water of streams, lakes, and ponds

GREEN DRAKE NYMPH IMITATION (Sens)

Hook: Size 12, 3X long
Silk: Cream
Tail: Cream, pale, webby saddle hackle, tips trimmed short
Body: Pale-cream fox fur (fluffed out generally)
Hackle: Cream webby hackle, two turns (clip off top fibers)
Wing Pads: Very small, light marginal wing feather of hen pheasant (clip to shape)
Finish: Whip and varnish

Figure XXVI A. Green Drake Nymph Imitation (Sens).

Emergence: May 25 to June 15; into July in more northern streams; Noon to middle of afternoon, rarely after twilight. Michigan, from noon on
Dun Size: Body: ¾ inch. Wings: ¾ inch. Tails: three, 1 inch
Dun Color: Body, head, and thorax mottling of brown, black, and cream. Abdomen: cream banded with brown. Legs: Cream tan. Wings: faint greenish tinge or gray tan, sometimes olive mottling
Standard Dun Patterns: Green Drake, Rat-Faced McDougal. Sizes 8 to 10

Figure XXVI B. Standard Dun Patterns.

Ovington Dun: Two slim brown-white hackle fiber tips. White wool body tied thin, banded with brown tying-silk. Cream brown and green-dyed hackle mixed in. Gray or black and white hackle tips wings

Figure XXVI C. Ovington Dun.

Standard Spinner Pattern: Coffin fly. Gray Wulff patterns, greenish tinge pattern

Figure XXVI D. Standard Spinner Pattern.

Ovington Variation: Black tails, white body, black and white mixed hackle

LIGHT CAHILL

Order: *Emphemeroptera*
Family: *Heptageniidae*
Genus: *Stenonema*
Species: *Canadensis* and several similar appearing together
Nymph Size: Clinger

Nymph Shape: Flat, short, and wide
Nymph Color: Body: dusty light tan. Legs: dusty buff. Wing pads: dusty gray. Tails: Dirty buff
Habitat: Fast water and heads of pools

LIGHT CAHILL NYMPH IMITATION (Sens)

Hook: Size 12 Mustad Viking 94840
Silk: Primrose yellow
Tail: Three wisps of mandarin flank feather fibers (half body length)
Body: Mixture of cream-tan fur with touch of yellow wool worked in, spun loosely
Hackle: Cream tan or pale ginger; two turns (clip to shape)
Finish: Whip and varnish
Emergence: June 1 to July 15, varying according to locality; some hatching well into July. (Small species sometimes in August in the north.) Late afternoon until dusk
Dun Size: Body: ⅜ inch. Wings: ½ inch. Tails: two, ½ inch
Dun Color: Body: cream buff. Wings: cream dusty (yellowish). Legs: light tan
Standard Dun Patterns: Light Cahill, Cream Bivisible, Red Fox, Red Quill, sizes 12–14.
Ovington Dun Pattern: Light-tan hackle fibers. Cream fox fur, body multicolored tan to yellow mottled hackle feather fibers. Gray hackle spun on front of fly and clipped for wings
Ovington Spinner: Dark-brown hackle fibers. Light-brown tying-thread body. Brown and yellow hackle. White tied in front and clipped for wings for bivisible effect.

LITTLE MARRYAT OR PALE EVENING DUN

Order: *Ephemeroptera*
Family: *Baetidae*
Genus: *Ephemerella*
Species: *Dorothea-Needham* (*Invaria* group)
Nymph Type: Clamberer
Nymph Size: Body: ¼ inch. Tails: three, ³⁄₁₆ inch
Nymph Shape: Moderately round
Nymph Color: Body: dirty-cream tan. Legs: tan with yellow cast. Wing pads: dark-tan gray. Tails: three, gray tan
Habitat: Fastest water of aerated streams, small clear brooks (hatch often comes into main stream from tributary)

LITTLE MARRYAT OR PALE EVENING DUN NYMPH IMITATION (Sens)

Hook: Size 14 Mustad Viking 94836
Silk: Primrose yellow
Tail: Three mandarin flank-feather fibers (tips)
Body: Cream-tan fur with a touch of yellow wool worked in
Hackle: Cream to pale ginger, two turns of shot hackle (cut off top fibers)
Finish: Whip and varnish
Emergence: June 10 to July 10 (later in northern streams or during high water or cold spells. Twilight until after dark)
Dun Size: Body: ¼ inch. Wings: ¼ inch. Tails: ¼ inch

Dun Color: Body: medium tan. Legs: tan. Wings: cream. Tails: light tan
Standard Dun Patterns: Pale Evening Dun, Little Marryat
Ovington Pale Dun: Tails: brown hackle fibers. Tan body of tying thread or tan hackle quill. Gray hackle point wings, tan-yellow hackle. A good pattern though not an imitation is same but with white hackle-tip wings. Light-tan bivisible is also very good tied on a 16 long-shank light-wire hook.

BROWN DRAKE OR LEADWING COACHMAN

Order: *Ephemeroptera*
Family: *Baetidae*
Genus: *Isonychia*
Species: Bicolor
Nymph Type: Swimming or free-ranging type
Nymph Size: Body: ⅝ inch. Tails: three, ½ inch
Nymph Shape: Oval, round, and streamlined
Nymph Color: Body: dark rusty brown. Legs: dark rust. Wing pads: dark brownish-black. Tails: dark rust brown
Habitat: Broad-water flats with rocks and holes

BROWN DRAKE OR LEADWING COACHMAN NYMPH IMITATION (Sens)

Hook: Size 12, 3X long
Silk: Rust
Tail: Two tiny dark rusty brown webby hacklet tips
Body: Thick bronze peacock herl ribbed counterclockwise with fine black silk
Hackle: Dark rust brown, two turns only (clip off top fibers)
Wing Pads: Small, dark brown-black black-duck upper wing covert feathers cut to shape. Ovington version of pads: brown yarn end tied on top of body
Finish: Whip and varnish
Emergence: June 15 to July 10: New York, Pennsylvania, Michigan, Maine. Dusk until dark, or earlier on cool days
Dun Size: Body: ⅝ inch. Wing: ¹¹⁄₁₆ inch. Tails: three, ½ inch
Dun Color: Body: dark tan. Legs: buff yellow to amber. Wing: dark gray-green or generally olive. Tails: buff
Standard Dun Patterns: Brown Drake, Brown Quill, Mallard Quill, Leadwing Coachman. Sizes 8 to 10.
Ovington Dun: Brown hackle tails, tan yarn ribbed with dark brown. Multicolored black-brown-green hackle, no wings.
Ovington Spinner: Black tails, black and brown wound-tying thread. Black hackle white wings tied of hackle fibers in front and cut to wings

GIANT STONE FLY

Order: *Plecoptera*
Family: *Pteronarcidae*
Genus: *Pteronarcys*
Species: *Dorsata*
Coloration: Light mottled brown, gray, and black
Size: 1¼ inches to 1½ inches
Habitat: Medium-fast sections of streams
Emergence: June through September across the country in usual trout belt

GIANT STONE FLY ADULT IMITATION (Sens)

Hook: Size 4, 3X long
Silk: Brown
Tail: Mottled turkey feather section of wing feather
Body: Rabbit fur (gray) tied with guard hairs sticking out. Rib with yellow yarn
Hackle: Long rusty dun
Wings: Mottled turkey wing feather fibers tied double, tent shaped over body rather than flat
Finish: Whip and varnish

Figure XXVII A. Giant Stone-Fly Adult Imitation (Sens).

GIANT STONE FLY NYMPHAL IMITATION (Ovington)

Two strands of brown turkey feather fibers or any brown feather fibers. Light yellow body of fur, topped by brown hackle fibers, ribbed with gold. Wing pads: brown hen pheasant breast feather (small). Hackle: multicolored brown-black-yellow tied palmer halfway down body. This stone in various size from 12 to 8 are good for all stone-fly imitations. Pick one similar to hatched cases on the rocks for seasonal use

Figure XXVII B. Giant Stone-Fly Nymphal Imitation (Ovington).

OVINGTON PATTERNS

Black-Nosed Dace: Hook: 12 3X long, also up to size 4, weighted or unweighted. Body: white floss gold ribbed and lacquered to harden. (All-tinsel body for murky water.) Light red yarn, sparse, tied in at throat under yellow hackle fibers. Jungle-cock feather cheek. Wings (no longer than hook bend): top, brown woodchuck; middle, black bear; bottom, white calf. Fly head black with white painted dot at eye. Alternate dace streamer pattern same except for wings. Black and white, brown and white hackle tips and amber peacock strands on top.
Small-Stream Shiner: Same as dace body but with palmer-tied white hackle (soft and long, cut off except top)
Streamer Bucktail: Same as dace body but mixing fur and streamer hackle feathers together as "wings."

Marabou Streamers: Silver and gold alternate banded body. Black and white, brown, black, and white, brown and white feathers for the three varieties, no longer than twice the length of hook shank. All hook sizes.

Quill Spinners: When unidentifiable spinners are about, there are three general phases of colors: black-brown, brown-tan, tan-gray. All tails black, body alternate winding of each color combination with same variant hackles. Add white hackle and cut for wings. These also serve as multicolored "wingless" dry fly.

Midges: Black silk, black hackle, brown silk, brown fibers, gray silk, gray hackle. All tied sparse. Size 20 hooks

Spiders: Gray, brown, black, and mix for variant. Black bodies. Size 14 to 20 hooks

INDEX

aquatic insects: *see* caddis May fly;
  Stone fly; insects: aquatic
aquatic insect imitations: *see* flies:
  artificial
artificial nymphs imitations
  development, 20; *see also*
  Appendix IV (Trout Flies), 315 *ff.*

bait: presentation, 149; worm, 260;
  see also minnows
bamboo rods: *see* Appendix I
  (Equipment), 289 *ff.*
bass, stream, 48, 80
big-stream angling: *see* stream: big
bivisible flies, 104, 129, 271
boulders, fast-runs problem, 249-56
bridge-pool problem, 162-8, 169-80
bucktail flies, 5, 8, 28, 36, 41, 58, 88,
  121, 157, 167, 177, 197, 206, 211,
  253, 255, 264; weighted, 30

caddis May fly, insect, 9, 66, 69,
  70, 124, 125, 150, 192, 241, 235
Cahill fly, 19, 78, 140, 259; dark, 19,
  78; light, 24, 85, 88-9, 91, 153,
  175; insect, 91, 153, 175, 240,
  247, 259
casting technique, 10, 17, 19, 25, 32,
  37, 53, 87; rollcast, 7, 18, 25,

34, 157, 206, 270; curve cast, 11;
  mend cast, 26, 54, 60, 88; high
  and long, 35; short: *see* short
  casts; *see also* Appendix II
  (Casts), 295 *ff.*
center-rock problem, 4-14
Coffin fly, 109
control, fly-line: *see* line: lure
  control
corner-bend problem, 74-81
curved-center-current problem, 40-5

dace minnows: *see* minnows: dace
dead-drift method: *see* downstream:
  drift
deep-center-current problem, 21
deep-flat-water problem, 196-201
downstream: drift, 10, 12, 29;
  retrieve, 37
drag, fly-line problem, 197; *see also*
  Appendix III (Working the
  Flies), 308 *ff.*
dressing, fly: *see* flies: sparse
  dressing
drift fishing: *see* downstream: drift
dropper fly rig, 9, 18, 19, 99, 205,
  208, 212, 220, 227, 247
dry fly: high-riding, 72; downstream,
  246; fishing (general): *see* flies:

artificial, and Appendix IV
(Trout Flies), 315 *ff.*
duns: *see* insects: aquatic

early-season fishing, 10, 42, 49, 50,
66, 94, 112, 120, 140, 165, 182,
129, 240, 272
eddies: *see* rock eddies

fast runs: *see* boulders, fast runs
fast water: *see* water: fast
feeding, subsurface, 277
fishing: partners, 135-77; technique:
see casting technique,
upstream mend cast
flashing (fish underwater), 274-86
flat-water fishing: *see* shallow-flat-
water problem
flies: artificial patterns, 10, 11, 20,
21; bucktails: *see* bucktail flies;
dry fly, 34, 40, 62, 103, 129, 246;
streamer, 36, 123; Marabou, 38,
71, 72; caddis: *see* caddis May
fly; wet fly, 75-6; spiders, 113,
175; spentwings, 113; sparse
dressing, 166; Cahill: *see* Cahill
fly; *see also* Appendix IV (Trout
Flies), 315 *ff.*
fly fishing: tackle, 28, 44, 59, 103,
123, 226; terminal rigs, 11, 123;
rods, 28, 44, 62, 226; leaders,
28, 44, 59, 62, 103, 165; lines,
122, and *see also* tapered line;
see also casting technique; flies:
artificial; manipulation; retrieves,
fly; Appendix I (Equipment),
289 *ff.*
fly pattern: choice, 4, 21, 27-8, 30,
36, 40, 41, 43, 51, 54, 58, 66-7,
71-2, 76, 78, 88, 105, 113, 121,
129, 135, 151, 157, 166, 183,
199, 211, 239, 259-60;
presentation: *see* presentation,
line and fly; manipulation: *see*
manipulation, fly
footgear, wading: *see* wading:
footgear
fore and aft cast: *see* Appendix II
(Casts), 295 *ff.*

glasses, polaroid, 254
Gray Fox: *see* insects: aquatic
Green Drake fly and insect, 80, 100,
103, 106, 108, 143, 192, 199,
210, 231

hairwing flies: *see* bucktail flies
hatches: *see* insects: aquatic
hatching nymph imitation, 17
head-of-pool problem, 93-100,
112-18, 128-38
Hendrickson: insect, 16, 66, 124,
191, 253; fly, 17, 24, 66, 143,
191, 207, 231; Light, 17, 24,
143, 207; Dark, 160-1; *see also*
Appendix IV (Trout Flies), 315
ff.
high water: *see* water: high
*How to Take Trout on Wet Flies
and Nymphs,* 160; *see also*
Introduction

insects: aquatic, hatches, 19, 152,
240; species, 21, 27, 42, 43, 89,
103, 106, 107; Gray Fox, 88,
140; Stone fly, 35, 133, 182, 213,
235

killing fish, 72

landing fish, 116, 200
late season: *see* season: late
leaders: size, 9, 16, 25, 29, 58, 99,
103, 123, 132, 165, 191, 227;
strength test, 62; *see also*
Appendix I (Equipment), 289
ff.
Leadwing Coachman: fly, 40, 78,
151, 208, 212, 220, 247; insect,
40, 152, 220
ledge-pool problem, 148-53
left-hand bend cast, 12, 117; *see
also* Appendix II (Casts), 295 *ff.*
life cycle, insects: *see* May fly: types,
dun-to-spinner change
Light Cahill fly, 24, 105, 140, 145,
175, 271
line: lure control, 6, 17, 35, 52,
74, 84, 116, 122, 129, 177, 187,

200, 213, 233, 240, 247; retrieve: *see* downstream: retrieve; *see also* presentation, line and fly; slack line; Appendix II (Casts), 295 *ff*.

Little Marryat fly, 27, 28

little-streams problem, 258-65

long-line fishing, 8, 35, 108, 197

low water: *see* water: low

manipulation, fly, 5, 35, 117, 128, 192, 198, 204, 213, 233, 246, 247; line, 17, 79, 84, 157, 174, 179, 183, 197, 220, 226, 233-4, 240, 254, 260

Marabou fly, 71, 153; *see also* flies: artificial

March Brown: fly, 24, 78, 141, 143, 175, 220, 240; insect, 24, 124, 175, 220, 240

May fly: artificial nymph types, 21; dun-to-spinner change, 42; spinner imitation, 43, 166; nymph study, 105; insect group, 142

medium-type water: *see* water: medium-level

mending the cast: *see* Appendix II (Casts), 295 *ff*.

Mickey Finn fly, 173-5

midge flies and insects, 129, 130-1, 176, 207, 239

midseason: *see* season: mid

midstream rock, 4-13

minnows: fishing, 12; dace, 36; live bait, 94; *see also* bait; flies: artificial

natural drift, 5, 16, 18, 53, 55, 174, 179, 183, 238; *see also* Appendix III (Working the Flies), 308 *ff*.

netting fish, 200

night fishing, 100, 134-6, 213

night flies: *see* night fishing

nymph: fishing, 19-20; types, 106

Pale Evening Dun, 27

Palmer tied flies, 104

Parmachene Belle fly, 186

pattern selection, fly: *see* fly pattern: choice

playing the fish, 116

presentation, line and fly, 16-17, 25, 32-3, 53-4, 74, 79, 84, 92, 104, 108, 117, 122, 183, 197, 220, 233, 246-7, 254; *see also* Appendix II (Casts), 295 *ff*., and Appendix III (Working the Flies), 308 *ff*.

Quill Gordon: fly, 8, 141, 197, 205, 210, 233; insects, 124, 141, 145, 197, 205, 210, 233, 235, 247

retrieves, fly, 41-2, 51, 61, 77, 85, 117, 158-9, 215, 234

right-hand mend cast, 12; *see also* Appendix II (Casts), 295 *ff*.

rise: trout, 26, 274-86; dun hatching, 278; spinners, 280

road problem, 244-7

rock eddies, 224-38

rod, stiff-tipped, 207; *see also* fly fishing: tackle; Appendix I (Equipment), 289 *ff*.

rollcast, 8, 18, 33-4, 53, 59, 61, 114-15, 157, 226, 234, 240, 269; *see also* casting technique

Royal Coachman fly, 35, 130, 195, 212, 226, 231

salmon, Atlantic, 28, 52, 259, 285

season: mid, 32, 156; late, 50-1, 53, 56, 240, 272; early, 49, 50, 66, 120, 140, 165, 182, 240, 272

shallow-flat-water problem, 190-3

sharp-angle-pool problem, 66-72

shelving-riffle problem, 48-56

short casts, 9, 32, 87, 129, 220, 247, 260, 271

sinkers: *see* Appendix I (Equipment), 289 *ff*.

slack line, 17, 25, 33, 52, 84, 105, 108, 111, 150, 177, 197, 200, 233, 246

slow water: *see* water: slow

smallmouth bass: *see* bass, stream

snag, stream problem, 182-7

spentwing flies: *see* flies: artificial

spider fly, 113, 175; *see also* flies: artificial
spinner, 280; *see also* insects: aquatic
split-riffle problem, 84-92, 229
S-shaped-pool problem, 156-61
step-pool problem, 266-72
Stone fly, 125, 135, 205, 213, 235; insect, 36, 85, 133, 205, 213, 235; *see also* insects: aquatic
stopcast: *see* Appendix II (Casts), 295 *ff*.
stream: snag problem, 181; big, 196, 219, 250; tributary problem, 204-8, 210-16; split problem, 230-5; rejoin problem, 238-41; *see also* wading: stream
streamer fly, 36, 187, 255; *see also* flies: artificial

tackle: *see* fly fishing: tackle, rods, leaders
tail-of-pool problem, 102-9, 120-4, 140-5
tailing, shallow-water, 275
tailing rise, trout, 102
tapered line, 25; *see also* Appendix I (Equipment), 289 *ff*.
temperature: *see* water: temperature
terminal tackle: *see* dropper fly rig

three-center-rocks problem, 24-30
tributary fishing: *see* stream: tributary problem
two-center-rocks problem, 15-22

upstream-and-across cast, 8, 104, 105, 190, 233, 254, 269
upstream mend cast, 41, 52, 54, 105, 233, 254, 269; *see also* Appendix II (Casts), 295 *ff*.
undercut-bank problem, 58-63

wading: stream, 33, 36, 44, 60, 95, 120; footgear, 251; staff, 254
waste-water problem, 218-22
water: high, 4, 193, 196; temperature, 9, 16, 80; low, 11, 86, 207; waste, 33, 218; medium-level, 42, 141, 190, 211; fast, 84, 120, 156, 265; slow, 182, 196, 224
weighted flies: *see* flies: artificial
wet-fly fishing, 74; *see also* Introduction; Appendix II (Casts), 295 *ff*.
worm fishing: *see* bait: worm
Wulff fly, 157, 187, 199, 226

zigzag retrieve, 11, 29, 52, 100, 122, 178; *see also* retrieves, fly

Mr. Ovington, who was born in New York City in 1917, is known to anglers and shooters the country over for his role as MC of the radio, and later television, show, *The Rod and Gun Club of the Air*, Mutual, 1945–53, to sportsmen for his seven books on angling, and, in the New York Metropolitan area, for his New York *World-Telegram and Sun* hunting and fishing column *Outdoors*, which he wrote from 1959 to 1964. He is presently at work on his forthcoming book, *Tactics on Bass*. Mr. Ovington's fishing itinerary has taken him from Labrador to Argentina. He is married and lives with his wife and three children in California, where he is the Head of the Natural Resources Group, a division of the Public Policy Research Organization of the University of California at Irvine.

A NOTE ON THE TYPE

The text of this book is set in Caledonia, a Linotype face
designed by W. A. DWIGGINS, the man responsible for so
much that is good in contemporary book design and typography. Caledonia belongs to the family of printing types
called "modern face" by printers—a term used to mark the
change in style of type-letters that occurred about 1800. It
has all the hard-working feet-on-the-ground qualities of the
Scotch Modern face plus the liveliness and grace that is
integral in every Dwiggins "product" whether it be a simple
catalogue cover or an almost human puppet.

Composed, printed, and bound by
The Book Press, Brattleboro, Vermont
Typography and binding design by
HERMANN STROHBACH